Students' Book

Advanced

Matters

JAN BELL
ROGER GOWER

Longman

CONTENTS CHART

LANGUAGE BANK

(Areas of grammar included for revision and extension)

WRITING BANK

INTRODUCTION *To the teacher*

These are some notes to help you before you begin. The Students' Book contains ten core units, a **Language Bank** containing optional grammar activities and a **Writing Bank** containing extra writing activities. Each core unit consists of three sections. In most units one section focuses primarily on **Reading**, one section focuses on **Grammar** and one section focuses primarily on **Listening**. In the **Reading** and **Listening** sections there are 'cycles' of activity, focusing on **Speaking** (including pronunciation), **Vocabulary** and/or **Writing**. Throughout the skills sections there is integration of the four main skills and in the grammar sections most activities lead to speaking or writing activities. At the end of each unit there is a **Language Reference** section which provides a summary of the grammar covered in each unit.

Listening and Reading sections

The other cycles of activity in the **Listening** and **Reading** sections (**Vocabulary** etc.) may be loosely linked in topic to the texts, but to give variety and a change of pace they are often independent. This has the added advantage that they can be taught as 'one-offs' or re-integrated into a different part of the course. Where appropriate there is reference to the supporting revision and extension activities in the **Language Bank** and controlled writing practice in the **Writing Bank**.

The **Vocabulary** cycles include practice of such areas as topic (e.g. the language of business), collocation, connotation and phrasal verbs. The **Speaking** cycles focus on such areas as speaking for communication (e.g. roleplay), pronunciation (e.g. sentence stress and weak forms), reply questions and different uses of the word *just* in spoken English. The **Writing** cycles give practice in such areas as letters, reports and instructions. Many of the activities are freer 'process-writing' activities and link to the more controlled writing activities in the **Writing Bank**. We recommend that activities in the **Writing Bank** are integrated as and when needed, in the class or individually on a self-study basis.

Grammar sections

This section presents and practises areas of grammar that have probably had little attention at lower levels (e.g. complex sentences; ways of giving emphasis through sentence structure; less common ways of talking about the future) and areas of grammar where a variety of forms are brought together (e.g. the perfect aspect; narrative forms). The areas of grammar are explained in the **Language Reference** at the end of the unit. In each section there is reference to an appropriate series of revision and extension exercises in the **Language Bank**. These exercises can be incorporated into lessons or given as self-study according to need.

Language Bank

The optional activities in this Bank include areas of grammar which are likely to be 'known' and are included for revision (items such as conditionals, relative clauses and reported speech). Where the grammar is likely to be relatively unknown and is included for extension, yellow grammar boxes give learners on-the-spot help. There is also a general diagnostic activity at the beginning of the Bank to help learners identify areas of strength and weakness, with reference to where appropriate practice can be found in *Advanced Matters*.

Writing Bank

This Bank consists of writing activities which are usually more controlled and with more input than those within the units and are linked to text formats such as journal articles, summaries, brochures, e-mail and letters. At the beginning of the Bank there are Writing checklists to support the 'process-writing' activities in the units.

Teaching with *Advanced Matters*

Advanced Matters Students' Book can be adapted to suit different individual needs and different teaching programmes. The way the Students' Book has been arranged in terms of sections, cycles and optional Banks gives teachers and learners maximum flexibility. The course can be extended or supplemented by drawing on the revision and extension grammar activities or the extensive vocabulary practice in the Workbook, and on the many ideas and activities (some of which are photocopiable) in the Teacher's Book.

We hope you will enjoy the course.

Jan Bell and Roger Gower

PERFECT WORLD

READING: An ideal day

Before reading **1** Imagine your ideal day.

a) Choose places in the world you would go to in the morning, in the afternoon and in the evening.

b) Decide what you would do in each place.

c) Find other students who would like to do similar things.

Reading **2** The article below is by Stephen Berkoff from a series which asks famous people to describe where in the world they would like to be at different times of the day. Berkoff is a British actor who has appeared in several films including *Beverly Hills Cop* and *Fair Game*.

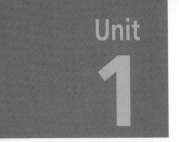

STUDENT A: You are going to read about his morning in Part A.
STUDENT B: You are going to read about his afternoon and evening in Part B.

A slow jog on Venice Beach;

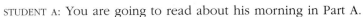

A

SUNRISE ON VENICE BEACH
I wake early at my hotel on Venice Beach, Los Angeles, dash downstairs and grab a coffee from Tom's Cafe next door. The sea is shimmering against the rising sun and the distant hills over Malibu are still a deep blue. I begin a slow jog to the Santa Monica pier, past the other early risers.

At the open-air gym I do a few dozen dips on the parallel bars and walk back as the scorched red dawn sets everything on fire.

BREAKFAST ON THE CÔTE D'AZUR
The morning air is sweet and scented with pine, oleander and roses from the garden and mixed with the distant aroma of the sea and freshly-ground coffee. From the terrace of my hotel I feast my eyes on the wide, shimmering Côte d'Azur in the south of France. It's the bluest sea I have seen, a deep aquamarine blue.

Breakfast arrives on the marble table-top: a basket of croissants, freshly-squeezed orange juice and earthy coffee. Afterwards I stroll past giant flowers with open trumpets and throw myself into the sea, which is as clear as glass and warmed by the sun.

LUNCHTIME AT GLEN COE
Since I am not really a lunch eater, I'd like to take a long walk along Glen Coe, one of the last wild places in Europe. The clouds hang low in the heavens and wild deer come down in the winter and sniff around the houses. The moor is covered in all the colours of Scotland – purple, russet, deep green – and the eye sees nothing but cloud-capped crags and soft hills. The mystery and the wildness of the place send the imagination reeling.

a) Read your part quickly and tick which of the things below he writes about.

	STUDENT A			STUDENT B		
	Venice Beach	Côte D'Azur	Glen Coe	Jaffa	Sydney	Rio
1 Things he does	✓					
2 The scenery						
3 Smells						
4 Food/drink				✓		
5 Atmosphere						

b) Read your part again and make notes under the same headings as 1–5 above.

c) Use your notes to tell each other about each place – say what he does, what he sees, what he feels and what his impressions are.

d) Which place seems to you:
- to have the best things to do?
- to have the best scenery?
- to have the best food and drink?
- to have the best atmosphere?

a samba in Rio

 B

AFTERNOON IN THE SOUK AT JAFFA
Jaffa has become almost a suburb of the growing city of Tel Aviv but the beach between the two is still worth a stroll. You watch the towers of the minarets get closer and closer, and when you arrive, although you are only a mile-and-a-half from the bustling city, you are plunged into another world: the endless alleyways and medieval staircases of Arabia.

The Arabic back-street cafes are the best places to eat humous and falafel plus hatzillim (aubergine, my favourite) and small delicious pickles and olives. In the market, open daily, I always find something and drag it back to London.

DINNER IN SYDNEY
A drive in warm air round the suburban back streets of Sydney reminds me of England in balmier days. After frolicking on Bondi Beach, I've built up an appetite for an evening meal at Doyle's famous fish restaurant.

From Doyle's the view is directly over the harbour to the twinkling skyline of Sydney, and breathtaking it is, too. The famous bridge winks its solitary centre light as you sit outside still tingling and glowing from the sea and sun. Doyle's has a calmness and gentleness of spirit, and although it has expanded since I first made its acquaintance in '78, I still feel totally at home.

LATE NIGHT IN RIO
You can't beat a nice caipirinha. A cane rum called cachaça is mixed with crushed limes and cracked ice, sprinkled with a liberal dose of sugar and served under a canopy of stars by the open-air pool of the Copacabana Palace Hotel.

Ronnie Biggs, stopping by for a drink, is in his usual ebullient mood. We decide to watch some samba – on top of one of the sugarloafs that so characterises Rio.

We take a cab to the cable car, and on our ascent are treated to a breathtaking sight of Rio stretched out before us. We enter the club in high and jubilant spirits.

We drink more of the firewater and in the end hop on to the floor for some samba. Then we'll admire the view again on the way down, a bit bleary-eyed this time.

Humous and falafel: both of these foods are made from chick peas
Ronnie Biggs: a famous robber 'exiled' from Britain

(From *The Sunday Telegraph*)

Speaking **3a)** Have you visited any of the places Berkoff writes about? Are there any you would particularly like to visit? Why?

b) Which of the things in Berkoff's day would you enjoy/not enjoy?

Vocabulary **4** Look back at the part of the text you read.

a) Underline up to five or six words or expressions you don't understand.

b) Work with other students who read the same part. Can they tell you what the words/phrases mean?

c) Find words which no one knows and split them between you. Guess their meaning from context and check in a dictionary. How are they pronounced?

d) Tell the other students in your group what 'your' words mean.

e) Now read the other part of the text. If you need help with vocabulary, ask a student who read it before.

5a) Mark the word stress on the adjectives in A and practise saying them.
Example: 'shimmering

A	B
1 shimmering	a) coffee
2 rising	b) gym
3 breathtaking	c) sun
4 freshly-ground	d) city
5 cloud-capped	e) orange juice
6 open-air	f) sea
7 freshly-squeezed	g) hills
8 bustling	h) sight

b) Match the adjectives in A with the nouns in B. Practise saying the adjectives with the nouns, putting the main stress on the noun. Example: *shimmering* '*sea*

6 Use similar headings to the headings in Exercise 2a) and some of the adjectives in Exercise 5 to talk about a place you've been to.

▶ **Language Bank page 158: Present verb forms**

WRITING: Describing places

1 Work in groups and look at the photos opposite. How would you describe each of the places? Examples: *fascinating, probably rather menacing at night.* Think of some possible advantages/disadvantages of each as a tourist attraction.

2a) Choose a place you all know (for example, the town you're in now) or a place you've all heard about. What are your impressions of the place? What makes it distinctive (the traditional festivals, the popular entertainment resorts)?

b) You are going to write a description of the place for one of these:
  – A tourist guide.
  – A travel brochure.
  – A personal letter.

1 List some phrases which describe the attractions of the place. Examples:
   – Tourist guide: *magnificent gourmet cuisine, long-established department stores.*
   – Personal letter: *the people are tall/dark/very friendly.*

2 Focus on one or two things that are worth a visit. What comes to mind when you think about them? Examples: *picturesque market, the pungent smells, the varied colours.*

3 Decide on the number of paragraphs, what will be in each and what order they will be in. You might want to do a bare summary of your description first.

4 Decide what main verb forms you will use (present, past or future).

5 Decide on a strong introductory sentence. Examples: *... is an outstanding area of natural beauty. We've just been to this fantastic place.*

6 Write a first draft as a group, using adjectives to bring the description to life.

7 Read another group's draft. Make any comments on the writing (for example, say why you like it) and ask at least two questions about the place. Example: *What are the beaches like?*

8 Rewrite your description and show it to other groups.

▶ **Writing Bank page 169: Describing places**
▶ **Language Bank page 141: Adjective word order**

SECTION 2   GRAMMAR: 'Unreal' use of the past

1a) Invent a context for each of these sentences. Who is talking? What are they talking about? Is the speaker talking about the past, present or future?

Example: Climb up that ladder? You must be joking. *What if* it collapsed!
A nervous man refusing to climb a ladder – now – because it might collapse – future.

1   *I'd rather* you were studying law than training to be a beauty consultant.
2   *I wish* I hadn't eaten that shellfish.
3   He acts *as if* he owned the place.
4   *Just suppose* you got the job, would you move to London?
5   *It's high time* you were in bed!
6   *Just imagine* we'd got married at university – what a disaster!
7   *If only* I could see her and tell her the news myself.

b)   Why do we use past forms in the sentences above? Check your answers in the Language Reference on page 17.

2a) Choose the verb form which best matches the context in brackets.

1   I wish I *would have/had/had had* some money with me – I *was/would be/would have been* able to get a taxi home.
    (You wanted to get home but you didn't have any money for a taxi.)
2   Suppose we *don't take/didn't take/hadn't taken* the car tomorrow, do you think we *get/would get/would have got* a lift home?
    (You are going to a party tomorrow and speculating about not taking your car. However, you know you will almost certainly take your car.)
3   If only you *had taken/would take/take* me out once in a while.
    (You want the other person to take you out.)
4   It's about time you *are/were/would be* on your way.
    (The time has come for you to go.)

b)   Which is often more emphatic: *I wish* in sentence 1 or *If only* in sentence 3?

c)   Have you ever been in any similar situations to those in Exercises 1a) and 2a)? For example: eaten things you wish you hadn't; not had any money to get home. What happened?

3   Put the verbs in the correct form, then compare the sentences a, b (and c) for each number (1–5).

Example: In 1, in what ways are the form and meaning of the structures *It's (high) time you …* and *It's time for you …* similar/different?

1   a)   It's high time you (*start*) .... applying for jobs. I'm not going to support you any more!
    b)   It's time for you (*think*) .... about getting a new car.

2   a)   I wish the postman (*hurry*) .... up. I'm waiting for a letter.
    b)   Do you wish you (*go*) .... to university when you had the chance?
    c)   I'm sorry I missed your birthday party. If only I (*not, go*) .... into town and (*get*) .... stuck in the traffic!

3   a)   I know you don't want to sell that painting – but what if you .... (*be*) broke, ... (*you sell*) it then?
    b)   If you (*eat*) .... any more of that ice-cream, it .... (*make*) you sick. Put it back in the fridge!
    c)   I don't mind you borrowing the car providing you .... (*get*) it back to me by tomorrow.

4 a) I'd rather you (*not lose*) .... your temper at the meeting. It made
  matters worse.
 b) I'd prefer it if you (*not phone*) .... after 10.00 pm in future.

5 a) Supposing the man (*get*) .... out a gun in that hold-up yesterday, what
  do you think the manager (*do*) .... ?
 b) Just imagine we .... (*win*) the lottery next Saturday, what do you think
  we .... (*do*) this time next year?

4 You are going to listen to people talking about their hopes and regrets.

a) Look at the cartoons. Can you guess what they are saying?

b) [⌨ 1.1] Listen and compare your guesses. Which speakers use an unreal
use of the past?

c) Which other hopes do people sometimes talk about (e.g. current political
situation, inventions)? Which other regrets do people talk about (e.g. being
born a man/woman, embarrassing situations, world history)?

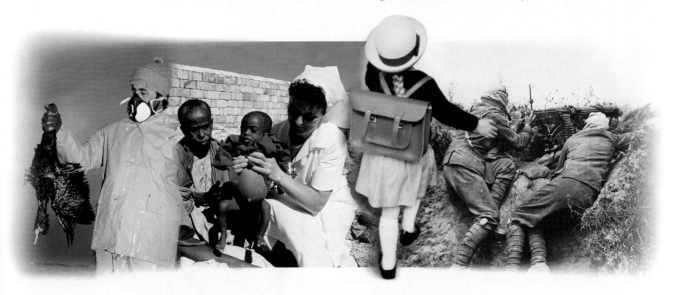

d) Prepare to talk about your own hopes and regrets.

e) Work in groups. Tell each other and give reasons.

▶ **Language Bank page 140: Grammar review; page 145: Conditionals**

SECTION 3   LISTENING: Genes 'R' Us

Before listening   **1**   Is there a young baby in your family? If so, what do you most like about him/her? Imagine you could 'design' your ideal baby (both physical features and character). What would it be like?

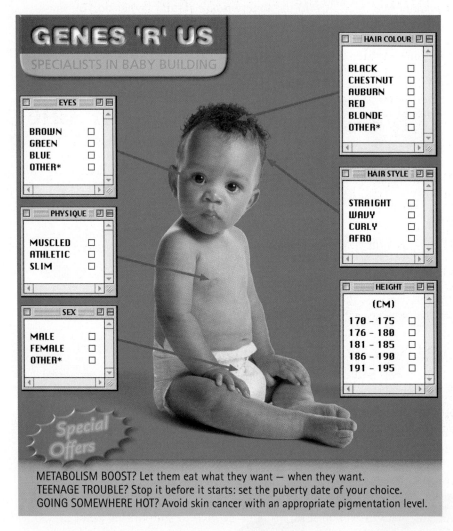

2   It will soon be possible scientifically to 'design' the babies we have. Which of these do you think are/would be a good thing to be able to do and why? (Some are already possible.) Do you think any should be illegal?

– Choose the sex of the baby.
– Choose the physical characteristics (eye and hair colour, skin pigmentation, height, body weight etc.).
– Operate on physical deformities before birth.
– Improve intelligence.
– Reduce violent behaviour.

3a) Read the dictionary definitions and information to help you with Exercise b).

gene /ˈdʒiːn/ *n* [C] information in the form of a pattern of chemicals [DNA] that is passed on from parents to children and controls one part of behaviour

genetics /dʒəˈnetiks/ *n* [U] the study of how the characteristics of parents are passed on to their children through genes

molecule /ˈmɒlɪkjuːl/ *n* [C] the smallest amount of chemical substance that can exist by itself

DNA /ˌdiː en ˈeɪ/ *n* [U] the acid which carries genetic information in the centre of a cell in all living things. This is responsible for characteristics being passed on from parents to their children

clone /kləʊn/ *n* [C] a living thing with exactly the same form as the thing from which it was produced

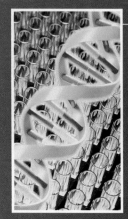

DID YOU KNOW:

• DNA is the molecule from which life grows? It is like a spiralling ladder made up of four chemicals (A,G,T and C).
• it takes 3,000 million letters of DNA to make a human being?
• there are about 100,000 different genes in a human being?

b) Read 1–5 below. Which in your view is the most and least valuable area of genetic research? Put them in order.

① **Gene science to predict the date of your death**

Life assurance companies are in turmoil over how to deal with latest advances in genetic research.

② **Human clones: Will they be developed?**

SINCE the cloning of Dolly, the sheep, America's chief of medical research has said he opposes any kind of ban on human cloning.

③ **GENETIC BREAKTHROUGH: SLIM HOPES FOR ALL**

A team of Californian scientists has isolated the gene that stops some people becoming fat, whatever they eat.

⑤ **Genes for sale**

Genetic material from kings, presidents and film stars is to be sold in watches, earrings and even phonecards. A breakthrough in the cloning of DNA from human remains – usually hair – means it can now be mass-produced.

④ **Chimpanzee egg fertilised with human sperm destroyed**

'Creature could have been used to do monotonous, routine or dirty jobs – or as an organ bank for transplants,' says biologist.

c) Compare your ideas with another student's, giving reasons for your order.

Listening 4 [🔊 1.2]   Listen to four extracts from a talk by Professor Steve Jones, Professor of Genetics at University College, London.

a) As you listen, match each extract with one of these topics.
A Scientists should take moral decisions during their research.
B It is acceptable to do genetic tests on unborn babies.
C Genetic research is moving too fast.
D Genetics threatens us with no more problems than medicine in general.

b) Which of the statements in a) does Professor Jones agree/disagree with? Which do you agree/disagree with?

c) Listen again. What reasons/examples does he give to support his point of view for each statement?

d) Answer these questions:
1 How can genetics help sufferers of cystic fibrosis?
2 Why do some parents support genetic research on the unborn?
3 What can we do now in genetics that we couldn't do 25 years ago?

e) Look at the tapescript on page 182 and find some phrases which show that the speaker is developing an argument.
Examples: *People often see … while I … Many people have said …*

f) Use some of the phrases you found in e) to say whether or not you are worried about what genetic scientists are able to do. Refer to the issues raised in Exercises 2 and 3 above and any other issues you know about.

g) What do you think about these statements?
– 'One of the advantages of being able to clone humans is that we could reproduce great people.'
– 'Criminals have the perfect excuse for their crimes: they get their behaviour from their parents and so cannot be held responsible.'

SPEAKING: Sentence stress and weak forms

1 In English, when we speak we stress the word (or words) that we feel contains the most information. That's why stressed words are usually (but not always) 'content words' (e.g. nouns) and unstressed words are usually 'grammar words' (e.g. articles).

a) Write the words in the box under the correct heading.

pronouns (e.g. *her*)	auxiliaries (e.g. *have, can*)	main verbs (e.g. *gave*)
adjectives (e.g. *happy*)	conjunctions (e.g. *because*)	adverbs (e.g. *slowly*)
prepositions (e.g. *by*)	demonstratives (e.g. *these*)	

CONTENT WORDS	**GRAMMAR WORDS**

b) Underline the content words in these sentences.
1 Do you know where the nearest bank is?
2 I like her because she's incredibly honest.
3 Drinking lots of water is supposed to be good for you.
4 Could you remind me of the name of that Russian writer?
5 I'll lend you the money as long as you give it back to me.

c) [1.3] Listen. One content word in each of the sentences above is stressed more than the others. Which one is it?

d) Practise saying the sentences.

2 When we stress words, changes can occur in the sounds of many unstressed words:

Where have *you been* → ***Where've*** … (contraction)
Was [h]e late? (sound disappearing)
I've been /bɪn/ *to* /tə/ *the cinema.* ('weak forms' of 'grammar' words, where the vowel reduces to /ɪ/ or /ə/)

There is a list of weak forms and their strong forms on page 192.

a) Read these sentences and underline the words you think will be contracted or 'weak'.
1 A: Why has she been told she must stop at home?
   B: Because she cannot take care of herself.

2 A: I would like to spend some time with you but I have to go.
   B: Where to?

3 A: What does it mean?
   B: Not a lot.

4 A: Where are they from?
   B: From Hungary. Do you know them?

b) [1.4] Listen and compare your answers.

c) Are there any words in which the sounds disappear or change? Listen again if necessary.

3 Look at the dialogues below.

a) For each, decide who A and B are and what is happening.

b) In context, which word do you think would be most stressed in each sentence and why?

c) Which words do you think are used in their weak form?

> 1 A: How can I help you?
>   B: I was wondering. Does the consultant see people in the evenings?
>   A: No, I'm afraid not. I could get you something in the afternoon.
>   B: OK. Could I see her on Thursday afternoon?
>
> 2 A: Come and look at the new brochure. What do you think of this cover photo?
>   B: Did Simon do it? He did, didn't he? I think it's the wrong image. I think we want something much more dramatic.
>   A: Really?
>   B: What do you think of it?
>   A: I like it.

d) [🔲 1.5] Listen and compare your dialogues with the dialogues on the recording. Discuss the reasons for any differences.

e) Practise with a partner either your dialogues or the dialogues on the recording.

SPEAKING: Telling anecdotes

1a) What is the funniest or most embarrassing situation you have been in when eating (e.g. spilling wine over an important guest; not having any money on you when paying the bill; eating someone else's food by mistake)?

b) [🔲 1.6] In Britain, avocado pears used to be unusual and exotic. Listen to Tony Robinson, an actor, telling the story of how, when he was 21, he tried to eat an avocado pear for the first time. Answer the questions.
1 Why was he confused when the girl put an avocado pear in front of him?
2 In what way did the girl 'help' him?
3 Why did he feel humiliated?

c) Imagine you are meeting Tony immediately after this incident. What advice would you give him for when he receives similar invitations in the future?

2 When we are thinking about what we are going to say or deliberately slowing down a story to build up anticipation we use 'hesitation devices' or 'fillers' (Examples: *eh, well, I mean ...*). When we want to make something less definite we use phrases like *sort of*.

a) Read the tapescript of Tony Robinson on page 182 and underline the hesitation devices.

b) What effect do they have in context?

3 Now work in pairs and choose either A or B.

A: Tell each other one or more of these.
1 Your first experience of eating/drinking something unusual. (Describe the situation and the sensation.)
2 Your first experience of flying.
3 Something amusing that has happened to you or somebody you know.

B: Tell each other your favourite joke with a storyline or tell each other an anecdote using the pictures below.

'UNREAL' USE OF THE PAST
Imaginary situations in the present/future

We use the past tense after certain expressions to talk about imaginary situations in the present or future. These are sometimes called 'unreal' or 'hypothetical' situations. Compare these two sentences:

*He looks/acts **as if he's** fifteen.* (He is probably fifteen.)
*He looks/acts **as if he were** fifteen.* (Imaginary. He's only twelve but has the appearance of a fifteen-year-old.)

NOTE:
We can use *were* instead of *was* in these sentences. In formal style *were* is more common than *was*.

Here are some similar constructions:

1 ***If we were** in Florida, I'd spend all day on the beach.* (but we're not.)

2 **I wish** │ *we had more money.* (but we haven't.)
   If only │
   NOT: *I wish/If only ~~we would have~~ more money.*
   If only is usually more emphatic than *I wish*.

Both of these are states. When somebody/something else keeps doing/not doing something (an action in the present) and we are sorry, dissatisfied or irritated we use *would*:

***I wish you would** shut up.* (You keep making a noise.)
***If only it would** rain.* (It's so dry!)

For ourselves we use *could* (not *would*):
***I wish I could** see the film.*

3 **(Just) imagine**   │
   (Just) suppose │ *we were swimming in the*
   Supposing   │ *Mediterranean.* (but we're not.)
   What if   │
   ***Suppose you had** more time, what would you do?*

4 ***It's time we went**.* (We can also say: *It's time for us to go* but NOT *It's time we ~~go~~.*)

5 ***I'd rather/sooner you didn't open** the window.* (=I'd prefer you not to open the window.)
   ***I'd prefer it if you didn't tell** Sue about this.* (=Please don't!)

   NOTE:
   After *I'd prefer* we can also use object + infinitive:
   ***I'd prefer you (not) to tell** Sue about this.*

   When it is about something we would like to do we use the base form of the verb without *to*:
   ***I'd rather/sooner** stay in tonight.*
   (But note ***I'd prefer to** stay in tonight.*)

6 ***I'll lend you the money providing/provided (that) you pay** it back.* (That's my offer – you're likely to pay it back.)
   ***I'd lend you the money provided/providing (that) you paid** it back.* (But you never do pay it back so I'm not going to lend you any.)

   NOTE:
   This has the same form as sentences with *if*.

Imaginary situations in the past

We use the Past Perfect to talk about imaginary situations in the past:

*He looked/acted **as if he was** fifteen.* (and he probably was.)
*He looked/acted **as if he had been** to the moon and back.* (Imaginary!)
***If we'd gone** to Australia, I'd have visited Ayers Rock.* (but we didn't.)

I wish   │ *I hadn't left university after my first year.*
If only │   (but I did.)

Imagine   │
Suppose   │ *you had fallen and hurt yourself.*
Supposing │   (what would you have done then?)
What if   │

***I'd rather you hadn't told** your husband everything* – he's very suspicious of me now.
***I'd have preferred you not to tell/have told** your husband everything.*
(It's too late – you did tell him everything – but I wish you hadn't.)

TEMPER, TEMPER

LISTENING: This brief madness

Before Listening **1a)** Read this newspaper headline and predict what you think the article is about.

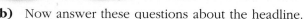

Driver courtesy day attempts to calm road rage

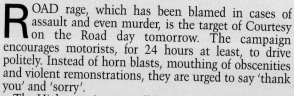

b) Now answer these questions about the headline.
  1 Can you think of situations in which people get angry (suffer 'road rage') while they are driving? What do they do?
  2 What do you think drivers are expected to do on a 'driver courtesy day'?

c) Read the article and check your answers.

ROAD rage, which has been blamed in cases of assault and even murder, is the target of Courtesy on the Road day tomorrow. The campaign encourages motorists, for 24 hours at least, to drive politely. Instead of horn blasts, mouthing of obscenities and violent remonstrations, they are urged to say 'thank you' and 'sorry'.

The Highways Agency will launch a 20 point plan for avoiding road rage. It discourages hogging the middle lane, queue jumping at road works and tailgating.

Other advice includes avoiding eye contact with other drivers, keeping windows closed and trying to 'stay calm and avoid challenges. Do not sound your horn, shout or swear'.

(From *The Guardian*)

d) Discuss these questions.
  1 Do you ever have incidents like these in your country?
  2 Why do you think things like this happen? Could anything be done to stop them?

Listening **2** [🔊 2.1] You are going to listen to three extracts from a radio programme called *Temper, Temper*. Listen to Extract 1, which includes an example of temper.

a) Answer the questions below.
  1 John McEnroe used to be a famous tennis player. Why is he angry?
  2 How can you tell he is angry?
  3 The presenter gives three other examples of situations in which people get angry (apart from road rage mentioned in the article above). What are they?
  4 Why does she think it is undignified for adults to be in a temper? Do you agree?

b) The presenter says that she lives in a culture which encourages us to *'let it all hang out'*.

    1 Is it the same in your country? Is it the same for both children and adults?

    2 What about people who never lose their temper? Is this normal? How do they express their anger?

3   In Extract 2, some people talk about how they feel when they lose their temper.

a) First discuss what happens to people, physically, when they lose their temper. What happens to parts of their body (e.g. heart, hands, skin)? What happens to their blood pressure?

b) Listen to Extract 2 and answer the following questions:

    1 How do these people feel when they get angry?

    2 Do you feel like any of the people interviewed when you get angry? In what ways are you the same or different?

    3 What is the *fight/flight* mechanism that is mentioned?

4   In the last extract you are going to listen to a doctor talking about anger.

a) Do you think the doctor will say that anger is good or bad for your health? In what ways?

b) Listen to Extract 3 and check your predictions.

c) Listen again and complete 1 and 2.

    1 People at a higher risk of dying earlier (from the ages of .... to ....) are ....

    2 Reasons for this: a) ....

                           b) ....

Vocabulary **5**   The nouns *temper, fury* and *rage* are all associated with being very angry. Some verbs go with (collocate with) all three of these nouns. Example: *fly into; be in; get into* a rage/temper/fury, but some verbs e.g. *lose* (your temper) or *shake* (with rage/fury) would sound strange with the other nouns.

The idiomatic expressions below all mean *lose your temper*.

a) Match the verbs in A with the nouns or adjectives in B. You can find examples of two of them in the tapescript for Extract 1 and one in Extract 2 (on pages 182–183).

A		**B**	
1	blow	a)	the handle
2	let	b)	your lid
3	fly off	c)	a tantrum/a fit
4	lose	d)	your top/a fuse
5	throw	e)	your cool/your rag/control
6	flip	f)	berserk/mad
7	go	g)	rip

b) On which word is the main stress in these expressions: the verb or noun/adjective?

6   Talk about yourself, using some of the expressions above:

1 What makes you very angry?

2 When was the last time you blew your top?

3 What things that you do make other people angry?

VOCABULARY: Collocation

When learning a language it is often very difficult to know which words collocate with which. For example, in English we say **make** (not *do*) *friends,* but **do** *your hair.* We say **strong** *and* **weak** *tea* but the opposite of a *strong wind* is a *light* (not *weak*) *wind.* The adverb *hard* collocates naturally with the verb *work,* as in to *work hard.*

A native speaker would know that whereas the words *fully understand* go naturally together the words *strongly understand* do not. This collocation would be understood, but it sounds strange. There is usually no reason as to why which words collocate with which – they just have to be learnt!

1   Solve the collocation puzzle by finding suitable words to fill the gaps in the sentences.

Across			
3	The .... majority of people voted 'yes'. *(adj)*	9	He was .... awake at 5 am. *(adv)*
4	When are you going to .... house? *(v)*	11	I .... regret what I said. *(adv)*
7	There wasn't a .... of truth in what he said. *(n)*	14	I .... believe there is life after death. *(adv)*
8	Hold .... while the bus is moving. *(adv)*	15	He complained .... about the meal. *(adv)*

Down			
1	6 is an .... number. *(adj)*	7	It was a .... of luck you were there. *(n)*
2	There was a .... of applause after his speech. *(n)*	10	Please try to write .... so I can read it. *(adv)*
5	There was .... fog so I couldn't drive. *(adj)*	12	You never .... attention in class. *(v)*
6	We can't really .... conclusions from this report. *(v)*	13	The baby was .... asleep. *(adv)*

2   When compiling a monolingual dictionary for students a wide range of spoken and written texts are examined so that the most common collocations can be included. So if you want to check your answers for the crossword a good dictionary, such as the *Longman Dictionary of Contemporary English,* should be able to tell you which words are commonly used with, for example, *asleep.*

> **asleep** /ˈsliːp/ *adj* [not before n] **1 sleeping:** *Quiet! The baby is asleep.* **fast/sound asleep** (= very deeply asleep) *You'll be fast asleep by the time we get home.* **2 fall asleep** to begin to sleep: *I always fall asleep watching TV.* **3 half asleep** not paying attention to something because you are tired

The collocations are usually shown in order of frequency – the most important collocations coming first. Notice that the common collocations are in bold and are followed by a definition and/or an example (in italics).

If possible, use a monolingual dictionary to look up the rest of your answers.

Verbs and nouns

3   Look at these five common verbs.

lose   run   make   break   take

a)   Work in pairs and think of as many nouns as possible which collocate with the verbs. Example: *lose = lose your way*

b)   Match the words from the box below to the verbs above. There may be more than one possibility.

the law	a bath	an excuse	part	track
a/the journey	a degree	a risk	a fuss	responsibility
your mind up	your memory	your balance	a car	a promise
arrangements	the news	offence	touch	the country
a business	a record	an effort	count	time off

c)   Work in pairs.
Each write one sentence using two of the collocations above.
Example: **I'd lost track** of how much it cost **to run my car**.

d)   Pass your sentence to the other person. They should use another two collocations to write a sentence which follows on as logically as possible.
Example: *When I realised how expensive it was, I* **broke the news** *to my wife and we* **made up our minds** *that we'd cycle instead.*

e)   Carry on for as long as you can until the 'story' is complete or you give up!

SECTION 2 GRAMMAR: Narrative forms

1a) Rearrange the jumbled pictures and decide on the story.

b) Tell each other the story.

c) Did you use mainly the active or the passive? The simple or the continuous? The present or the past? What are the verb forms commonly used in narrative?

d) Read a version of the story below and underline the best alternative of the verbs in italics.

e) Find an example of the following verb forms: Past Simple, Past Continuous, Past Perfect and Past Perfect Continuous, the Future in the Past.

Stephen Whitty (1) *chatted/had chatted/had been chatting* to a few old friends in a pub and (2) *already had/had already had/had already been having* a couple of beers with them before he (3) *realised/had realised/had been realising* he was late for dinner.

So, at 9 o'clock, he (4) *was leaving/left*. As he (5) *drove/was driving* home he (6) *was seeing/saw* in his mirror a police car following. He (7) *panicked/was panicking*, (8) *sped off/was speeding off* at 100 miles per hour and (9) *hid/was hiding* in a bush.

After he had been sniffed out by police dogs he (10) *was/had been tested* and (11) *was found/was being found* to be under the drink-drive limit.

However, Whitty, 24, (12) *was fined/had been fined* £1,000 for dangerous driving and (13) *was being/was banned* for a year. He also learned he (14) *would have to/was to/was going to have to* retake his driving test.

f) Look at the questions below and discuss your answers. Refer to the Language Reference on page 31 if necessary.

QUESTIONS FOR DISCUSSION

1 Past Simple or Past Perfect?
   a) In (2) why did you choose the Past Perfect in preference to the Past Simple (or vice versa)?
   b) What is the best choice for these sentences?
   I finished/I'd finished my breakfast when he came in.
   Before I went/had gone out I locked up the house.
   When I saw/had seen Paul I stopped for a chat with him.
   c) In which sentence are both alternatives possible?
   d) What is the difference in emphasis between the alternatives?

2 Simple or Continuous?
   a) Did you choose the Past Perfect Continuous in preference to the Past Perfect Simple in (1)? Why?/Why not?
   b) What is the difference in meaning between the sentences below?
   I had been writing letters all day and was worn out.
   I had written six letters.
   c) What made you choose the Past Continuous rather than the Past Simple (or vice versa) in (4)–(9)?
   d) What is the difference in meaning between these sentences?
   I was looking at the clock when Henry came in.
   I looked at the clock when Henry came in.

3 Future in the Past and Past habit
   a) Which of these did you choose in (14) – *would have to*, *was to*, or *was going to have to*? Why?
   b) What is the different use of *would* in these two sentences.
   1   *When we first met he **would** always send me flowers for my birthday, even when he had very little money.*
   2   *When he left I didn't know if I **would** ever see him again.*
   c) In what other ways could you express *would* in the sentences above?

---

2   Read the newspaper story below.

Glen and Linda Thomas (1) *were feeling (feel)* very excited as their jet (2) .... *(take off)* from Manchester airport en route to the Caribbean.
They (3) .... *(wait)* a long time for this day – their daughter, Karen (4) .... *(get)* married two days later on the beach in Antigua.
Unfortunately as soon as they (5) .... *(landed)* they (6) .... *(tell)* that they (7) .... *(not/be able to stay)* because of an imminent hurricane.
Because of this, the Thomas's (8) .... *(fly)* on to the Dominican Republic, where they (9) .... *(stay)* for four days. Meanwhile their daughter, Karen (10) .... *(try)* to switch her wedding to St. Lucia. When that (11) .... *(do)* her parents (12) .... *(agree)* to fly back to Gatwick to pick up a direct flight to St. Lucia. But at Gatwick they (13) .... *(find out)* that the wedding (14) .... *(delay)* for another 24 hours because of a storm. They finally (15) .... *(get)* to the church on time after they (16) .... *(spend)* 28 hours in the air.

(From the *Independent on Sunday*)

a) Change the verbs in brackets to the narrative form which you think is the most appropriate. Sometimes there may be more than one possibility. Be careful – there are some passive forms.

b) Discuss your answers in pairs and justify your choices. Refer to the Language Reference on page 31 if necessary.

▶ **Language Bank page 153: Narrative forms; page 154: The passive**

3 Work in pairs. Both of you have notes based on more news stories. (If you prefer, you can tell a story of your own.)

a) Look at your notes and decide what the story was. Think carefully about the choice of narrative verb forms.

b) Tell your stories to each other. Use your notes as little as possible and try to tell them as fluently as you can. Add any other details you wish to. Try to include some or all of the following:
- A variety of narrative verb forms.
- Linking words such as *then* and *however*.
- Conversational devices such as *just, I mean* or *sort of*.

STUDENT A

Two determined ambulancemen/go to house in a small village/put perfectly healthy person on stretcher/rush him to hospital.
He/protest/but they/ignore him.
'Real' patient (same name/live in the same village/suffer from anaemia) drive/to hospital. Not allowed/register/already registered!

STUDENT B

Married businessman/book in hotel with mistress/give false name Scott Anderson.
Unfortunate choice/man of this name wanted in connection with murder.
Hotel staff contact/police.
Armed officers/creep into bedroom/question/man.
Realise wrong man/apologise.
Man check out. Later hotel staff try/trace him/he and woman not pay bill for £100!

---

c) [🔲 2.2] Listen to the original stories on tape and compare your version.

▶ **Language Bank page 150: Linking expressions**

SECTION 3 READING: Consumer war

Before reading **1** Look at the headline and cartoon.

a) Have you had any experience of being a customer and having to 'fight' for your rights?

b) 'The customer is always right.' Is this true of attitudes in your country?

Oh what a lovely consumer war

The customer is always right – if you fight

Reading **2** Read the first part of the article. Ignore the gaps and numbers at this stage.

ANY DAY I am expecting a man from British Gas to come round and cut off my supply.
(1) *I can't wait!* It will be more fun than the time the man from Sainsbury's supermarket implied I was trying to cheat his company out of £30; better by far than last month's coffee and catfood war; and more delightful than my glorious sausage victory in the Ivy restaurant.
(2) .... Restaurants are good for this; supermarkets better.
(3) .... I'm sure there have been times in all our lives when we've been dying to tell such organisations where to go. (4) .... When the chips are limp and undercooked, the steak overdone and the salad looks as if it has been scraped off someone else's plate, do we tell the waitress what we think of the chef's food?

(5) .... Or what about when, as happened to me, British Gas sends one of its threatening final demands for a bill we've actually paid? Do we ring and spit with fury at their blithering incompetence? (6) ....

a) Insert sentences A–F into the appropriate gaps (1–6) above. The first one is done for you.

A Nothing, however, quite beats a serious humdinger with a faceless corporate monster like British Gas.

B There are few things which give me such pleasure, you see, as a really juicy row about consumer rights.

C Only in our dreams.

D Of course we don't. 'Very nice,' we say.

E I can't wait!

F But how many of us have the courage of our convictions?

b) Read the first part of the article again, and then the second part on page 26. Are the following statements true or false?

1 The writer likes having rows in supermarkets best.

2 He says he always complains about bad service.

3 If the girl on the British Gas hotline hadn't been so rude, the writer probably wouldn't have been aggressive with her.

I have been guilty of such acts of cowardice. Only the other day I consumed, without demur, a plate of soggy chips in a Greenwich pub. And I very nearly chickened out of confronting British Gas. It was the sneery tone of the girl on the consumer hotline that changed my mind. British Gas had no record of my payment, she insisted, and it was highly unlikely to be the company's fault. Maybe, she added with a sarcasm so heavy that you could hear the inverted commas, my cheque had been 'lost in the post'. I rang my bank. The cheque had gone through three weeks before.

By now the blood was up and I was most upset when, the next time I phoned the consumer hotline, it was not answered by the offensive young missie. Instead, I vented my spleen on some anonymous young man, feeling secretly rather bad about it until I realised that he was only marginally less obstreperous than the girl. He suggested that I had probably written the wrong customer code on my cheque and to prove I had paid I must ring my bank and ask them to send a duplicate. 'Oh no,' I yelled back gleefully. 'I've wasted quite enough time already. It's your problem. You solve it.' And having threatened immediate legal action should I be cut off because of British Gas's ineptitude, I slammed down the phone.

I could have handled the situation more subtly. And it might even be that if I do get cut off there will be no legal redress. But I still think it was worth it – both for the cathartic pleasure I derived from having a good old scream and for the sake of all the other customers who have been similarly mistreated.

Only in Britain would companies like British Gas dare to treat their customers with such ill-disguised contempt. And the reason is that they know they can get away with it. 'Don't get mad, get even,' they say in America, where the consumer is king. 'Suffer in silence,' respond the British.

c) Complete the sentences. Underline the correct words in italics in 2.

1 The writer was angry with British Gas because ....

2 He *regrets/doesn't regret* losing his temper with them because ....

3 He blames the attitude of British Gas on ....

3 Read the last part of the article.

My personal complaining debut was not happy. I grumbled to the manager of an Indian restaurant in Oxford that my curry clearly had been made with dry, stale meat from an old roast chicken. 'What do you expect for this price?' he replied. But restaurants that take some pride in their cuisine, like London's Ivy – which once replaced my spicy sausage because I had mentioned that it wasn't spicy – tend to be almost embarrassingly sympathetic.

Large, impersonal organisations such as supermarkets pose more of a problem. But it pays to stick at it. The other week, I kicked up such a stink about the supermarket's continued failure to provide me with Kenya coffee beans and Fisherman's Choice cat food that I was given five free tins of premium tuna.

I suppose, if I were ruthlessly honest, I'd have to admit that one exchanged sausage, five tins of tuna and the threat of a disconnected gas supply are not much to show for a lifetime's complaining. But in years to come, when I'm dangling my children on my knee and they ask, 'Daddy, what did you do in the Great Consumer War?' I'll be able to respond without a blush.

(From *The Daily Telegraph*)

a) Summarise the whole article in two or three sentences.

b) Compare your summaries in groups. Which is the best?

4   Work with a partner and try to work out the meaning of any of the following words and expressions in italics that you don't know.

1   tell such organisations *where to go*
2   I very nearly *chickened out of* confront
3   my cheque had been *'lost in the post'*
4   the consumer *hotline*
5   the offensive *young missie*
6   they know *they can get away with it*
7   *marginally less obstreperous*
8   it pays to *stick at it*

Speaking   **5**   What really annoys you about public services?

a)   Look at this list and add any others you can think of:
  –   Waiting a long time in banks, post offices etc.
  –   Rude shop assistants, waiters etc.
  –   Poor food in restaurants.
  –   Phone boxes that are out of order.
  –   Incorrect bills.
  –   Delayed or cancelled buses, trains etc.
  –   Organisations which don't answer the phone or forget to phone you back.
  –   Inefficient mechanics, builders etc.

b)   Put the list in order (1–8) according to how strongly you feel. Example:
  1 = It makes you furious.
  4 = It irritates you.
  8 = You don't mind.

c)   In groups compare your rankings and give reasons.

d)   Which, if any, of these things would you complain about?

e)   What would you do?

WRITING: Letters

1a) What kind of letters would you write in reply to 1–5 below? Example: *A letter of congratulations for (1).*

b) Make a list of any other types of letter which you personally write in your own language and/or may need to write in English.

① Chris and Vanessa are delighted to announce the birth of Katie Anna Brook (2.8kg) on 9th November

② Send your letters to Talkback

Tell us what really annoys you, what you think about any hot issues, what you would do to put things right. If your letter gets printed, a Talkback mug is yours! And there's a cool Comquest explorer computer (worth £59.99) for the star letter writer. This is where you write: Talkback, Haverstock House, London EC19 2YW

③ Melanie and Guy
request the pleasure of the company of
Sarah, Peter and Alex
at their Marriage in
Preston Registry Office at
12.00 noon on 8th April
with a Service of Blessing at
St. John Baptist Church, Broughton
at 1.00 pm
followed by a Reception at
The Claremont Hotel,
Blackpool Road,
Ashton, Preston

⑤ ROSE'S FLORIST
To Alice with love, Lizzie

④ Have a holiday in Manhattan!
★ ★ ★ ★ ★ ★ ★ ★ ★ ★ ★ ★ ★ ★ ★ ★
See all the sights from an amazing top floor apartment ★ Sleeps 6 ★ Available June–September.
To find out more write to Ricki Sommers
159 Bleecker Street
New York
NY 10772
USA

2 Look at the two letters opposite. What is the purpose of them and how are they different in style?

3 Find at least one example in each letter of a typical feature of formal/informal letters. Use these headings:
a) Grammar
b) Vocabulary
c) Punctuation
d) Layout

Northern Bank plc
23 Trinity Street
Glasgow
G82 5DS

Miss Lorna Charge
24 Ashdon Road
Glasgow
G84 7GT

19 May 1999

Dear Miss Charge,

I thought you would wish to be advised that at
close of business last night your account was
£249.68 overdrawn; no credit has been received
since 2 April 1999.

Please deposit funds to correct the position
within 7 days, or, if this is not possible, please
contact me to discuss how we can best help you.
Borrowing without our agreement does incur charges
in accordance with our published tariff; an early
response will ensure that further charges are kept
to a minimum.

Yours sincerely,

J. Emmett

Mr J Emmett
Manager's Assistant

---

23 Calabria Street
Irvine
CA 92620
14th Dec

Dear Lorna,

A quick note – long overdue! – to say thanks for your lovely letter. It arrived ages ago, but in the excitement and hassle of getting here and settling in I don't seem to have had two minutes to put pen to paper.

We've now moved all our stuff in – the boxes from Britain finally turned up! – so we feel a bit more at home. I have to say I have been feeling dreadfully homesick for my home, friends and family but there are compensations (the swimming pool and lovely weather, for a start!).

We also wanted you to be one of the first to know that I'm expecting a baby – due in May! So I'm feeling as sick as a dog, as well as homesick (but very excited, too)!!

When you last wrote you were just about to go off to university. I bet you're having a great time! You will drop us a line soon and give us all your news, won't you? Are you coming over at Easter, by the way?

Lots of love,

Karen

PS Alex sends his love.

---

4 You are going to choose one of the contexts in Exercise 1 or letters in Exercise 2, and write either a formal or informal letter in response.

1 Before you write, think carefully about who you are writing to because this will influence your choice of language style. Think also about what the purpose of the letter is, and organise your letter clearly so that it will achieve the desired aim.

2 After you have written your letter use the Checklists on page 163 of the Writing Bank for guidelines on how to improve your work. If necessary, revise and redraft the letter.

▶ **Writing Bank page 172: Letters: formal**

SPEAKING: Roleplay

1   Imagine you are in this situation and have missed an important appointment because your car is blocked in.
What would you say to the person who left the car there? Would you be polite, angry or sarcastic?

2   Read the dialogue below.

a)   Find an example of where the man is being sarcastic, and where he is obviously furious.

b)   Guess what the woman is saying? How would you react?

MAN: Oh, so you've decided to come back, then! That's very kind of you!
WOMAN: ....
MAN: A problem? Oh no, no problem. I've just been trying to leave my own house for the last hour and because of you my son has now missed his dental appointment.
WOMAN: ....
MAN: Sorry? Sorry? Is that all you can say?
WOMAN: ....
MAN: It's beyond me how anyone can *not* see the notice. It's large enough! In any case, anyone can see this is private property, if you can be bothered to look.
WOMAN: ....
MAN: I couldn't actually care less where you had to go. I've a good mind to phone the police.
WOMAN: ....
MAN: Don't you dare tell me I'm overreacting.

3   [🔲 2.3]   Listen to the dialogue and write down what the woman says.

4a) Listen again. How do the people sound when they are being sarcastic, angry and apologetic? Describe the difference in tone.

b)   Practise reading the dialogue in pairs.

5   Use some of the language above to roleplay the following situation. Use as many of your own ideas as possible.

STUDENT A: You are sick and tired of your neighbour's noise – crying baby, loud music, their son's piano practice, dog barking, etc. Phone to complain.

STUDENT B: Look at page 179.

NARRATIVE FORMS

Past Simple

The Past Simple is used to talk about:

1 Completed actions or situations which took place at a particular time or over a definite period of time in the past. It is used with definite time expressions such as *on Tuesday, three months ago, in 1992* etc.:
   *I **went** to London last week.*
   *I **worked** for a computer company when I was younger.*

2 Repeated situations in the past:
   *I **travelled** to work by bus every day for a year.*
   NOTE:
   When we talk about habit in the past we can also use *used to* and *would*.

3 Two actions which happen quickly one after the other:
   *When I **saw** him I **crossed** the road to avoid speaking.*
   i.e. NOT the Past Perfect in this case.

NOTE:
The Past Simple is also used to talk about 'unreal' situations in the present and future.

▶ Language Reference page 17: 'Unreal' use of the past

Past Continuous

The Past Continuous is an 'aspect' of the past tense, not a separate tense. In many languages 'aspect' (showing how we look at an action or state in terms of the passing of time) is not expressed by a verb form but by an adverb or by other means.

Like all continuous forms the Past Continuous is used:

1 To emphasise actions which were in progress, and often interrupted by events:
   *At lunchtime yesterday I **was sitting** on the beach when I was stung by a wasp.*

2 For background descriptions to events:
   *We went for a picnic. The sun **was shining** brightly.*

3 For changing states:
   *... but it **was getting** windy.*

4 For temporary situations:
   *I **was finishing** my sandwiches and **enjoying** the sunshine.*

5 For repeated actions – often with an element of criticism implied. You must use *always* in this case:
   *He **was always smoking** in the house.*

6 For past intentions, which are not always carried out:
   *I **was hoping** to have a game of squash but it looks as though it's too late.*

NOTE:
The Past Continuous is also used:

1 To talk about the future in the past:
   *I **was meeting** Fred the next day.*

2 For tentative requests:
   *I **was wondering** whether you could lend me a fiver. Any chance?*

Past Perfect Simple

The Past Perfect Simple is used to talk about an action or situation which happened before a specific time in the past. We use this form if the order of events needs to be emphasised:
*When we got there the train **had left**.*

NOTE:

1 If a time clause makes the sequence clear, the Past Simple is often preferred:
   *The train **left** before we got there.*

2 It is not necessary to use the Past Perfect if one action follows immediately on from (often as a result of) the other:
   *When the thief **saw** the policeman he ran off.*

3 It is not advisable to keep repeating *had* in subsequent clauses. One is usually sufficient to establish the time sequence:
   *It **had been** a very busy day. I'**d got up**, written three letters, made a couple of phone calls and checked my report – all before 9 am.*

Past Perfect Continuous

Like other continuous forms this is used when we want to focus on the activity itself or its effect on us rather than the completed action. It has continued up to the moment we are thinking about:
*When John got back from work I was worn out because I'**d been writing** letters all day.*
(Compare: *By the time John got back from work I **had written** six letters,* where the focus is on the completed activity.)

Future in the Past

When we are talking about the past we sometimes want to talk about something which had not yet happened – which was still in the future.

There are a variety of verb forms to choose from. When we decide which one to choose we follow the same criteria as when we choose a 'normal' future form. The forms are usually 'changed' like this:
is going to → was going to:
*My friend **was going to** come and visit the following week, so I took a few days off work.*

will → would:
*He said he **would** help me move.*

The Present Continuous → the Past Continuous:
*My sister **was getting** married in July so I changed my trip to August.*

It is also possible to use *was to, was about to, was on the point of + -ing*. However, *was to* tends to be more common in formal or literary language:
*Jane rose very early on the day **she was to** be married.*

READING AND WRITING: Crossed wires

Before reading

1 [📼 3.1] Listen to Bernie and find out what makes him unusual.

a) Is there any logic in the associations he experiences?

b) His condition is called synaesthesia (/sɪnɪsˈθiːzɪə/). Does he say anything to suggest that he thinks synaesthesia is a pleasant condition?

2 Work in pairs. You are going to read an article about synaesthesia from a scientific journal.

a) Divide these words between you and look them up in a dictionary.

unobtrusive *(adj)*	to handle (a machine) *(v)*	module *(n)*
tentative *(adj)*	to be distinct (from) *(v)*	to unveil *(v)*
quest *(n)*	to wire (an electrical system) *(v)*	

b) Tell each other the meaning of the words you looked up.

THE SWEET SMELL OF PURPLE

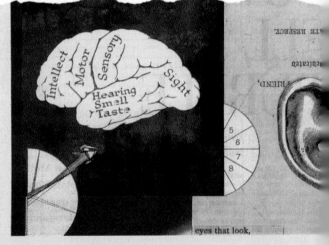

eyes that look,

MURIEL still remembers when her father painted the family house. The paint was white. But it smelled unmistakably blue. Then there's Kristen, who tastes words, complete with texture and temperature.
5 Often the spelling affects the flavour. The name 'Lori', for instance, tastes like a pencil eraser, but the name 'Lauri' tastes lemony.

These two women have synaesthesia, which means that their senses mingle. A stimulus to one
10 sense gives rise to entirely unexpected responses in others. A scent, in Muriel's case, triggers not only smell but colour. Grass might smell purple – or roses grey. The taste of chocolate might bring on a prickly feeling, of pins jabbing into flesh. Sounds, too, evoke
15 colours and shapes. One synaesthetic can picture the green loops of a helicopter's drone; another is assaulted with red daggers on hearing a bell.

Most people with the condition – there are an estimated one in 25,000 – simply hear letters,
20 numbers and words in colour. To them, it is a natural, unobtrusive part of life, like seeing. Synaesthetics aren't impaired, don't 'suffer' and for the most part enjoy their little gift. Amusing and quaint though it is, synaesthesia, neurologists agree,
25 is rather unimportant – at least, it would be if it hadn't fired a debate that goes to the core of how the brain works.

The problem is that synaesthesia is not easily explained. How does this sensory mix-up happen?
30 And where in the brain does it take place? According to the widely-accepted view, the various functions of the brain, senses included, are handled in specialised neural 'modules'. Each module consists of a number of areas of the brain wired together by neural
35 pathways and centred on the cortex, the sheet of tissue that forms the outer shell of the brain and is

Reading 3 Read the article *The Sweet Smell of Purple* from a scientific journal.

a) Find answers to these questions.
1 What exactly is synaesthesia?
2 How is it different in different people?
3 Why has the condition become important to scientists?
4 How is it assumed that the brain normally deals with the senses?
5 How does the British team think synaesthetics' brains differ from 'normal' brains?

b) Compare your answers with another student.

c) Which of these are true according to the text?
1 Some synaesthetics can taste the names of people.
2 The condition is an irritating sickness.
3 Everyone agrees that different sensory activities are dealt with by different parts of the brain.
4 Everyone agrees that the brains of synaesthetics are biologically different from 'normal' brains.

NEW SCIENTIST

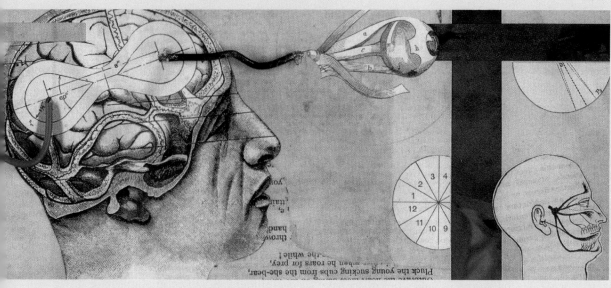

the seat of rational human thought. Information to do with hearing, for instance, is processed in one module, while vision is processed in another.

But synaesthesia seems to defy this segregation: at least two senses are interacting. When Muriel 'smells' the colour of paint, does the activity take place in the brain's 'smell centre' or in the module for vision? Or somewhere else? Is there something special about her brain or could any old brain do this?

A team of psychologists and neurologists in London, headed by Simon Baron-Cohen of the Institute of Psychiatry, has been looking at the condition for six years. They have come to the tentative conclusion that the brains of synaesthetics are biologically distinct. 'In people with synaesthesia,' suggests John Harrison, a neurologist at Charing Cross Hospital and a leading member of the team, 'perhaps unusual pathways link centres of the brain that process what we hear to areas processing what we see.' In other words, their brains are cross-wired. 'It's a perfectly good explanation.'

But not according to an American neurologist, Richard Cytowic of Capitol Neurology, a private clinic in Washington DC. The brains of synaesthetics may not be fundamentally different at all. Far from being a hierarchy, dominated by a 'rational' cortex where functions such as sensory perception are localised and separated, the human brain may be a much more integrated unit. It may be that the neural structures beneath the cortex co-ordinate communication in the brain and decide on the importance of the information being processed. And the quest to explain synaesthesia, he says, has helped to unveil it.

(From the *New Scientist*)

Speaking 4 Ask each other some of these questions.

1 What colours do you associate with: warmth, sadness, anger, jealousy, your country?
2 Do you know any synaesthetics? Would you like to be one? Why?
3 Are there any professions in which synaesthesia would be:
   a) a drawback?
   b) an advantage? (e.g. Artists who have tried to link the senses include the composer Scriabin who saw musical notes as colours and the painter Kandinsky who saw colours as sounds.)

Yellow, Red, Blue 1925, KANDINSKY, © ADAGP, Paris and DACS, London 1999

Before writing 5 You are going to write a summary of the article and you will need to know the words in italics below to have a good understanding of it. Some have a similar meaning. Choose the best synonyms from the box and put the verbs in the correct form.

| influence *(v)* stinging attractively handicap *(v)* attack *(v)* |
| suggest contradict cause *(v)* unusual |

1 the spelling *affects* the flavour (line 5)
2 a stimulus *gives rise to* unexpected responses (line 10)
3 a scent *triggers* a colour (line 11)
4 bring on a *prickly* feeling (line 13)
5 sounds *evoke* colours (line 14)
6 is *assaulted with* red daggers (line 17)
7 synaesthetics aren't *impaired* (line 22)
8 amusing and *quaint* (line 24)
9 if it hadn't *fired* a debate (line 26)
10 seems to *defy* this segregation (line 40)

Writing a summary

6 A summary contains the most essential points of the text without losing the clarity or the emphasis of the original.

a) Look again at the article and put these descriptions of each paragraph in the correct order.
A: Asking about the reason
B: Outlining the latest research findings
C: Opening with examples *(paragraph 1)*
D: The opposing view
E: Stating a problem with the scientific explanation
F: Generalisation linked to the examples
G: Explanation of examples

b) Complete these summaries of each paragraph using one or more words.

1 One synaesthetic's early ………. is of her father ………. the house. ………. the paint was white, she ………. it as blue.

2 Synaesthesia is where there is a ………. for one sense but there is a different ………. in another.

3 The majority of synaesthetics hear through ………. and are ………. with their condition. The reason synaesthesia is ………. to scientists is that it shows how the brain ………. .

4 The condition is ………. to understand. It is thought that the nerves in the ………. link together in different segregated units in order to deal with the different ………. . These ………. link to the outer tissue of the brain called the ………. , which is probably where human beings think.

5 One of the reasons synaesthesia ………. lots of questions about the brain is that it is not clear, for example, which unit deals with colour – is it the ………. unit or the ………. unit?

6 Simon Baron-Cohen and a group of psychologists and neurologists in London ………. people with synaesthesia and they ………. that it is possible that for synaesthetics the links in the nerve centre ………. differently from the rest of us.

7 ………. , Richard Cytowic, in Washington DC, believes the brain is more ………. and it is the ………. not the ………. which direct ………. .

c) Work in pairs and compare your answers.

d) What are the most important pieces of information in the summary in Exercise 6b)? Try to reduce the summary to about half its length (100 words). If necessary, make notes first.

e) Show your summary to other students. How could yours be improved?

▶ **Writing Bank page 177: Summary writing**

VOCABULARY: The senses

1a) When you first think of these do you think of a smell, a taste, a sight, a sound or a feeling?

| coffee | the sea | your mother's name | happiness | the place you work |

b) Which is your favourite/least favourite?

	Favourite	Least favourite
SOUND	*water in a stream*	
SMELL		
TASTE		
SIGHT	*snow on mountain tops*	
FEEL		*fur*

c) Do you believe in a 'sixth sense'? What about telepathy, intuition or déjà-vu? Why/not?

2 Match these adjectives with one or more of the senses.

Example: *musty = smell*

| musty | sour | fragrant | booming | fluffy | stirring | cuddly |
| fuzzy | rancid | mouldy | pungent | squeaky | drab | |

a) What do you associate with each adjective?
Example: *sour = unripe fruit*

b) Think of two more adjectives for each sense.

3 Match the words in A with at least one of the situations in B, giving reasons for your choice. Use a dictionary to help you.

Example: *1 = k) You see a flash of lightning in a thunderstorm.*

	A		**B**
1	flash	a)	people dancing in the room above you
2	clatter	b)	racing car accelerating
3	glint	c)	a dog trying to find drugs
4	stench	d)	a librarian tidying papers in a quiet library
5	thump	e)	a fire of burning rubber
6	rustle	f)	a getaway car driving off and the face of the thief
7	roar	g)	church bells
8	glimpse	h)	dropping tools on a marble floor
9	sniff	i)	wine-tasting
10	peal	j)	mountain stream in the moonlight
		k)	a thunderstorm
		l)	a smoking compartment in a train after everybody gets off
		m)	clearing away cups and saucers
		n)	passing through a small town on a fast train
		o)	trees in a breeze

4 Describe the sights, sounds, smells, tastes and the things you touch in one of these situations. Use some of the words in Exercises 2 and 3 if possible.
– A visit to an exotic market place.
– A forest fire.
– A firework display at a carnival.
– A mountain walk.
– A house the morning after a party.
– A childhood memory.

5 Work in pairs.

a) Ask your partner the questions from the questionnaire.

b) Which answers in the class are most similar to the ones you received?

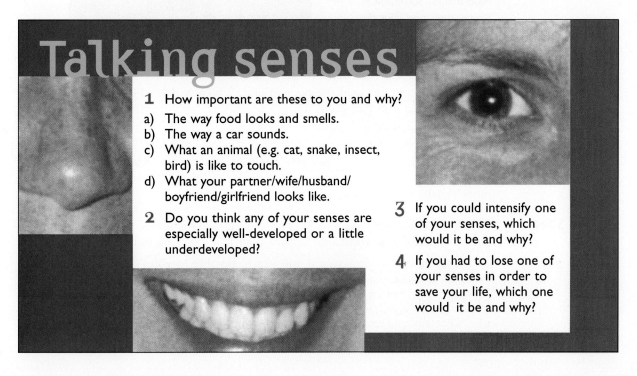

Talking senses

1 How important are these to you and why?
a) The way food looks and smells.
b) The way a car sounds.
c) What an animal (e.g. cat, snake, insect, bird) is like to touch.
d) What your partner/wife/husband/ boyfriend/girlfriend looks like.

2 Do you think any of your senses are especially well-developed or a little underdeveloped?

3 If you could intensify one of your senses, which would it be and why?

4 If you had to lose one of your senses in order to save your life, which one would it be and why?

SECTION 2   LISTENING: *Smithereens*

Before listening   **1**   Read the poem *Smithereens* by Roger McGough, a popular modern poet.

> **smithereens** /ˌsmɪðəˈriːnz/ *n* (plural) a lot of small broken pieces

a)   What do you think the poet means when he says:
1   he collects smithereens?
2   he picks up the leftovers?
3   he pockets eavesdroppings and stores them away?
4   he makes nice things out of them?

Smithereens

I spend my days
collecting smithereens.
I find them on buses
in department stores
and on busy pavements.

At restaurant tables
I pick up the leftovers
of polite conversation.
At railway stations
the tearful debris
of parting lovers.

I pocket my eavesdroppings
and store them away.
I make things out of them.
Nice things, sometimes.
Sometimes odd, like this.

b)   Work with a partner and compare your answers.

c)   You are going to read the poem aloud. Which words will you stress? Where will you pause?

d)   Practise reading the poem.

Listening   **2**   [🔊 3.2]   Listen to Roger McGough introducing and reading the poem. How does his reading compare with yours? (e.g. Does he read it more quickly or more slowly than you? Does he stress words you didn't?)

Speaking   **3**   You are going to listen to Roger McGough talking about how he writes his poetry. Imagine you were able to earn your living writing poetry.

a)   What kind of poems would you like to be able to write (e.g. love poems, poems about places)?

b)   What kind of daily routine would you have? (e.g. Would you write at night?)

c)   What advantages and disadvantages would there be in this kind of life?

d)   Find another student who has similar ideas.

Listening **4** [3.3]   Listen to Extract 1 from the interview.

a) Answer the questions.
1   What experiences has he written about?
2   What is his daily routine?
3   In what way is he similar/different to the poet you imagined you were in Exercise 3?

b) Listen again. Which of these does he say? Say in what way the other sentences are incorrect.
1   He is a serious poet.
2   His humorous poems are only for children.
3   Things he sees on TV can stimulate an idea for a poem.
4   A poet is like a sheep.
5   The only day he doesn't write a poem is on the day of a poetry reading.
6   He writes a poem as soon as he wakes up.
7   He is totally useless at everything except writing poems.

5 Listen to Extract 2 and answer the questions.

1   What does he feel makes a poem different from prose?
2   Are many British people interested in poetry?

Speaking **6** Discuss some of these questions.

a) Can you remember any poems from childhood? What do you think of them now? Have you ever written any poetry?

b) Who are the most famous creative artists in your country at present (e.g. poets, painters, musicians, novelists, film-makers)? Are they:
– original?
– classical and traditional?
– popular with young people?

Wisława Szymborska

Quentin Tarantino

Linda Brava

c) Tell each other about one you like and one you dislike. (What is their subject matter? Why do you like/dislike them?)

d) Which creative artists do you like from other countries?

SPEAKING: Rhythm

1 In English, stressed syllables are usually longer than unstressed syllables.

a) How many syllables are there in each of these words?
1 birthday   4 mosquito
2 return   5 sentiment
3 immigration

b) Underline the stressed syllable in each.

c) Match the following words with the words above according to their stress patterns.
A depressing   D character
B harbour   E giraffe
C disillusion

d) [3.4]   Listen and check.

2a) [3.5]   Listen to these sentences and match the rhythm of how they are said with the words in the box below.

Example: *Go away!* = *lemonade*

1 It's later than that.
2 Do you have to?
3 I don't care what you think.
4 I'll call you at seven.
5 I know what this is.

| exemplification | intelligently | indistinguishable |
| tuberculosis | immigration | |

b) [3.6]   Listen and check.

c) Practise saying each pair.

3 English speech is similar to music in that it has a beat and is created by the alternation of stressed and unstressed syllables.

a) [3.7]   Listen. In terms of rhythm, what do 1–5 have in common?
1 Bread tea soup wine
2 Bread and tea and soup and wine
3 Some bread, some tea, some soup, some wine
4 Some bread and some tea and some soup and some wine
5 Some bread and then some tea and then some soup and then some wine

b) What is the stressed syllable in each of the words below?
1 radishes oranges lettuces cabbages
2 potatoes tomatoes papaya sultanas

c) Now try repeating the rhythms in a) 1–5 but using the nouns in b).

4a) [3.8]   Listen to this dialogue. Which are the two most stressed syllables in each line?

A: What did you say to him?
B: Told him I hated him.
A: Why were you rude to him?
B: Maybe I wanted to be.
A: How was he looking today?
B: Not as he should have been.

b) Work in pairs and practise saying the dialogue with the same rhythm as on the recording.

5 Work in groups.

a) Look at the photographs. How is the idea of love different in each photograph? Which do you think is the strongest? Which do you most identify with?

b) Read the first part of a poem by the Liverpool poet Adrian Henri and think of other situations you associate with the idea of 'love'.

> *Love is ...*
> *Love is feeling cold in the back of vans*
> *Love is a fanclub with only two fans*
> *Love is walking holding paintstained hands*
> *Love is*
> *Love is fish and chips on winter nights*
> *Love is blankets full of strange delights*
> *Love is when you don't put on the light*
> *Love is*

c) Now try to write some lines to finish the poem using a similar rhythm.

SECTION 3   GRAMMAR: Verb patterns

Verb + verb/verb + *that*

1a) Match the verbs in the box with these constructions.

A + -*ing*	B + *to*	C + -*ing/to* (little change in meaning)	D + -*ing/to* + bare inf. (change in meaning)	E + object
avoid *(avoid drinking)*	promise *(promise to help)*	continue *(continue playing/to play)*	remember *(remember posting/to post)*	let *(let me stay)*
resent	want	like	forget	make

agree	help	want	struggle	avoid	make	leave off
regret	burst out	neglect	let	deserve	forget	involve
like	try	face	continue	resent	choose	threaten
admit	promise	mean	remember	know	begin	

Check any you are uncertain about in a dictionary.

b)   What is the difference in meaning between these sentences?
    1   I saw him steal the car.
    2   I saw him stealing the car.

c)   What other verbs can be used instead of *see* in both of the sentences in b) (e.g. *notice*)?

2   Some verbs followed by -*ing* or an infinitive (+ *to*) can also be followed by a *that* clause.

Example:
*The union **agreed to** call off the strike.*
*The union **agreed (that)** they would call off the strike.*

Change these sentences in any way necessary to include a *that* clause after the verb in italics.

1   I *remember* visiting my grandmother every weekend.
2   Tony's *decided* to apply for the job.
3   This *means* you having to fill out a new form.
4   She *admitted* being under 18.
5   He *pretended* to be asleep.
6   My brother *suggested* our going by bus.
7   They *claim* to have discovered a cure for the disease.
8   Sarah *denied* being involved in the accident.

   ▶ **Language Bank page 161: Verbs + -*ing/to*-infinitive/*that***

Verb patterns with reporting verbs

3 When we say what people have said we often try and convey things like their attitude and their tone of voice through 'reporting verbs'.

Example: *'Tell me now,'* he **whispered**.
We can also add an adverb to make it more vivid.
Example: *'Tell me now,'* he whispered **chillingly**.

a) [3.9] Listen to the utterances a–j on the recording and match them with the verbs in 1–10.

1 '.........*d*.........,' he begged.
2 '.................,' shrieked Tania.
3 '.................,' Kirk stammered
4 '.................,' Tania grumbled.
5 '.................,' the man demanded.
6 '.................,' the man insisted.
7 '.................,' he murmured.
8 '.................,' urged Tania.
9 '.................,' she boasted.
10 '.................,' groaned Kirk.

b) Listen again. Which of the adverbs in the box describe how the utterances in a) were said on the recording?

affectionately	nervously	angrily	desperately	excitedly
irritably	defiantly	repeatedly	menacingly	calmly

c) If you were reporting the utterances in Exercise 3a) not using direct speech, how could you do it? Use any other words necessary to make it sound as natural as possible.
Example: *'Please, please let us go,'* he begged. → *He desperately begged the man to let them go.*

4 Reporting verbs have different dependent prepositions.

a) What is the preposition after these verbs?

1 Alison argued .... the personnel manager .... her salary.
2 The goalkeeper apologised .... the referee .... swearing at him.
3 Pete complained .... not being appreciated.
4 The driver in the red car was blamed .... the accident.
5 The Government has hinted .... a big tax cut.
6 The man confessed .... stealing the van.
7 He accused his wife .... lying.
8 We pleaded .... the union not to go on strike.
9 She insisted .... the truth of her story.
10 The director congratulated me .... my success.

b) Check your answers in a dictionary.

▶ **Language Bank page 161: Reported speech**

5 Work in pairs. Read the extract from a detective novel about a sports star, Kenneth Fleming, who is murdered in the cottage he has moved into on his own. On his first night in the cottage Kenneth telephoned his mother. Rewrite the extract, mixing indirect speech with direct speech to describe the phone call vividly.

Begin like this:

> *As soon as he'd moved all of his stuff into the cottage Kenneth phoned his mother to tell her where he was. He knew she had been worried and heard relief in her voice. 'I'm so glad, my dear,' she admitted and asked him affectionately if he had everything he needed ...*

'I'm in.'

'I'm so glad, my dear. You have everything you need?'

'I suppose so. Yes I have. I suppose so.'

'What is it, Ken? Is something wrong with the cottage? You had no trouble getting in?'

'No trouble. It's just ... Nothing. Only ... I'm blithering on. Sounds like I'm going mental, doesn't it?'

'What? What is it? Tell me.'

'I didn't expect to feel ... out of sorts, somehow.'

'Ill?'

'I keep waiting to hear Stan and Jean's voices — them arguing with each other. It's odd they're not here.'

'It's natural you should miss them. Don't be hard on yourself.'

'I suppose I do miss them.'

'Of course you do. They're a large part of your life.'

'It's just that I phoned them and ... Hell, I shouldn't be weeping on your shoulder about this. You've been good to me.'

(Adapted from *Playing for the Ashes* by Elizabeth George)

1 VERB PATTERNS
Verb + verb/verb + *that*

1 The verbs *see, watch, hear, notice, feel* can be followed by these structures:
   a) Verb + object + *-ing* form:
      I saw/watched/heard him stealing *a car.*
      (The act of stealing was in progress when I saw him.)

   b) Verb + object + bare infinitive (without *to*):
      I saw/watched/heard him run *away.*
      (I saw/watched/heard the action from beginning to end.)

   c) *See, hear, notice, feel* (but NOT *watch*) can also be used with a *that* clause:
      I saw (that) *he was having dinner.*
      I heard (that) *he was working for the UN.*

2 Some verbs can be followed by a *to*-infinitive or a *that* clause with the same meaning.
   Examples: *agree, arrange, claim, decide, demand, be determined (I was determined that ...), expect, hope, prefer (formal: I would prefer that ...), pretend, promise, swear, threaten:*
   He pretended to be *asleep.*
   He pretended (that) *he was asleep.*

   NOTE:
   Some verbs can have a difference of meaning:
   *She **learned to** live with the situation.* (= learn how to)
   *I **learned that** the letter never arrived.* (= discovered that)

3 Some verbs can be followed by an *-ing* verb or a *that* clause.
   Examples: *appreciate, deny, mention, resent, suggest:*
   I suggest waiting *five minutes.*
   I suggest (that) we (should) wait *five minutes.*
   *Do you **deny breaking** the vase?*
   *Do you **deny (that) you broke** the vase?*

4 Some verbs followed by *-ing* or a *to*-infinitive cannot be followed by a *that* clause.
   Examples: *avoid, can't stand, enjoy, look forward to, be committed to, dedicate one's life to* (+ *-ing*)
   choose, refuse, want (+ *to*-infinitive)

5 In some (usually formal) *that* clauses we can use *should* or the 'subjunctive' (which can have the same form as the present or past simple):
   He insisted that we (should) bring/we brought *a picnic.*
   She recommends/recommended that I (should) see/I saw *a doctor.*
   I propose that you (should) be/you are *chairman.*
   I suggest (that) we (should) wait *five minutes.*

   NOTE:
   The third person 'subjunctive' can be used with or without 's':
   I suggest (that) he go/goes *now.*

Verb + object + *to*-infinitive

Some verbs can be followed by an object + *to*-infinitive.
Examples: *ask, beg, challenge, dare, encourage, forbid, force, invite, order, persuade, remind, request, send, teach, tell, urge, warn:*
*The doctor **advised me to take** a long holiday.*
*She **invited me to stay** with her.*

NOTE:
Some but not all of these verbs can be followed by a *that* clause:
*He **advised me that** I should take ... (but NOT ~~invited~~ me that ...)*

Other patterns

The following patterns apply to these verbs:
*He **admitted (to) making** a mistake. (He admitted that he **had** made ...)*
*I've **known her (to) get** very upset.*
*Will you **help me (to) start** the car?*
(to is optional)
*I **made him clean** his room. (without to)*
BUT:
*He **was made to** clean the car. (to in the passive)*
***Let me come** with you. (without to)*

NOTE: *Let*, meaning *allow*, has no passive form and we have to use *be allowed to* instead: *he was allowed to ...*

2 REPORTING VERBS

When we report what people have said we use a variety of verbs and adverbs:
*'Well done!' **exclaimed** Tom.*
(In indirect speech, this could be reported as: *Tom **congratulated her warmly** on her success.*)

Useful reporting verbs include:
acknowledge, advise, agree, allege, announce, argue, beg, boast, claim, comment, complain, confirm, declare, explain, hint, implore, inquire, insist, maintain, object, observe, plead, point out, protest, reiterate, state, stress, underline, warn

NOTE:
1 Many reporting verbs can be followed by a *that* clause:
   *He **implied/added** that all was not well.*

2 You will need to check in a dictionary which are *transitive* (followed by an object) or *intransitive* (not followed by an object) or both:
   *Nothing will **persuade me** that/to ... (transitive)*
   *She **admitted that** she was defeated. (intransitive)*

3 You will also need to check on dependent prepositions:
   *apologise (to someone) **for/about**, accuse (someone) **of***

4 To give a text more colour we often use verbs which describe how the person speaks:
   stammer, shriek, groan, screech, yell, squeal, mumble

ANOTHER COUNTRY

GRAMMAR: Giving emphasis

Reading

1 In the newspaper article below, Giles Coren, an ex-university student, gives his opinions on 'gap years'. In Britain a gap year refers to a year off between leaving school and starting higher or further education, or between finishing your education and starting work.

Traditionally, students have used this year to travel and experience life in other countries, often by working there.

a) What advantages and disadvantages do you think there might be in having a 'gap year'? Is it common in your country?

b) Would you like or would you have liked the opportunity to travel and work in other countries for a year at this age? Give a reason.

2a) Read the text and compare what Giles says with your ideas.

There is absolutely nothing at all to be said for taking a year out between school and university and using it to
5 travel the world. Supporters of the gap-year fraud claim that it broadens the mind. As if a broad mind were of any use at all in settling down to the miserable
10 grist of a workaday existence – in life it is only those with the very narrowest horizons who survive.

The first disaster was that my
15 chosen university insisted that I took a year off.

'You will be very welcome in 1989,' they said. 'But you need to mature.' 'Mature?' I was not
20 a cheese. Did that venerable begowned gentleman actually believe that to pick up an exotic disease or lose my right arm wrestling with an alligator in the
25 Amazon would in some way make me keener to read Spenser?

I will never know. All I do know is that I had the prospect

30 of 15 months before I started university with nothing to do and no money. I really didn't want to travel.

What is more, even if I had
35 wanted to go away I couldn't have afforded it.

It is the private income posse who travel. Dosh from Daddy. They will say that they 'worked'
40 for their round the world air ticket meaning 'I earned nine pounds for walking the neighbour's dog and my parents paid the rest.' It is they, and only
45 they, who go away.

But, and here is the point, I learnt more about life, death and the nature of humanity in the 15

months that I spent working in
50 London than anyone who came back from the depths of South-East Asia. Far more enlivening to work a till in Harrods and see what happens to a posh woman
55 in a Hermes scarf when her credit card won't work.

Whatever you do in your gap year you do not mature but merely age. And wherever you
60 spend your time it is wasted. However good you might think your gap year was, if you hadn't taken it you would be a year younger now.

Spenser, Edmund: a 16th century English poet

(From *The Times*)

b) Which of these titles do you think would be the best one for the article? Why?
- Diseases and alligators: The risks and rewards
- Foreign travel: No way to bridge the dreaded gap
- A gap year: Time off well spent?

c) Which of Giles's opinions do you agree or disagree with?

d) Comment on the tone/attitude of the article. Is it cynical? Light-hearted? Funny? Find words or phrases to justify your choices. Example: He is quite cynical (*it is only those with the very narrowest horizons who survive* – line 11).

Emphatic words and expressions

3 In the article Giles uses the following words and expressions.

absolutely	at all	only	actually	do	really	even

a) Look back at the text to see how these words are used to make his writing more emphatic.

b) Look at the sentences below and add one of the words from the box where you see the symbol *. There may be more than one possibility.

1 A: Shall we go?
  B: Go!? I've * just arrived!

2 A: It was a nice wedding, didn't you think?
  B: Yes, but I'm afraid I didn't like Lisa's dress * .

3 A: Did you get a lot of work done while I was out?
  B: I finished it! I * managed to sort out my papers.

4 A: 'Bye. I * hope you'll enjoy the film.
  B: I'm sure we will. See you later.

5 A: Was the film good?
  B: It was * brilliant!

6 A: How are you getting on with Hannah these days?
  B: I can't believe it. She's * invited me to lunch!

7 A: Does this look OK?
  B: Yes, great. I * like you in red.

c) [4.1] Listen to the sentences for one possible interpretation, and practise reading them.

4a) Look at the Language Reference (1, 2 and 3) on page 59 for examples of other emphatic words and expressions. Then rewrite the sentences in italics to include the word in brackets.

Example: That was a wonderful meal! *I hadn't realised what an amazing cook you were.* (such) – *I hadn't realised that you were such an amazing cook.*

1 I think they must be going out together. *Every time I see him, he's with her.* (whenever)
2 *I've told you many times not to do that.* Stop it! (over)
3 That was Joe on the phone. *He's getting increasingly worried about his job situation.* (more)
4 Nobody's helping me this time. *I'm doing it on my own.* (myself)
5 *No, I'm not at all tired.* Let's go a bit further. (least)
6 There was a big drama today! *The producer got up and walked out.* (just)
7 *I enjoyed seeing you yesterday.* (did)

b) [4.2] Listen to the recording and compare the sentences to your own. Listen to both the grammar and pronunciation.

Grammatical emphasis

5   Another way of giving emphasis is to change the focus of a sentence or clause. A common way in both writing and speaking is to use 'cleft sentences'. These are sentences beginning with:

1 *It is/was ... that/who ...* or 2 *What/all ... is/was ...*

Examples:
it is *only those with the very narrowest horizons* ***who*** *survive.* (line 11)
(instead of *only those with the very narrowest horizons survive.*)
All *I do know* ***is*** *that I had the prospect of 15 months ... with nothing to do ...*
(line 28) (instead of *I will never know. But I do know that ...*)

a)   Look at lines 37–38 and 44–45 for two more examples of the first construction (*It is ...*).

b)   How would you say these in a less emphatic way?

6a) Look at the sentence and complete the unfinished sentences.

Tim phoned me yesterday from London. (neutral word order)

1   It was yesterday that *Tim phoned.*
2   It was me that ....
3   It was Tim who ....
4   It was London that ....
5   What Tim did was ....
6   Where Tim phoned from ....

b)   Which structures focus on the verb and which focus on the noun/adverb?

c)   Where does the main stress fall in the different sentences?

d)   [4.3]   Listen and check.

7   Work in pairs and rephrase these sentences to bring a different part of the sentence into focus. Practise saying them.

Example: You need a holiday! What ***you*** *need is a holiday.*

1   My mother taught me how to cook.
    It ....

2   I'd love to be on a beach.
    Where ....

3   Come on! I'm only asking for £5!
    All ....

4   I reversed into a wall and bent the bumper.
    What happened ....

5   I normally leave my bike at the station and get the train.
    What ....

6   No, in fact *I* didn't see you, John did.
    It ....

8   Work in pairs. Use the words and structures introduced in this section to talk about things you feel strongly about. (Examples: things you love, need, want, are worried about, frightened by etc.) Give your opinion on issues such as the Internet, computer games for children, traffic in towns, drugs, etc.

▶ **Language Bank page 146: Emphasis: inversion**

VOCABULARY: *Just*

Just look at that – isn't that just amazing?

1a) The word *just* is very common in spoken English. It has many uses. For example, it can:
– be used for emphasis (like *simply* or *absolutely*)
– mean *only*
– mean *exactly*
– be used as a softener when asking for something

What do you think the meaning of *just* is in each of the sentences below?
1   A cup of tea's just what I needed. Thanks!
2   I just couldn't say a word!
3   It'll just take a few seconds.
4   Can I just use your pen a second?
5   Could I use your pen just for a second?
6   That meal was just fantastic!
7   Just at that moment the bell rang.
8   I just called to say I love you.

b)   [🔊 4.4]   Listen to the sentences above and then practise reading them. Notice that the *t* in *just* disappears in the sentences above if there is a consonant following, e.g. *just what I* /dʒəswɒtaɪ/ or it links to the vowel if there is one following, e.g. *Just at* /dʒəstət/.

c)   Work in pairs and build up a dialogue following the notes below. Try to include *just* in each sentence.

   A: You want to try out B's new computer.
   B: Agree, but emphasise that you need to use it in ten minutes.
   A: Say how wonderful it is and how it's exactly what you were looking for.

d)   Now continue the dialogue using your own ideas, trying to use *just* where possible.

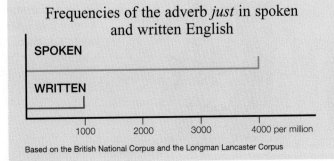

Frequencies of the adverb *just* in spoken and written English

SPOKEN

WRITTEN

1000   2000   3000   4000 per million

Based on the British National Corpus and the Longman Lancaster Corpus

This graph shows that the adverb *just* is much more common in spoken English than in written English. This is because it is very commonly used in spoken English to mean 'exactly' or to mean 'a short time before or after'. It also has special uses in spoken English and is used in a lot of common spoken phrases.

SECTION 2 — SPEAKING: Shifting stress

1 Although it is usually 'content' words that we stress in spoken English (see Unit 1 page 14) we can, in fact, stress any word in a sentence, including 'grammar words', in order to bring something into focus. This often contrasts with or corrects what someone else has said.

a) [📼 4.5] Listen to the following sentences. Underline the word that is most stressed in each sentence. Ignore the words in italics for the moment.

1 He told me Peter was going to buy a new car.
- *not a motorbike*
- *not a second-hand one*
- *not Fred*

2 I wish you hadn't told her about the money.
- *I wish someone else had*
- *I wish you'd written to her*
- *I wish you'd told her husband*

3 I think he said he worked in France.
- *but I'm not sure*
- *not lived there*
- *not Germany*

b) Which of the statements in italics would be the most obvious extension of the sentence with the stress you chose?

2a) Mark the stressed word in the replies below.

Example:
A: *Have you eaten any of that chocolate yet?*
B: *I've eaten <u>all</u> of it!*

1 A: Did you see that scary film last night?
  B: No, but I heard about it.

2 A: Do you work for Ian?
  B: Well ... I work with him!

3 A: Was there a lot of traffic on the motorway?
  B: No, surprisingly, only when we came off.

4 A: When's Tessa expecting her baby?
  B: She's had it, actually.

b) Why did you stress those specific words?

3a) Underline the words you think carry the main stress in the following dialogues.

1 A: Have you seen my keys anywhere?
  B: They're probably on the shelf.
  A: Which shelf? I can't see them.
  B: No, not that shelf. The top one. Where you usually put them.
  A: Do I? Ah, there they are. Thanks a lot.

2 A: I can't decide whether to get him a shirt or a CD.
   B: But he's got millions of shirts.
   A: Yes, but not nice ones. Look at these.
   B: Get him a CD.
   A: Yes, but which CD? The problem is, I don't know what he's got. No, I think I'll get him a shirt. Now, shall I get him a plain one or a striped one?

b) [🖭 4.6] Listen and compare with the recording.

4 Read the following sentences and think how you might finish them. The word to be stressed is the one in italics.

1 I suppose I *could* go, ...
2 I'm looking forward to the actual *holiday*, ...
3 She's very *sweet*, ...
4 The *son* is very nice, ...
5 I've left the bike at the *back* of the house ...
6 I'm afraid that's *his* problem, ...

VOCABULARY: Emphasising adjectives

1 The adjectives in Box A are sometimes called 'scale' adjectives (we can use adverbs such as *very* or *a bit* to make them stronger or weaker e.g. *very busy*). Those in Box B are sometimes called 'limit' adjectives (they are already 'emphatic adjectives' so they cannot be made stronger or weaker. However, they can be emphasised using adverbs such as *absolutely* e.g. *absolutely exhausted*).

A

cold	small	tired	important	sure	shocked	funny	angry
long	bad	silly	interesting	busy	happy	noisy	

B

hilarious	deafening	minute	fascinating	interminable	crucial
ecstatic	convinced	appalled	livid	exhausted	disastrous
freezing	hectic	ridiculous			

a) Match each adjective in Box A with a stronger one in Box B and mark the stressed syllable in words of more than one syllable.
Example: *cold/'freezing*.

b) In pairs, write down as many adverbs as you can that can go with 1) 'scale' and 2) 'limit' adjectives.

2   Look at the adverb and adjective collocations below.

a)   Match the adverbs on the left with the adjectives they usually collocate with on the right.

> NOTE: *Quite* has two meanings. If it is used with a 'scale' adjective (e.g. *quite **difficult***) it means *a bit* and if it is used with a 'limit' adjective (e.g. *quite **impossible***) it means *completely*.

| 1 | really | happy | 2 | completely | disgusted |
| | absolutely | furious | | a bit | tired |

| 3 | quite | amazing | 4 | extremely | livid |
| | utterly | difficult | | absolutely | angry |

| 5 | pretty | relaxed | 6 | quite | funny |
| | totally | good | | very | convinced |

b)   Compare these adverbs with the ones you thought of in Exercise 1b).

3a) [🔲 4.7]   Listen to somebody talking about a summer school she attended.

> The lessons were quite interesting but the school was absolutely filthy and totally disorganised. And the flat we were staying in was fairly modern and rather nice but the other people who shared it were absolutely awful and incredibly noisy.

b)   Practise reading the extract above, giving the adverbs which go with the 'limit' adjectives more emphasis by stressing them and raising the voice a little.

c)   Work in pairs. Agree with the following statements, using an adverb and a 'scale' or 'limit' adjective. Think about how you say them.

Example:
You look very tired.   I believe the house is minute.
Tired? I'm absolutely exhausted!   *Yes, it's quite small.*

1   Was the disco really loud?
2   Did you think that programme was funny?
3   I believe you had a hectic holiday.
4   I was appalled by the news, weren't you?

d)   Think of some other examples of your own.

4   Work in pairs.

a)   Describe things, places or people you know. Try to use at least one 'scale' and one 'limit' adjective, together with the appropriate adverb.

Example: Someone you like/dislike.
My brother's best friend is incredibly tedious.

1   A place you've been on holiday.
2   A room you like/dislike.
3   A CD you love/hate.
4   A meal out you've had recently.

b)   Talk about things that:
1   you find quite difficult to do.
2   make you feel very relaxed.
3   you think is/are absolutely amazing.
4   make you rather upset.
5   you are utterly convinced about.
6   you are completely disgusted by.

SECTION 3 LISTENING: *Italian neighbours*

Before listening **1** Tim Parks, a writer, has lived in Italy since 1981 and is married to an Italian. Look at the photos above. What differences do you think there are between living in Italy and living in your own country? Or, if you are Italian, between living in Italy and another country?

Listening **2** [4.8] You are going to listen to Tim talking about living in Italy.

a) Listen to Extract 1 of the interview and find answers to the questions.
  1 What does Tim say is difficult for foreigners about living in Italy?
  2 What relevance do the following people and places have to this difficulty?
    – the local doctor
    – Naples
    – the university
  3 What is his attitude to the difficulty? Does he find it irritating or amusing?

b) What is it/would it be like to live in a place like this? Fun? Irritating? Give reasons.

c) What is your country's attitude to official rules?
  1 Do people habitually break them?
  2 Do people always want them changed or revoked?
  3 Are there any you think should be changed? If so, why?

d) What are the things which a foreigner living in your country would find difficult? Give examples.

e) Listen again, focusing on the anecdote about the taxi driver. Then imagine you are Tim and tell the story, using the cues below to help you.
Tell it either in the present tense (as he does) or in the past. Try to use some of the conversational expressions that he does e.g. *actually, I mean, well, and so on, just, you know.* (See the tapescript on page 185.)
  1 Naples/famous/chaotic traffic
  2 first time/visit/come/from airport/in taxi
  3 driver/go/too fast/go through red lights
  4 stop/at red light/ask why stop
  5 this/light you stop at/we know that

3a) Listen to the first part of Extract 2. What is Tim saying about national stereotypes?

1 They don't exist – every person is different.
2 There is some truth in them but they are exaggerated.
3 They are surprisingly true.

b) Do you agree with his view on national stereotypes? Why?/Why not?

4 You are going to listen to the second part of Extract 2.

a) Can you guess what the British think the Italians are like? Can you guess what the Italians think the British are like?

b) Listen and make notes on how the Italians see the British and vice versa.

c) How do your notes compare with your predictions in Exercise 4a)?

5 How would you define the 'national character' for your nationality? Is it the same as the stereotypical view which people have of people in your country?

READING: *Notes from a small island*

Before reading　Bill Bryson is an American writer, married to an English woman, who lived in Britain for nearly twenty years.

1　In the following extract from his book *Notes From a Small Island* Bryson makes these observations of the British people:
– They are the happiest people on earth.
– They are so easy to please.
– They have a curious attitude to pleasure.
– They have a tireless, dogged optimism.

a) Why do you think he says these things? Have you got any experiences to back them up or contradict them?

b) Do any of these observations surprise you, based on what you know about the British?

Reading　**2a)** Read the text and find more information about the observations in Exercise 1 (e.g. What makes him think the British are the happiest people on earth?).

b) In what way do you think Bryson's life became 'immensely richer'?

3a) What do you learn about Americans from the text?

1 What is alien to the American mind?
2 What, for them, is the whole purpose of living?
3 What is a birthright for them?

b) Do you think Bryson is serious in his comments on the Americans? Can you think of any other characteristics you could attribute to Americans?

One of the charms of the British is that they have so little idea of their own virtues, and nowhere is this more true than with their happiness. You will laugh to hear me say it, but they are the happiest people on earth. Honestly. Watch any two Britons in conversation and see how long it is before they smile or laugh over some joke or pleasantry. It won't be more than a few seconds.

And the British are so easy to please. It is the most extraordinary thing. They actually like their pleasures small. That is why, I suppose, so many of their treats – teacakes, scones, crumpets, rock cakes, rich tea biscuits, fruit Shrewsburys – are so cautiously flavourful. They are the only people in the world who think of jam and currants as thrilling constituents of a pudding or cake. Offer them something genuinely tempting – a slice of gateau or a choice of chocolates from a box – and they will nearly always hesitate and begin to worry that it's unwarranted and excessive, as if any pleasure beyond a very modest threshold is vaguely unseemly.

'Oh, I shouldn't really,' they say.

'Oh, go on,' you prod encouragingly.

'Well, just a small one then,' they say, and dartingly take a small one, and then get a look as if they've done something terribly devilish.

All this is completely alien to the American mind. To an American the whole purpose of living, the one constant confirmation of continued existence, is to cram as much sensual pleasure as possible into one's mouth more or less continuously. Gratification, instant and lavish, is a birthright. You might as well say 'Oh, I shouldn't really' if someone tells you to take a deep breath.

I used to be puzzled by the curious British attitude to pleasure, and that tireless, dogged optimism of theirs that allowed them to attach an upbeat turn of phrase to the direst inadequacies. – 'well, it makes a change', 'mustn't grumble', 'you could do worse', 'it's not much, but it's cheap and cheerful', 'it was quite nice really' – but gradually I came round to their way of thinking and my life has never been happier.

I remember finding myself sitting in damp clothes in a cold cafe on a dreary seaside promenade and being presented with a cup of tea and a teacake and going 'Ooh, lovely!', and I knew then that the process had started. Before long I came to regard all kinds of activities – asking for more toast in a hotel, buying wool-rich socks at Marks & Spencer, getting two pairs of trousers when I really only needed one – as something daring, very nearly illicit. My life became immensely richer.

Speaking **4** Work in groups and discuss any experiences you have of living or holidaying in a different culture.

a) Was it as you had expected? For example, did the people conform to the stereotypical image you may have had of them?

b) What did you particularly enjoy or dislike about being there?

c) In what ways was life there very different to being in your own country?

5 If you could choose somewhere else to spend a few years, which country would you choose? Why? Which would you definitely not choose? Give reasons.

6 Discuss these views on national characteristics. Do you agree with them?

– 'When you meet somebody of your own nationality you can usually tell at once what they're like (their background, politics etc.). You can never really do this in a foreign culture.'

– 'When you are fluent in another language you feel different and freer than you do when you're speaking your own language.'

– 'Language reflects national character more than anything else. For example, the Italian language reflects the importance Italians attach to formal presentation and appearance.'

– 'In the modern world with global communications it is unnecessary and undesirable for us to hold on to our national character.'

Vocabulary **7** *Actually* is a very common expression, used by both Bryson and Parks.

a) Match each of the examples of what they say with the uses in the box.
1 *They (the British) **actually** like their pleasures small.*
2 *(there is) ... a difference between the official way of doing things and the way things are **actually** done.*

SOME USES OF *ACTUALLY*

a) to correct information or expectations
b) to confirm information or expectations
c) to clarify/give extra information
d) as a softener, before bad news
e) for emphasis, to introduce surprising information
f) to mean 'in reality'

---

b) Match the other four uses in the box with the sentences below.
1 A: Has Fred sold his car yet? B: Yes he has, actually.
2 I'm in a hurry so I won't stop. Actually, I'm meeting Richard.
3 A: Are you still on for Friday. B: Well, actually, we're not going to be able to make it, I'm afraid.
4 A: When are you off on holiday? B: Well, actually, we're not going now.

c) Add *actually* to each of the sentences in italics below.
1 A: Did you enjoy the film?
   B: *Well, I didn't go in the end.*
2 A: *Rumour has it that she walked out of the meeting!*
   B: Really! Why?
3 A: I'm intending to do my tax return this weekend.
   B: *Yes, but will you **do** it?*
4 A: Surely it isn't going to rain again!
   B: *I'm afraid it is.*
5 A: Have you got a second, Jim?
   B: *Well, I'm afraid I'm just on my way out.*
6 A: That's our new neighbour, Harriet Walker.
   B: Oh yes, I know her. *Her son's in Hannah's class.*

d) [📼 4.9]   Listen to the exchanges on the recording and practise saying them.

> NOTE: *Actually* (or *actual*) does NOT mean at the present time. We say *I am* **currently** *working part-time*, or *I am working part-time* **at the moment** (NOT *I am* ~~*actually*~~ *working part-time*).

e)   Work in groups.
1   Write down five sentences about other people in the group.
2   Read out your sentences to each other.
3   Correct or confirm the information you are given about yourself, or add extra or surprising information.
Examples:
Well, actually, my exam's in ***June***, *not July.*
Yes, I ***do*** *go windsurfing, actually. Who told you?*
Yes, you're right, I ***am*** *22. Actually, it's my birthday tomorrow.*

WRITING: Report writing

What a racket

A Best Buy tennis racket may not win you Wimbledon, but it could improve your game

Long summer nights and the smell of freshly-mown grass are sure signs that the tennis season has arrived. If you play tennis regularly, and think it's about time to treat yourself to a new racket, use this guide to help you pick the right one. We've tested a range of rackets costing from £50 to £130.

Positive Health Choices

For you to fully understand the potential benefits of making desirable lifestyle changes, including regular, moderate exercise, it is important to consider your present lifestyle and current fitness level. A baseline of information about yourself helps you to focus clearly upon your personal goals and provides a start point from which to measure improvements in your health and fitness.

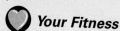 **Your Fitness**

Being in good shape gives to us all a great feeling of personal well-being. Our fitness is something that we can all improve, no matter what level we're at.

* You scored well in the Strength and Stamina Tests. Well done.

* Your body fat is within the acceptable range and therefore not likely to be a health risk to you.

The following pages provide you with a full profile of your individual lifestyle and your fitness scores and ratings.

1a) What are the reports above about? What is the aim of each?

b)   Have you had to or do you have to write or read reports? If so, what kind?

c)   Has anyone written a report on you, something you did or have been involved with?

2   Linking expressions can make your writing clearer and easier to follow. Check how well you can use them by completing the sentences below. If you find you need revision of both types of linking expressions there are more exercises in the Language Bank on pages 150–152.

1   The prices were much too high. Consequently, ...
                                                            However, ...
                                                            Moreover, ...

2   I really enjoyed the disco, although ....
                                            despite ....
                                            much as ....

3   It's a beautiful country. Yet, ...
                                    In addition, ...
                                    Nonetheless, ...

4   I decided I'd hand in my notice in case ....
                                                unless ....
                                                as soon as ....

5   I missed the plane. As a result, ...
                                        Furthermore, ...
                                        All things considered, ...

6   I couldn't think of a good excuse. Otherwise ....
                                                    Even so ....
                                                    Instead ....

3   You are going to write a short report.

a)   Choose one of the ideas below or an idea of your own. Think about who your readers will be.

1   The local council has asked students at your university to prepare a report on shopping facilities in your town, with a view to opening new shops based on your recommendations.

2   Write one of the following for your college newspaper:
   – A report on a hotel you have stayed in.
   – A report on a meal you have had in a restaurant.
   – A report of a place you have visited (e.g. a university in another country; a museum in a different city).

The Rainforest Cafe, London

b)   Give your report to someone else to read, and ask for their suggestions for improvement.

▶ **Writing Bank page 175: Report writing**

GIVING EMPHASIS

There are many ways in which we can give emphasis when we write or speak.

1 EMPHATIC WORDS AND EXPRESSIONS

It is important to note carefully the position in the sentence of the emphatic words in bold in these examples.

With adjectives

It was **really** tasty/**very** tasty **indeed**!
It was **absolutely/simply/just/utterly/quite** marvellous!
She's a **great deal/far/much/even** cleverer than him.
Leave him alone. He's **only** small.
It's not **at all/in the least** interesting.
That was **bloody** awful. (Note that 'bloody' is sometimes regarded as taboo language.)

NOTE:
1 **So** is used to emphasise an adjective (with or without a noun) or an adverb:
   She's **so** annoying. He speaks **so** fast I can't understand.
   It is also used before much, many, few, little:
   You've got **so many** toys/**so much** patience/**so little** time.

2 **Such** is used before a noun, with or without an adjective. It can be followed by a/an:
   She's **such an** annoying woman./It's **such** awful weather.

With verbs

She **actually/even** cooked us breakfast.
I **only** touched it./I've **only** just arrived.
I **totally** disagree./I agree **entirely/absolutely**.
He **strongly/really** objected to the plan.
She **just/simply** disappeared without trace.
I don't like that **at all/in the least/in the slightest**.

In the following examples the auxiliaries do, was and have are used to create emphasis:
I **do** hope you'll like it. If she **did** come, I didn't see her.
I **was** there. Didn't you see me? I **have** enjoyed seeing you!

With nouns and pronouns

It was my **own** idea. I thought of it **myself**.
I like them all; **even** Jim.
I've got **absolutely** nothing **at all** to say.
He's **only** a child.
It's **actually/really** his, not mine.
I haven't got any money **whatsoever**.

NOTE:
Reflexive pronouns can be used to emphasise subject or object:
The manager **himself** spoke to me.
Do you actually get to see the woman **herself**?

2 WHO, WHAT, WHEN, WHERE, HOW, WHY (EVER); NO MATTER

1 These words can act as a subject or object in their own clauses:
   Whatever you did, I'm sure it was fine.
   Whoever did this it's a disgrace.

   A clause with whoever etc. can also act as a subject or object of the verb in another clause:
   Whoever committed this crime will be found out.
   I'll do **whatever** I want.

2 They can also emphasise questions:
   Whatever is going on? **Why ever** have you bought that?

NOTE:
Other expressions can also be used with questions for added emphasis:
What **on earth** has happened?
What **the hell** does he think he's doing?
How **in the world** can I do that?

3 REPEATING THE VERB, INTENSIFIER, ADJECTIVE ETC.

I tried **and tried** and got more **and more** tired.
I was very, **very** angry.
I rang you over **and over** again yesterday.

4 CLEFT SENTENCES

Cleft sentences are so called because the sentence is divided into two parts, with the emphasis on one part, giving it extra importance.

It + is/was + subject/object + relative clause

1 In cleft sentences beginning with the preparatory it the words to be emphasised are joined to the relative clause by that (or who etc.) The word or phrase to be emphasised comes after it is/was.
   A 'neutral' sentence such as My friend sent a letter to the boss yesterday can shift its focus to a noun or adverb (not a verb) depending on what comes after it:
   It was **my friend** who sent a letter to the boss.
   It was **yesterday** that my friend sent a letter to the boss.

2 This structure is very useful when clarifying information that has been misunderstood:
   A: Here's your tea.
   B: Well, actually **it was coffee** (that) I ordered.
   When we are writing we can't use our voice to stress particular words to make a point as we do when we are speaking, so cleft sentences are particularly useful here.

NOTE:
If the word to be emphasised is a pronoun, many people prefer to use the more informal It's me who's responsible or It was him that did it rather than the more formally correct It is I who am responsible or It was he that did it.

What or all + subject + verb + is/was

1 The structure with what (the thing that) or all gives special focus to the verb and following clause – especially verbs such as like, hate, need and want:
   I hate sugary drinks. → **What I hate is** sugary drinks.
   All I want is to get a bit of peace and quiet.
   What I saw was absolutely fascinating.
   All I know is she is guilty!

2 Do or did are often used to focus on the verb:
   She usually leaves her car at the station. →
   What she usually does is (to) leave her car at the station.
   They eventually phoned the police. →
   What they eventually did was (to) phone the police.

3 Even more emphasis can be given to the sentence as a whole by using what happened was before the clause:
   What happened was (that) they eventually phoned the police.

BUSINESS OR PLEASURE?

LISTENING: Commercial breaks

Before listening

1a) How does each of the advertisements below try to appeal to us?

b) Have you ever bought or would you buy any of the products?

2a) [🔲 5.1] Listen to these short extracts from a discussion about advertising. One of these is *not* referred to. Which is it?
– an advantage of advertising
– music in ads
– the kind of people ads are aimed at
– images that make us uncomfortable
– the ability of advertising to make you choose a product

b) Discuss answers to these questions:
1 Is there anything they say you agree or don't agree with? Give reasons.
2 Think of your three favourite advertisements. Which medium (TV, print, radio) is each in ? What makes them attractive to you (e.g. the humour)? What kind of people are they aimed at (e.g. the young)?
3 Does advertising make you buy things? If so, what?
4 Do you mind being manipulated by advertisements? Give reasons.

Listening 3 Trevor Beattie has created a number of successful advertisements including numbers 1 and 2 below.

a) [▭ 5.2] Listen to Extracts A–E and match each extract with the questions we asked him below:
1 Is there anything you won't advertise?
2 What makes an advertisement effective?
3 Does advertising make people buy things they don't want to buy?
4 How far do you think of your audience when you create an ad?
5 Are advertisements sometimes more popular than the products they sell?

b) Listen again. What does Trevor Beattie believe? Make these false statements true and give reasons for each. Use some of the expressions in the box.
1 A successful advert always fits into an accepted formula.
2 A good advert can succeed without us being aware of the product.
3 Advertising is like any other creative art.
4 Doing cigarette adverts is fun.
5 Advertising can make us loyal to a product.

stand out from the crowd	not in the business of	stay in your mind
get (the) message across	feel a bit odd about	(not) live up to it
(not) make any sense at all	brainwashed	

⑤ Even though his Max ice cream was full of dairy goodness, Timmy showed no mercy.

New MAX ice cream from Wall's gives kids double the fun: the delicious dairy goodness and real fruit puree will tickle their taste buds while the strawberry sauce pen will help turn tea time into an epic adventure. Couldn't your kids murder a Max ice cream?

④

ALWAYS COOL. Coca-Cola ALWAYS COCA-COLA.

ALFA SPIDER.
EVER HAD A RECURRING DREAM?
YOU WILL.

Speaking **4**   Discuss answers to some of these questions.

1   Do you believe advertising is an art form? Give examples.

2   Should any of these advertisements be banned? Can you think of any others?
- cigarettes/alcohol
- subliminal advertising (ads which influence people's unconscious minds)
- fashion ads which use drug addicts as models and war scenes to provoke a reaction

3   What are some of the benefits of advertising? What are some of the disadvantages?

5   Think of an advert for each of these:
- A family car.
- A fizzy drink.
- Aftershave.
- A cat food.

If you were advertising them, how would you do it? How could you make your advertisement different?

VOCABULARY: Commercial English

1a) What areas of business and commerce do you know most about (e.g. finance, import and export)?

b)   Think of some expressions you know that are used in a commercial context and share them with another student (e.g. interest rates, profit and loss).

c)   Read these extracts from the business and finance pages of British newspapers and try to match them with A–H on page 63.

① **The Guinness group announced record pre-tax profits of £975m yesterday and launched a take-over bid for its nearest rival.**

② Rank announced a slump in profits, down from £515m to £65m on a 9% rise in turnover to £2.1bn.

③ **National Express, the bus company, is to give away £30m of its shares to 4,000 employees as a loyalty bonus.**

④ **The decision by the US Federal Reserve to increase interest rates by 0.25% came as no surprise.**

⑤ **Another Italian fashion designer is planning to float his company on stock markets in Milan and New York this spring.**

⑥ Inflation is now predicted to rise sharply by the end of the year.

⑦ Investors in Enterprise Zone Trusts receive income tax relief on the investment, with no upper limit.

⑧ The US trade deficit jumped 8.7% to $114.2bn, despite a fall in its deficit with Japan.

A: It is expected that prices are going to go up.

B: It is a business which the public will be able to buy shares in.

C: A country has spent even more than before on buying from abroad than it has earned from selling abroad.

D: A business has made so much money that it is trying to buy another company.

E: People are getting generous advantages from the Government.

F: A company is making less money than before, despite earning more money.

G: A country has increased the cost of borrowing money.

H: A business is giving something extra to its staff.

d) Work with another student.

1 STUDENT A: Look at sentences 1–4 on page 62.
   STUDENT B: Look at sentences 5–8.

2 Underline the words/phrases you would expect to see mainly in a commercial context. Try to guess any you don't know and then check your guesses in a dictionary. Do you want to change any of your answers in Exercise c)?

3 Explain your sentences carefully to your partner.

2 Try to answer these questions.

1 When you buy food in a supermarket are you buying wholesale or retail?
2 Is it usually better to be in the black or in the red?
3 Do you ever buy things on credit? If so, what?
4 When is trade usually at a low level: during a consumer boom or a recession?
5 Is someone's net income higher or lower than their gross income?
6 Which companies go bankrupt: those that make huge losses or huge profits?
7 When there is high public expenditure are taxes usually high or low?

3 Which is the correct word in context?

1 The recent *inflation/interest rates/devaluation* of the dollar has had a strong effect on the financial markets.
2 There are not enough women in top *direction/management/superintendence* in this country.
3 It's the performance of small firms in *the private sector/the private enterprise/state-owned industry* that make for a healthy economy.
4 The government avoided raising direct *VAT/taxation/duty* – it attacked goods and services instead.
5 Britain built up her wealth by *bargaining/trading/exchanging* with other countries.
6 The firm has once again failed to balance its *budget/forecast/estimate* and spent more than it has received.

Speaking **4a)** Would you rather have your own business or work for someone else? What are some of the advantages/disadvantages of setting up your own business?

b) Work in groups. Decide on the small business your group will set up (e.g. restaurant, hairdresser) and give it a name.

c) Decide on: location; potential clients; 'key selling points' (i.e. what makes your business different); and the image you want to convey.

d) Will you make a special introductory offer to new customers? (If so, what?)

e) Write a short Web page for the Internet announcing your new business.

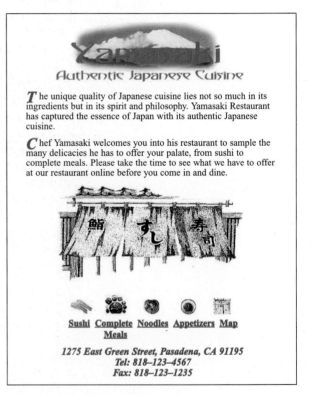

f) Show your page to other groups and tell them about your company. Which company is likely to be the most successful?

▶ **Writing Bank page 166: Business formats**

SECTION 2   GRAMMAR: Future forms

1   Most of the structures underlined below can be used to talk about the future.

a)   However, in these contexts five of the sentences (including the example) are *not* primarily talking about the future. Which are they? What are they saying?

Example: *Number 1: the speaker is sure the people left before now.* (predicting what has already happened)

1   It's no use phoning now – they<u>'ll already have left</u>.

2

> **Cyclists <u>to be offered</u> family cars, says Chinese Government**

3   <u>Will you be watching</u> the match after dinner?

4

> **<u>SEE YOU IN COURT</u> VOWS FERGIE TO EX-HUSBAND**

5   If you <u>will keep bickering</u>, I have no sympathy with you.

6

> Scientists in Finland <u>are about to reveal</u> details of the world's first anti-gravity device.

7

> **VIRGO** <u>The full moon will expose</u> deep feelings and turn you into a werewolf.

8   Hurry up! <u>We're waiting</u> for you.
9   When <u>does the plane from Moscow get in</u>?

10

> <u>Rainfall may be heavy</u> and thundery at times.

11   Come Christmas, we<u>'ll have been living</u> here for nearly twenty years.
12   <u>Shall we go</u> for a pizza?
13   When <u>are you going to break</u> the news?
14   There's no need to hurry – they<u>'ll be having</u> breakfast.
15   Oh dear – the car <u>won't start</u>.
16   Get a move on! The match <u>will have started</u> by the time we get there.

b)   Find an example for each of these in a).
A   Making a suggestion. Example: *12*
B   Predicting the future with certainty.
C   Predicting the future without certainty.
D   Talking about an intention.
E   Talking about a timetabled event.
F   Talking about something not yet started but completed by a point in the future.
G   Making a promise/threat.
H   Talking about an official plan.
I   Making a polite enquiry about a person's plans.

▶ **Language Bank page 148: Future forms**

2 Work in pairs. Discuss the difference in meaning between the sentences in each group below. Why does the speaker choose this particular future form?

Example:
a) All right then. I'll meet you tomorrow.
b) Don't worry. I'll be meeting you tomorrow anyway.
a) Agreeing to something at the time of speaking.
b) Talking about a meeting already fixed – expected to happen in the normal course of events. No personal intention.

1 a) What will you be doing this time tomorrow?
   b) What will you have done this time tomorrow?

2 a) Will you be cooking dinner this evening?
   b) Are you going to cook dinner this evening?
   c) Will you cook dinner this evening?

3 a) Do you want to come out for dinner?
   b) Will you be wanting to come out for dinner?

3 Check on less common future forms in the Language Reference on page 73. Then choose the most likely alternative(s) for the context.

1 I can't come now – a) we'll be having b) we're about to have c) we'll have dinner.
2 a) Will you have finished b) Are you finishing c) Do you finish your report by 5.00?
3 a) You'll be getting b) You'll have got c) You're to get back before nine. I don't want you staying out late.
4 When you see him what a) are you to tell b) are you going to tell c) do you tell him?
5 a) She tells me b) She's about to tell me c) She'll have told me who she was with last night. Don't interrupt!
6 She looks very pale – do you think she's a) fainting b) going to faint c) due to faint?
7 a) I'll be giving b) I'll have given c) I'll give the CD back to you, I promise.
8 This time next week a) we'll have sunbathed b) we are on the brink of sunbathing c) we'll be sunbathing in Mexico.

4 Work in pairs and make short exchanges from the cues using any appropriate future forms. Make the dialogues as natural as possible. First think of what you're going to say, then practise – trying not to refer to your notes.

1 A: There's someone at the door.
   B: That/be/my father. I/play tennis with him later. Why don't you join us?
   A: No. I/go. I/just finish the newspaper. I/meet Sue for lunch.
   B: You/come back later? We could get some work done.
   A: No, you/not finish your game of tennis by the time I'm ready to start work.
   B: OK.

2 A: I understand the company/collapse.
       What/happen? Do you think/we/all be out
       of work?
   B: Well, the chairman/meet/the directors later
       this afternoon. I expect we/tell tomorrow
       morning. Will you/work/at home? I/give
       you a ring.
   A: No, I/meet/a client in Manchester
       tomorrow morning. I expect I/finish with
       her by lunchtime but I/not be/home till
       about six.
   B: I/ring you in Manchester?
   A: Good idea. I/give you the number.

5a) Make notes under these headings but include one thing under each heading
that is definitely not true. Try to include a variety of different forms.

PERSONAL: My long-term plans and intentions
GENERAL: My beliefs and predictions for the future

b) Work in groups. Take it in turns to tell each other. The others must guess
        which things are not true.

c) Who seems most similar to you in their personal future? Whose predictions
        for the future are most similar to yours?

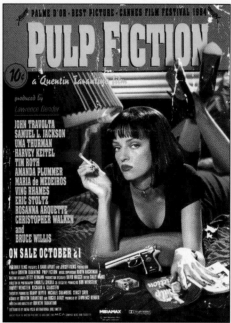
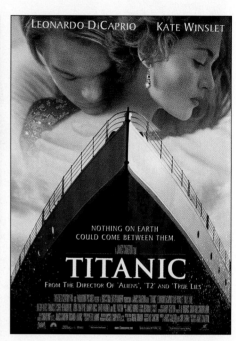

SECTION 3	**READING: Blockbusters**	

Before reading **1** These are some of Hollywood's most successful films. Have you seen any of them? If so, which ones do you like/dislike?

a) Do you prefer films from your own country? If so, which ones?

b) Which is your favourite film of all time? What do you like most about it? (e.g. the actors? the special effects? the plot? the music?)

2 One of the classic Hollywood films is *Gone with the Wind,* made in 1939. Have you seen it? Do you know the plot? Which is it: 1, 2 or 3 below? If you haven't seen the film, you will find the correct answer on page 179.

1 A headstrong girl gives up her father's property for the man she loves.

2 A ruthless girl marries three times but is killed in the American Civil War.

3 An egotistic girl survives the American Civil War but loses the only man she cares for.

Reading **3** The film was based on the novel by Margaret Mitchell, published in 1936, one of the biggest best-sellers of all time.

This is an extract from early on in the novel, in a scene between the main character, Scarlett O'Hara, and Ashley Wilkes. Scarlett is sixteen years old and in love with Ashley but Ashley is in love with Scarlett's cousin, Melanie.

Read the extract and put these sentences in the gaps.

A: 'Sir, you should have made known your presence.'

B: She did not want to be fair, although she knew what he said was true.

C: Then he was gone before she could speak again, closing the door softly behind him.

D: 'And you, Miss, are no lady.'

E: What was the word she wanted? She could not think of any word bad enough.

F: 'This,' said a voice from the depths of the sofa, 'is too much.'

G: 'You're afraid to marry me!'

GONE WITH THE WIND

'Why don't you say it, you coward! (1) *You're afraid to marry me!* You'd rather live with that stupid little fool who can't open her mouth except to say "Yes" or "No"...'

'You must not say these things about Melanie!'

' "I mustn't" be damned to you! Who are you to tell me I mustn't? You coward, you cad, you——You made me believe you were going to marry me——'

'Be fair,' his voice pleaded, 'Did I ever——'

(2) .... He had never once crossed the borders of friendliness with her and, when she thought of this, fresh anger rose, the anger of hurt pride and feminine vanity. She had run after him and he would have none of her. He preferred a whey-faced little fool like Melanie to her. Oh, far better that she had followed Ellen and Mammy's precepts and never, never revealed that she even liked him – better anything than to be faced with this scorching shame!

She sprang to her feet, her hands clenched, and he rose towering over her, her face full of the mute misery of one forced to face realities when realities are agonies.

'I shall hate you till I die, you cad—you lowdown—lowdown——' (3) ....

'Scarlett—please——'

He put out his hand toward her and, as he did, she slapped him across the face with all the strength she had. The noise cracked like a whip in the still room and suddenly her rage was gone, and there was desolation in her heart.

The red mark of her hand showed plainly on his white tired face. He said nothing, but lifted her limp hand to his lips and kissed it. (4) ....

She sat down again very suddenly, the reaction from her rage making her knees feel weak. He was gone and the memory of his stricken face would haunt her till she died.

She heard the soft muffled sound of his footsteps dying away down the long hall, and the complete enormity of her actions came over her. She had lost him forever. Now he would hate her and every time he looked at her he would remember how she threw herself at him when he had given her no encouragement at all ... .

Her hand dropped to a little table beside her, fingering a tiny china rose-bowl on which two china cherubs smirked. The room was so still she almost screamed to break the silence. She must do something or go mad. She picked up a bowl and hurled it viciously across the room towards the fireplace. It barely cleared the tall back of the sofa and splintered with a little crash against the marble mantelpiece.

(5) ....

Nothing had ever startled or frightened her so much, and her mouth went too dry for her to utter a sound. She caught hold of the back of the chair, her knees going weak under her, as Rhett Butler rose from the sofa where he had been lying and made a bow of exaggerated politeness.

'It is bad enough to have an afternoon nap disturbed by such a passage as I've been forced to hear, but why should my life be endangered?'

He was real. He wasn't a ghost. But, saints preserve us, he had heard everything! She rallied her forces into a semblance of dignity.

(6) ....

'Indeed?' His white teeth gleamed and his bold dark eyes laughed at her. 'But you were the intruder. I was forced to wait for Mr. Kennedy, and feeling that I was perhaps persona non grata in the back yard, I was thoughtful enough to remove my unwelcome presence here where I thought I would be undisturbed. But, alas!' He shrugged and laughed softly.

Her temper was beginning to rise again at the thought that this rude and impertinent man had heard everything – heard things she now wished she had died before she ever uttered.

'Eavesdroppers——' she began furiously.

'Eavesdroppers often hear highly entertaining and instructive things,' he grinned. 'From a long experience in eavesdropping I——'

'Sir,' she said, 'you are no gentleman!'

'An apt observation,' he answered airily. (7) ....

(From *Gone with the Wind* by Margaret Mitchell)

4a) Put the names of the characters (Scarlett, Ashley or Rhett) in the gaps and complete the sentences.

Example: *Scarlett* was angry because she had assumed that *Ashley was going to marry her.*

1 .... feels ashamed because ...
2 .... hits .... , who then ...
3 .... is so angry that ...
4 The whole conversation has been heard by .... , who ...

b) Answer the questions.
 1 In what way was Scarlett not 'fair' to Ashley?
 2 What do you think caused the 'desolation in her heart'?
 3 What does the phrase 'stricken face' tell you about Ashley's feelings?
 4 What effect do the 'two cherubs' have on Scarlett?
 5 What do phrases like 'exaggerated politeness', 'laughed softly', 'answered airily' tell you about Rhett Butler's character?

Speaking **5a)** Which character or characters do you have most sympathy for in this situation? Why?

b) How would you have reacted in Ashley's position?

c) What advice would you give Scarlett?

6a) In what way did this modern film bring Shakespeare's *Romeo and Juliet* up-to-date?

b) Imagine you are making an up-to-date remake of *Gone with the Wind* which would appeal to young cinema audiences. You want the film to be very popular and make a lot of money. The film could be about an imaginary civil war in an imaginary country.
 – What would the characters look like?
 – How would you organise the action?
 – How would you change these lines of dialogue for a modern audience?
 I shall hate you till I die, you cad – you lowdown – lowdown ...
 Feeling that I was perhaps persona non grata in the back yard, I was thoughtful enough to remove my unwelcome presence here ...
 – How would the scene continue?

c) Work in groups of three.
 – Compare your ideas and agree on the ones you want to use.
 – Decide who will play what character.
 – Act out the scene.

SPEAKING: Reacting

1   When do we use 'reply questions'?

Example: A: *We went to the cinema last night.*
           B: ***Did you****? What did you see?*

a)   [■ 5.3]   Listen. The intonation of the reply questions in these examples is different because of the different moods of the speakers. In which dialogue does B express:

A surprise?
B boredom?
C worry/concern?
D anger?
E doubt?

b)   Look at the tapescript on page 186 and mark the reply questions to show the pitch movement.

Example: *Did you?*

2   [■ 5.4]   Sometimes our reactions can be whole sentences with a question tag. Listen to five short dialogues. Which mood do you think the second person in each dialogue expresses? Choose from the list in 1a).

3   Work in pairs.

a)   How many different contexts can you think of for these dialogues? Practise saying them with the correct intonation for each context.

1   A: I saw Sue with another man last night.
    B: Did you?

2   A: So you've left him, have you?
    B: Yes, I have.

b)   Think for a minute about each of the following situations. (e.g. Who is the person talking to you? Why do they say that?) Take it in turns to be the person telling and the person reacting. Try to use reply questions and question tags where appropriate. You might also want to use some of the expressions in the box on page 72. Continue the conversations naturally.

1   A: I really can't decide what to do with my life ...
    B: (Try to persuade A to become a teacher.)
    A: (You are reluctant.)

2   A: God, you look pale this morning ...
    B: (You feel OK.)

3 A: You missed a great gig! (... was brilliant!)
    B: (You are surprised and interested. It was your favourite musician but you didn't know he/she was playing.)

4 A: There was this noise upstairs in the middle of the night ... (You were alone. You investigated.)
    B: (You don't believe the story.)

Pull the other one!	Did I really?	Do you think so?
I suppose so.	Go on, tell me more.	It can't be helped.
You're having me on!		

c) Choose two of these situations. Take turns to be A and B. B should react (e.g. express surprise, annoyance etc.) and ask questions to find out more.

1 A: I'm sorry I've got bad news for you ... (e.g. *Your English exams have been brought forward .../I've just smashed up your car ...*)
    B: ....

2 A: Next year, I'm going on holiday to ...
    B: ....

3 A: Listen. (e.g. *Don't take any notice of your doctor ...*) What I think you ought to do is ... (e.g. *change your diet ...*)
    B: ....

4 A: I see you're having problems with that computer. (e.g. *Can I help you?*)
    B: ....

5 A: I want to tell you about something really interesting that happened to me the other day ...
    B: ....

1 THE FUTURE
Future Continuous/Perfect/Perfect Continuous

1 Future Continuous: when we are sure something will be in progress at a specific time in the future:
It'll be raining by three o'clock. (The rain will start before three and probably continue after three.)
Note that this form takes away personal intention: *I'll be going* to the hospital anyway. *I'll* give it to him.

2 Future Perfect: when we are sure something will be finished before a specific time in the future:
We'll have decorated the kitchen by next Tuesday. (We will start decorating before Tuesday – perhaps it's already started. On Tuesday it will be finished.)

3 Future Perfect Continuous: when we say 'how long' (duration) and that the action/state may not be finished:
On Tuesday *we'll have been decorating* the kitchen for two weeks. (We started more than a week ago. On Tuesday we will not be finished. We might have to continue after Tuesday.) When we use this form we focus on the activity in progress.

NOTE: *Will* can also be used:
1 to express certainty about the present or past:
Don't call Julie now: she*'ll be* at work/she*'ll have gone* to work.

2 to express willingness or refusal:
I won't lend her any money: she never pays it back.

Fixed/planned events

For fixed/planned events we can use:
1 the Present Simple:
The shop *opens* at 9.00 – not before.
I *start* work on Monday.

2 *be due* (*to* + base form) *Due* is an adjective which means 'expected at a particular time':
The shop's *due to* open at 9.00.
What time *is* the bus *due*?
(Be careful: a common meaning of *be due to* + noun is *owing to/the result of*: The crash *was* entirely *due to* pilot error.)

3 *be set* (*to* + base form) to show that we have made the necessary preparations/got something ready:
He's *set* to run in the marathon later this year. (= made the necessary preparations)
All *set*? (= ready to leave)
The festival is *set to* attract thousands of visitors. (= a positive thing likely to happen, usually found in newspapers)

4 *is/are to* + base form to talk about formal arrangements (e.g. in a radio commentary):
The Queen *is to drive* down the Mall and then go through the Palace gates.

Things that are close to happening

For events that are close to happening we can use:
1 *be about to* + base form – one of the most common and useful expressions:
She looks as if she's (just) *about to* burst into tears.
The expression is common in sentences such as *was about to ... when ...* :
He *was about to leave* when he saw a man in a car.

2 *be on the point/verge/brink of* + -ing (noun) – these are less common:
They're (just) *on the point/verge of* pulling out of the deal.
The talks were *on the point/verge/brink of* collapse.
He was *on the point/verge of* leaving London when her brother phoned.
Which expression you choose is mainly a matter of collocation. For example, we can say *on the brink of extinction* (i.e. a negative change in situation) but we can also say *on the brink of success*. However, *on the brink of* is less common in positive situations.

Saying/Asking what should be done

We can use:
1 *Is/are* + infinitive in a few limited contexts:
– an adult giving an order to a child:
You *are to* sit in the corner of the room and not say a word.
– in a dramatic context when we ask (ourselves) out loud for help:
What a disaster! What *am I (supposed) to* do? (It can sound exaggerated in everyday contexts!)

2 *Will* for direct instructions:
Will you do as you're told?

Softening what we say

1 We use the Future Continuous to give the impression we are distancing ourselves:
Will you be wanting to borrow my car? (polite enquiry)
It sounds as though we are not really worried whether the answer is 'yes' or 'no'. Compare: *Do you want to borrow my car?* – an offer or a direct request for information; *Are you going to borrow my car?* – what's your intention?

2 We use the Future in the Past to 'soften' a changed plan:
I *was going to* come with you tomorrow but unfortunately something's cropped up. (Compare: I can't come with you tomorrow.)

2 QUESTION TAGS

Question tags are normally used:
1 to ask for confirmation:
You live in China, *don't you*?

NOTE:
The intonation often falls on the tag if we are reasonably sure of the answer.

2 when we want to 'soften' an order:
You won't tell him, *will you*? (i.e. *Don't tell him!*)

3 to react to what the other person is saying:
So you passed your driving test, *did* you? Great!

In 1 and 2 above, positive statements usually have a negative tag and negative statements usually have a positive tag. In 3 above a positive tag is used after a positive statement.

To form tags, the auxiliary and the subject pronoun in the statement are usually reversed. Exception: *I'm lucky, aren't I?* Where there is no auxiliary a form of the verb *do* is used.

NECESSITY: THE MOTHER OF INVENTION?

LISTENING: Great inventors

KATCHA BUG

Catch That Spider!

If you can't bear anything creepy crawly but can't bear to kill them either use the award-winning Katcha Bug. Just put the top over the insect and twist it around. When the spider is trapped pop it outside.
The long handle means you never have to get close!

Katcha Bug   £5.99

Whistle for your keys! ▲

Never lose your keys again. Just whistle, and Keyfinder will beep and flash, helping you to find your keys immediately.
Key Finder Keyring £5.95

BARK*BUSTER*

Trains Pets Fast!
An effective way to stop dogs barking. Simply point the **Barkbuster** and press the button. Your pet will hear a high frequency

harmless sound pulse. Say a firm "No" and your pet will associate the sonic pulse with barking. Behaviour improves after only a few sessions.

NO!

Barkbuster £19.99

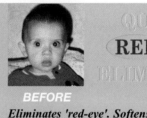
QUASAR RED EYE ELIMINATOR

BEFORE   *AFTER*

Eliminates 'red-eye'. Softens the deep shadows of direct flash.

Quasar Compact is a plastic product and should last the life of the camera.
Packs flat for ease of storage in camera bags. Ultra lightweight and quick to assemble. Each unit can be used many times over.

DISCOVER THE BENEFITS OF QUASAR NOW!

Before listening

1a) Would you buy any of the recent inventions above? Why/not?

b) Which inventions in the last hundred years or so do you think have been the most necessary or useful to mankind? Which do you think have been useless?

c) What do you wish had never been invented? Why?

d) Do you know about any inventors? What did they invent?

2 Brenda Kean has recently become a full-time inventor.
These are some of the questions we asked her. Can you guess what she says in reply to 1 and 2?

1 What qualities do you need to be an inventor?
2 Once you've invented something, what is the next stage?
3 How did you get the idea for your first invention?
4 Which inventions do you admire the most?
5 What would you most like to have invented?

Listening **3a)** [🔲 6.1] Listen to Extract 1.

1 Which question in Exercise 2 is she answering?
2 Which of the things on the opposite page did Brenda invent?
3 What do you think Brenda means by *necessity is the mother of invention*? In what way is this relevant to her?

b) Listen again and complete the information.

1 Two examples of inventions by women are ....
2 Before she was an inventor Brenda used to be ....
3 She was asked by a manufacturer in Sweden to ....
4 She couldn't use .... because ....
5 When she used the flash on her camera ....

c) What did Brenda do next? Use these words to help you.

silver foil lid	Chinese meal	hood shape	elastic bands
bounced the flash			

4a) Listen to Extract 2. Which of the questions in Exercise 2 is she answering? Were your ideas the same as hers?

b) Listen again and choose the best answer.

1 A patent
   a) is like a business contract.
   b) protects your ideas from being copied.

2 If you sell your ideas to another company they
   a) don't take much risk.
   b) get most of the profits.

3 If you license another company to make your product you
   a) get a fee and nothing else.
   b) get money according to the number you sell (i.e. royalties).

4 Brenda made the product herself
   a) because she wanted to see if she could do it.
   b) just because she needed the money.

5a) Listen to Extract 3. Did you agree with Brenda about the qualities needed to be an inventor?

b) Listen again. What do you think Brenda would agree with?
An inventor must be:

logical	creative	self-sufficient financially	sensitive
pushy	quick at solving problems	determined	
convinced of what she's doing			

6a) Listen to Extract 4. Which questions go with these answers?

1 The cat's eyes that you get in the middle of the road, or those new glasses.
2 The dishwasher – I loathe washing up.
3 Something that empties the dishwasher and stacks it away in the cupboards.

b) Discuss the following questions:

1 Which invention do you most admire?
2 What would you most like to invent/to be invented?
3 Can you think of anything that could be invented that would help to make our world 'greener'?

SPEAKING: Linking words together

1a) Look at the sentences below:

– Necessity‿is the mother‿of‿invention.
– I'm‿as blind‿as‿a‿bat‿and‿as deaf‿as‿a post.

1   When we speak, the consonant sound at the end of one word (e.g. /v/ at the end of *of*) often links to the vowel sound at the beginning of another word (e.g. /ɪ/ at the beginning of *invention*).

2   In addition, an 'extra' sound sometimes links two vowel sounds (e.g. a semi-vowel /j/ sound helps link the vowel sounds /iː/ and /ɪ/ together in *necessity is* /nəsesətiːjɪz/ and a /r/ sound helps link the /ə/ (or schwa) sounds in *mother of* /mʌðərəv/).

NOTE:
There is also a /w/ sound, used to link vowel sounds, as in *here you are* /hiːəjʊwɑː/.

b) [🔲 6.2]   Listen to the sentences above.

c) Practise reading the sentences aloud. Link consonants to vowels or vowels to vowels in order to achieve a better rhythm.

2   Read the story.

> My friend wasn't‿in when‿I arrived home, so I went to see my neighbour to ask if I could use her phone. Unfortunately she wasn't in either. As far as I'm concerned there isn't anything worse than being locked out. Luckily I saw an open window and decided to try and get in that way.

a) [🔲 6.3]   Listen to the story read aloud.

b) Mark in the linking of consonants to vowels as in the examples above.

c) Look at the sentences again and mark the extra sound links with /r/, /j/ and /w/.

d) Listen again to check.

e) Practise reading the story aloud.

f) Think of a couple of sentences to end the story. The picture may give you ideas. Write them down and mark in the linking sounds.

3 The sounds /d/ and /t/ often disappear in connected speech when they come at the end of a word and when there is a consonant sound before and after the sound. Example: *east wind*

a) [📼 6.4] Listen to the dialogue below. Cross out any letters which are not pronounced.

A: Next, please.
B: I'm just looking actually. OK, a coffee and a salad sandwich.
A: Is that coffee with milk?
B: No, black. And a Coke. A very cold one, please.
A: There you go. Pay at the till.

b) Practise reading the dialogue in pairs.

4a) [📼 6.5] Listen and complete the dialogue below.

A: .... going to ....
B: .... get away .... six ....
A: .... I'll .... car.
B: .... cooking?
A: .... always do ....
B: Well, ... don't .... Why .... salad .... ?
A: .... me. .... six .... entrance.

b) Mark all the possible links between words in the dialogue. Show any extra sounds, and any sounds which might 'disappear'.

c) Compare your work in pairs.

d) Practise reading it in pairs.

e) Listen to the tape again.

f) Read the dialogue once more.

VOCABULARY: Phrasal verbs

The term *phrasal verb* is used here to refer to any base form of the verb (e.g. *get*) which is followed by a single particle (e.g. *up*) or two particles (e.g. *up to*). There are over thirty particles, and some of the most common are those of direction or location (e.g. *up, down, on, off, in, out*).

1 Sometimes the particles can help you to guess the meanings of phrasal verbs.

Up, for example, can mean (among other things):
A increasing or improving.
B completing or ending.

a) Match each group of sentences with meaning A or B.
  1 I tore up the letter and threw it in the bin.
     They pulled up at the front door and got out.
     Eat up your dinner!
     We've used up the last drop of milk.

  2 I picked up a bit of Spanish on holiday.
     They've done their house up really beautifully.
     Will you blow up my balloon for me?
     Turn the radio up, please. I can't hear the news.

2 All the following phrasal verbs are a combination of the verb *to be* and a
particle. Match the sentences in A with the responses in B. Example: *1 = c)*

A

1 I'm *off*.
2 Lucy's job application has to be *in* today.
3 Are you still *on* for tomorrow?
4 I think the milk's *off*.
5 When are the sales *on*?
6 The meeting's *off*.
7 Jim seemed very *down* yesterday.
8 Sales figures are *up* this month.
9 The computer is *down*.
10 Do you realise the oven is *on*?

B

a) Can't wait!
b) Cancelled or just postponed?
c) See you tomorrow!
d) Oh no, I need to send an e-mail.
e) Not until after Christmas.
f) Good, this means we should get a pay rise.
g) Shall I post it for her?
h) Yes, he's not very well.
i) It smells disgusting.
j) Yes, it's just warming up.

3 A verb can be combined with particles such as the ones below to have a
variety of different meanings.

on	off	up	down	in(to)	out

a) Substitute the more formal word in brackets with *put* and one of the
particles from the box.
Example: *She <u>put out</u> her cigarette as soon as she saw the sign. (extinguished)*

1 Can you .... all the family for the weekend? (accommodate)
2 I hope I'm not .... you .... your work? (distracting)
3 Are we .... you .... too much if we come to stay? (inconveniencing)
4 She had to .... a 10% deposit on the house. (pay)
5 She .... a proposal for a new course. (submitted)
6 The school are .... a production of *Alice in Wonderland*. (giving)
7 The dog was very old and in pain so the vet said it would be kinder to
   .... him .... (give him a lethal injection)
8 I don't want to .... the kids .... but the exam is really difficult!
   (discourage)
9 She .... a lot of time on that report. (spent)

b) In some of the sentences above why is the verb separated from the particle?

c) In the other examples the verbs and particles can also be separated. Where
will the particle go?

▶ **Language Bank page 156: Phrasal verbs (grammar)**

4 Some phrasal verbs have different meanings, both idiomatic and non-idiomatic. (e.g. **put down** *your pen on the table* or **put down** *a riot*). These different meanings are often exploited humorously in jokes.

a) Complete the jokes below, using a phrasal verb from the box.

see through	pick up	go out	drop off	put out	fall out

Example:

1 Have you heard the one about the woman who was picked up for speeding?
She was so heavy that the policeman broke his arm.

2 Can you .... the cat, please?
Why? Is it on fire?

3 Why do children in an aeroplane always agree?
Because they don't want to ....

4 Why are ghosts bad at telling lies?
Because you can always .... them.

5 I can't sleep at night.
Sleep at the edge of the bed and you'll soon ....

6 What did one candle say to the other?
Are you .... tonight?

b) What are the two different meanings?

5 Work in groups.

a) Write down three other phrasal verbs that you know and which are not used above.

b) Subdivide into pairs. Put your verbs together and write a short story, using these six phrasal verbs at least once and as many of the phrasal verbs in this section as you can.

c) Read out your stories to the whole group and decide which is the best.

SECTION 2   GRAMMAR: Participle clauses

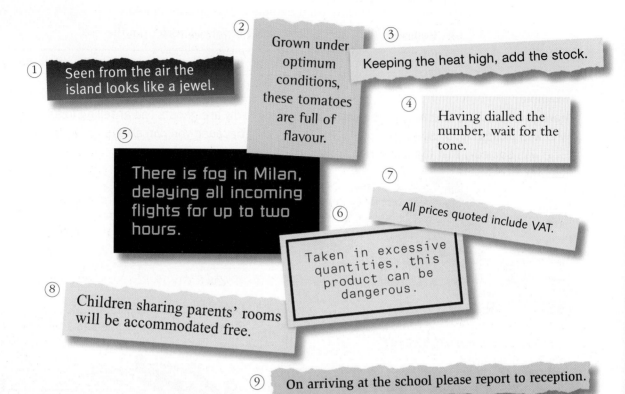

① Seen from the air the island looks like a jewel.

② Grown under optimum conditions, these tomatoes are full of flavour.

③ Keeping the heat high, add the stock.

④ Having dialled the number, wait for the tone.

⑤ There is fog in Milan, delaying all incoming flights for up to two hours.

⑥ Taken in excessive quantities, this product can be dangerous.

⑦ All prices quoted include VAT.

⑧ Children sharing parents' rooms will be accommodated free.

⑨ On arriving at the school please report to reception.

1   Look at the sentences. Where do you think each one comes from?
Example: *1 could be from a travel brochure.*

2   All the sentences contain participle clauses (verb forms with *-ing* or *-ed*). Participle clauses do not normally need the subject or the verb *to be*. They don't need conjunctions, prepositions etc. either, except when the meaning without one of these words would be ambiguous (as with *on* in 9).

a)   Which of the following words – *if, while, so* (*that*), *because, when, after* – could be used to expand each of the sentences in 1–6 above?
Example: ***When*** *seen from the air, the island looks like a jewel.*

b)   Which sentence(s):
1   refer(s) to things happening at the same time? Example: *3*
2   refer(s) to things happening one before another?
3   show(s) an event which is the reason for or result of another event?
4   is/are like a relative clause?
5   show(s) a condition?

c)   Expand sentences 7 and 8 to make them into sentences with a full relative clause.

d)   Participle clauses tend to be used more in written than spoken language. How would you say sentences 1–6 and 9 if you were speaking? Example: *When you see it from the air the island looks like a jewel.*

▶ **Language Bank page 159: Relative clauses**

3   Rephrase the following sentences to make participle clauses. If there is a conjunction in brackets, use it.

Examples:
I didn't know what to do, so I phoned my parents for advice.
Not knowing what to do I phoned my parents for advice.
Plant them early in the season otherwise they won't come out this year. (*unless*)
Unless planted early in the season, they won't come out this year.

1   After I'd invited Peter to dinner, I remembered I was going out.
2   She stood in the doorway and sheltered from the rain.
3   He knew I was afraid of flying so he'd bought me some tranquillisers.
4   Open the box and then put it in the fridge straightaway. (*once*)
5   I left my last job two months ago and I now realise how unhappy I was. (*since*)
6   I met her a few times but never got a chance to speak properly to her. (*despite*)
7   As soon as he arrived at the airport he gave her a quick ring. (*on*)
8   I ran all the way to work and got there on time. (*by*)

4   Look at the cued sentences below, which were taken from newspaper extracts.

a)   Make complete sentences from the cues. There is one participle clause in every sentence.
Example:
A revolutionary new radio/not require electricity/predict/sell millions all over the world.
*A revolutionary new radio not **requiring** electricity is predicted to sell millions all over the world.*

1   A man/pull/from the wreckage of his car by a passerby/tell/ yesterday of the horror of his experience.
2   Disappoint/by the result of his last match, top tennis player Rios nevertheless/decide/to fight on.
3   'Know/him as I do, I/not think/ he/spend/the Lottery money wisely,' /say/the winner's ex-wife, Lolita.
4   Fleur Williams, /know/to millions since she/appear/as Tanya in the soap-opera, Mill Street, /just say/she/divorce/her husband of six months.
5   Vanessa Redgrave, currently/appear/in a West End production of *Uncle Vanya*, /interview/on Channel 4 this evening.
6   Their native habitats be/destroy, the common newt/have/to adapt to different environments.

b)   Work in pairs. Think of any recent news items in your country and make one or two sentences about each of them, including at least one participle clause.

SECTION 3   READING: Stop the world!

Before reading **1a)** Work in groups.

1 Which of the things in the picture do you use?
2 Make a list of any other modern gadgets or appliances which you use at work or home. Example: a microwave oven.
3 Individually, decide how important they are to your everyday life. Put them in order 1-10 (10 being the least essential).
4 Discuss your list with others in the group and give reasons for your choices.

b) Do you think modern technology has a positive or negative effect on life at work and home? Give reasons.

Reading **2** Look at the first text opposite. The article identifies two problems of modern life – too much information and an increase in shyness.

a) What do you think is causing these problems? Discuss with a partner.

b) Read the text and check your predictions.

c) Read the text again and answer these questions.
1 What physical symptoms does 'information overload' cause?
2 Why is prioritising so important?
3 What is meant by 'the urgency culture'?
4 What does the professor mean by a new 'ice age'?
5 What are we not doing as we concentrate on sending out information?
6 Why are people reluctant to start an everyday conversation nowadays?

d) Explain the words or expressions in italics by saying the sentence in another way.
1 The fax is *spewing out* a 50-page (line 1)
2 *No wonder* information-overload syndrome is (line 5)
3 unable to *handle* (line 16)
4 blamed the information *tidal wave* for (line 18)
5 *let alone* to decide on (line 25)
6 Computers have *eroded* (line 49)

e) Discuss the following questions in groups.
1 Do you agree that computer technology can be detrimental to our lives? Have you, or has anyone you know, had any experience of this? Should we and could we change this aspect of our culture?
2 How could we deal more effectively with a large amount of information?
3 Is 'small talk' becoming less common in your country?
4 Do you think men or women are more affected socially by the impact of technology?

STOP THE WORLD!

The fax is spewing out a 50-page document, the answering machine is flashing six messages, the mobile phone is ringing again, there are 20 e-mails to respond to and the Internet has found 11,000 articles
5 on the subject you are researching. No wonder information-overload syndrome is the latest ailment to strike office workers.

A survey commissioned by Reuters Business Information found that half of 1,300 managers
10 questioned were suffering from information overload and that new technology, instead of making their job easier, was causing stress, less job satisfaction and a greater degree of illness, such as headaches and stomach pains. Almost half the managers believe the
15 Internet is making the situation worse and admitted they were unable to handle the amount of information they receive on a daily basis. An even higher number blamed the information tidal wave for a deterioration in their home life and personal
20 relationships, and said that dealing with so much information frequently meant staying late at work or having to take work home.

Our ability to generate information has simply exceeded our ability to review and understand most
25 of it, let alone to decide on priorities. And prioritising is vitally important when you consider how much information we are exposed to – more information has been produced in the past 30 years than in the past five milleniums. The fact that not all of it is of
30 equal importance means that it needs to be sifted first. Likewise, it is crucial that we avoid getting caught up in the urgency culture, where everything has to be done 'by yesterday'.

The growth of computer technology is also fuelling
35 a worldwide 'epidemic' of shyness, the psychologist Professor Zimbardo said yesterday. He believes we are at the beginning of a new 'ice age' of non-communication. The growing use of e-mail and the disappearance of jobs such as shop assistants means
40 that face-to-face conversations are becoming a rarity and it may well soon be possible to go through the entire day without talking to another person directly. Less and less time is spent on personal hobbies, holidays and with friends and relations.
45 We are sending information but not conveying emotion. Zimbardo's theory is that there is much less small talk – the recounting of the inconsequential trivia of social life that forms the social glue which holds communities together. Computers have eroded
50 the opportunity for small talk and this means that people now feel they need a serious reason to start an everyday conversation.

3a) The article below is about the Amish. Do you know anything about them?

b) Read the article. In what way(s) is Amish culture very different to the life described in the article above?

The Amish are a church community of around 150,000 people living in 22 states of the USA who believe they have been called by God to live a life of faith, humility and service. Keeping large-scale technology and its influence at a distance, they believe that they are living examples of an alternative type of modernity. Some of the main characteristics of their life are summarised below.

Isolation: The philosophy of separateness pervades their entire life, and their distinctive language and clothes create symbolic boundaries. Just as the way we dress may reflect our role and status in society, their clothes, far from being a costume, are an expression of their deepest convictions, symbolising submission and humility. Amish must marry Amish, and even their schools are separate. Technology which threatens this isolation is not permitted.

Family life: The family and community are of paramount importance to the Amish, who support and care for other members of the community, obviating the need for any kind of personal insurance or pension. They lead a monogamous and patriarchal life, with large families and no divorce. Although they are a people apart they are also a people together.

Simplicity: The Amish invariably live in rural communities, making their living in farm-related activities, for which they are renowned. Manual labour and hard work are prized and they have little regard for labour-saving devices. Their main form of transport is by buggy, and the horses which pull them exemplify key values to the Amish such as tradition, time, nature and sacrifice. Education and training is basic, avoiding intellectualism and anything which encourages a desire for power and lack of humility.

c) Based on what you have read, which of the following do you think the Amish would reject: computers, washing machines, fridges, television, cars, tractors, modern medicine, telephones? Why?

d) Read the second part of the article on the next page and check your predictions.

Although perceived as very traditional, the Amish have integrated modern technology into their life where they feel it will enhance their lifestyle. For example, whereas electricity is forbidden in the home, because of the risk of 'hooking up to the world too much', they do use things such as electric fences (to contain cattle), tractors and power saws in their farming. Petrol engines power equipment such as water pumps and washing machines, and bottled gas heats water and operates fridges, stoves and lights.

Other examples of selective adoption are the car and telephone. Car ownership is strictly forbidden, since mobility is a threat to their lifestyle, but the Amish do at times travel in cars, trains and buses driven by others when they want to go further afield than their horse-drawn buggies permit. Similarly, the Amish bond by face-to-face interaction and although they feel that the phone acts as a separator and that alleviating their isolation would be a direct threat to their unity, they did permit, in 1980, the use of community phones. The fact is that phones are very useful – to make contact with doctors (perhaps ironically the Amish frequently use the services of modern medicine) or to order supplies, for example.

The Amish have discovered that the more modern the world becomes the more they are forced to alter their behaviour, attitudes and lifestyle. They selectively have chosen how modern they actually want to be in rejecting computers and accepting chain saws. By taking charge of their destiny and making choices they have been able to maintain their core values while compromising with the changing world.

4   Read both parts of the article about the Amish again.

a)   Decide whether the following statements are correct. If they are not, correct them.
1   The Amish wear a special costume in order to attract tourism.
2   They are not allowed to marry outside the Amish community.
3   The Amish are dependent on other people in the community.
4   The Amish always live in the country.
5   All labour-saving devices are forbidden.
6   The Amish usually travel by horse-drawn buggy.
7   They are not allowed to use modern medicine.
8   The writer believes that the Amish compromise their beliefs by using some modern technology.

b)   What do you think?
1   Is it possible to 'stop the world'? Give reasons. What aspects would you like to stop?
2   Are there any aspects of modern life or technology which you or your family are opposed to and consciously resist?
3   What would you like and dislike about living in the Amish community?

Speaking and writing

5   Imagine you are writing a short informal article about the Amish community for a newspaper.

a)   Try to summarise the two parts of the article in as few words as possible, while keeping the main ideas.

b)   Compare your version with other people's.

c)   Think of a title for your summary.

▶ Writing Bank page 177: Summary writing

6   Imagine you are going to present a TV news bulletin based on your Amish article.

a)   Work in small groups. Decide what you are going to say.

b) Present the bulletin to the rest of the class. One of you should be the newsreader. Other members of the group can also be interviewed on the programme (e.g. an ex-Amish member or a visitor to the Amish community).

7 Write a 'headline' about something which has happened in your own life. It can be serious, or something completely trivial (e.g. *Chicken and rice for lunch again!*). People can ask you questions to find out more details about what happened. Report back to the rest of the class on interesting stories.

WRITING: Making instructions clear

1 When did you last read a set of instructions telling you how to do something?

a) Were they in a book or a brochure etc. or in an informal note from a friend?

b) Think of a situation when you might need to write to somebody telling them how to do something.

c) What makes a good set of instructions? Think of at least three criteria.

2 Look at the two sets of instructions below. One is a set of instructions from a leaflet and the other is an informal note. Do they fulfil your criteria for good instructions? Why/not?

(A)

1 Pour in sufficient water for the required quantity of espresso, plus 1 cup of water for the production of steam.

2 Pour about 100 ml of low-fat milk into a small narrow jug which must fit comfortably under the steam nozzle of the machine. The milk must be cool and a cold jug should be used.

3 As soon as the first drops of espresso run out, the frothing of the milk can commence. Opening the steam control knob a little, hold the jug under the steam nozzle so that the nozzle dips right into the milk. However, care must be taken that the nozzle does not touch the bottom of the jug, otherwise the flow of steam may be hindered.

(B)

Dear Diane,

How to operate our video machine!

- Turn on video machine, making sure there is a video cassette inside! Then, take the remote control, which should be on top of the TV and point at video before pressing video plus.

- Next you have to key in the number of the thing you want to record. By pressing video plus again you can check you've got it right because (hopefully!) you'll see the time and number on the screen.

- Finally, press menu button on controls, and don't forget to turn off the video!

Any more info. you may need in booklet on top of TV.

Good luck and happy watching. See you Friday.

Rob

3 Look at the instructions again.

a) The two writers have used different ways of organising their writing to try and make their message clear. What are they? Example: in A the instructions are numbered.

b) The writers have tried not to use the imperative form all the time, in order to avoid monotony. Find examples of the following in the texts:
1 a participle clause (with *-ing* or *-ed*), a relative clause (with *who/which/that*) and an adverbial clause (e.g. *By pressing*).
2 language used to give advice/warnings.

c) Linking words are particularly important in instructions.
1 Find examples of sequencing expressions (e.g. *Firstly, after*).
2 What are the functions of *so that* and *otherwise*? What other expressions could you use instead?

d) Which vocabulary do you think is more typical of more formal written English? How could you say it more informally (e.g. *sufficient* could be replaced by *enough*)?

e) What features of informal instructions would you probably not find in more formal written instructions (e.g. exclamation marks)?

4 Work in pairs.
STUDENT A: Rewrite the video instructions for a leaflet.
STUDENT B: Rewrite the coffee maker instructions as a note to a friend staying at your house.
Look at each other's work and see if you can make any improvements.

5 You are going to write instructions. Choose an idea of your own or one of the ideas below.
1 How to use a piece of technical equipment in your house or office.
2 How to play a game/sport that you like.
3 Give directions to your house from the town centre.
4 Give instructions on how to make something that you like eating or drinking, and which perhaps is typical of your country or region.

a) Think carefully about who you are writing to and why you are writing. The kind of language you use will depend on this. (Example: if you are writing to a friend in your class it will probably be an informal note.)

b) Before you start writing make notes on: what information you are going to include, how many paragraphs you will have and what order they will be in. Compare your notes with someone else. Then write up your notes in the form of paragraphs.

c) Give your instructions to somebody else to read, and read somebody else's. Are they clear? Are they detailed enough? Ask questions if you want to have something clarified.

▶ **Language Bank page 150: Linking expressions**

1 PARTICIPLE CLAUSES

In written English, and sometimes in spoken English, there is a tendency to shorten utterances by using present, past and perfect participles.

In the examples below, the subordinate clause in sentence A can be replaced by the participle clause in B:

A *While she was walking down the street she slipped.*
B ***Walking** down the street, she slipped.* (Present Participle)

A *If you take ginseng once a day, it will help.*
B ***Taken** once a day, ginseng will help.* (Past Participle)

A *Because I had done most of the course I was reluctant to give it up.*
B ***Having done** most of the course, I ...* (Perfect Participle)

Adverbial participle clauses

1 Adverbial participle clauses give information about *when* something happened, *why* something happened, *the result* of something happening and *the possibility* of something happening:

a) Time adverbials (describing actions which happen simultaneously or consecutively):
She cut her hand while she was gardening becomes:
*She cut her hand **gardening**.*

I closed the door quietly and then stepped outside becomes:
***Closing** the door quietly, I stepped outside.*

After we had paid the bill we left becomes:
***Having paid** the bill we left.*

b) Adverbials of reason and result:
Because/As/Since I had a lot of energy I decided to redecorate a room becomes:
***Having** a lot of energy I decided to redecorate a room.*

The dog rushed into the road and so/as a result the car swerved becomes:
*The dog ran into the road, **causing** the car to swerve.*

c) Adverbials of condition:
If/Provided it is watered at regular interval, this plant should do very well becomes:
***Watered** at regular intervals, this plant should do very well.*

2 Here are some conjunctions which are used with participles for clarification, but without a subject and the verb *be*:

TIME: *before, after, since, once, until, while, whenever:*
***Once** seen it is never forgotten.*

CONDITION: *if, unless, whether:*
***Unless** taken regularly, it will have no effect.*

PLACE: *wherever:*
***Wherever** played it's always very popular.*

CONTRAST: *while, although, despite:*
***Although** attacked by the media, he refused to resign.*

By and *on* are also frequently used:
*They managed to meet the deadline **by** working all hours.*
***On** hearing the alarm, leave the building immediately.*

3 In sentences with participle clauses the subject of the participle clause must agree with the subject of the main clause:
***Having been sick** all over the carpet **the cat** was thrown out.*
(*Having been sick* refers to 'the cat'.)
NOT *Having been sick all over the carpet **I** threw the cat out* (which would mean that I was sick, not the cat).

Relative participle clauses

These are sometimes known as 'reduced relative clauses'. They function in the same way as relative clauses but the relative pronoun (*who, which* etc.) and the auxiliary verb *be* (when used in a full clause) are left out:
Children who arrive late should report to the office.
*Children **arriving** late should report to the office.*

Cars which are made in Japan are usually very reliable.
*Cars **made** in Japan are usually very reliable.*

Any food which is not eaten will be taken home.
*Any food **not eaten** will be taken home.*

2 PHRASAL VERBS

Phrasal verbs (more accurately called 'multi-word verbs') are made up of a verb and a particle (e.g. *take off*). A particle can be either an adverb (*look something **up***) or a preposition (*look **after** something/somebody*). There are also verbs which are followed by both an adverb particle and a preposition (***get away with** something*).

The particle of a phrasal verb can be in two positions (e.g. ***get over** an idea* or ***get** an idea **over***) or inseparable (***get over** an illness*), depending on whether it is an adverb or a preposition.

Common verbs combine with all sorts of particles. One verb can combine with many different particles or prepositions (e.g. *put **off/on/back***) and one combination can itself have lots of different meanings (e.g. *take up*). The same phrasal verb can also be a different grammatical type. Example: *take off* can be transitive (*I took off my coat*) and intransitive (*The plane took off*).

Sometimes the meaning of a phrasal verb can easily be understood because it is literal (e.g. *She **turned round***) or because the particle simply reinforces or strengthens the verb (e.g. ***Hurry up***).

Other phrasal verbs are idiomatic in that when a particle is added it completely changes the meaning of the verb:
*I can't **make** the writing **out**.* (= read clearly)

Phrasal verbs tend to be informal and are often replaced by a single verb in a less informal context:
get up → rise; give in → surrender

A COMMON LANGUAGE?

VOCABULARY: Problem words

1a) Work in pairs. In what ways do you think the words in the box are sometimes 'difficult' for learners? Match them with A–F below. Use a dictionary to help you.

sympathy	refuse	/njuː/	guarantee	/weɪst/	accommodation	
lead	library	/sɔːs/	bank	height	bow	

A Spelling.

B Pronunciation.

C A 'false friend'. It looks or sounds similar to a word in another language but does not have exactly the same meaning (e.g. *actual* in Spanish means 'present/up-to-date/topical', but in English it means 'real' – *The estimate was 100 dollars; the **actual** cost was only 90.*).

D A word with the same spelling as another word but with different pronunciation and different meaning (e.g. the verb *row* /rəʊ/or/raʊ/).

E A word with the same spelling and pronunciation as another word but different in meaning (e.g. the noun *bear* and the verb *bear*).

F A word with the same pronunciation as another word but a different spelling and a different meaning (e.g. *write* and *right*).

b) Do you know any words in your language which are 'false friends' with English words?

2 Work with other students to complete this Problem Word crossword.

Across

2 In the church the couple walked down the /aɪl/.

4 Correct the word: He's very *sensible* to criticism.

6 Have you done your piano pract... ?

7 A different spelling for 7 Down to mean a 'small dried grape often used in making cakes'.

9 It means 'rubbish' but also to 'say no'.

10 Another meaning/spelling for 2 Across.

11 It means 'very small' when said like this: /maɪˈnjuːt/.

12 It means 'endure' but it's also an animal.

14 The spelling for 12 Across when it means 'empty'.

Down

1 Correct the word: This spare room is for *eventual* visitors.

3 A tricky-to-spell cutting device: /ˈsɪzəz/.

5 The material we use for writing is called station... .

7 Correct the word: This is not the *actual* issue of the magazine. It's an old one.

8 The spelling for *sees* when it means 'grab'.

13 Correct the word: She travelled *lonely*.

3a) What different meanings are there for these words Use a dictionary to help you. Example: *bat*

| bat *(n)* | shed *(v/n)* | lean *(v/adj)* | tender *(v/adj)* | hamper *(v/n)* |

b) Match the underlined words with the phonetics.

①

a) Her voice will <u>entrance</u> you.
b) Where's the nearest <u>entrance</u>?
1 /ɪnˈtrɑːns/ 2 /ˈentrəns/ Example: *a) = 1, b) = 2*

②

a) A kind nurse bandaged his <u>wound</u>.
b) He <u>wound</u> the scarf round his neck.
1 /waʊnd/ 2 /wuːnd/

③

a) The <u>wind</u> is blowing really hard.
b) Can you <u>wind</u> up the window, please?
1 /waɪnd/ 2 /wɪnd/

④

a) The Ferrari is in the <u>lead</u>.
b) That joke went down like a <u>lead</u> balloon.
1 /liːd/ 2 /led/

⑤

a) There is a <u>tear</u> in that shirt!
b) Is that a <u>tear</u> I see on your cheek?
1 /teə/ 2 /tɪə/

⑥

a) I can't stand the smell of <u>incense</u>.
b) This scandal is going to <u>incense</u> the public.
1 /ˈɪnsens/ 2 /ɪnˈsens/

c) What different words with different spellings can you make from the pronunciation?
1 /sent/ Example: *sent* and *scent*
2 /ˈmɔːnɪŋ/ 3 /weɪt/ 4 /kiː/ 5 /stiːl/ 6 /ˈberi/

4 Discuss answers to these questions.

1 What makes English easy to learn? What makes it difficult? (Remember that in English nobody has to learn whether a new noun is masculine, feminine or neuter and adjectives do not have to 'agree' with their nouns.)

2 What are the main problems for a foreign learner studying your language? The grammar? Vocabulary? Spelling? Pronunciation? Are there a lot of exceptions to the rules?

▶ **Language Bank page 142: Some problem areas of grammar, e.g. Adverb position and Articles**

LISTENING: A global language

Before listening

1 At the present time English is referred to as a 'global language' because it is used for communication by people from all over the world.

a) Which do you think is the correct alternative? Underline your guess. (The figures are all approximate.)

1 English is spoken by a) *100 million* b) *1.5 billion* people (both native speakers and non-native speakers).

2 a) *1 million–10 million* b) *100 million–a billion* people speak English as a foreign language.

3 a) *80%* b) *95%* of all information stored in electronic retrieval systems is in English.

4 There are between a) *1,000 and 2,000* b) *6,000 and 10,000* languages in the world.

5 In 100 years' time there will be a) *half the present number* b) *the same number* of languages in the world.

6 English has a) *250,000–400,000* b) *500,000–1 million* words, including technical, jargon and slang words.

7 The average native speaker of English has between a) *5,000 and 10,000* b) *20,000 and 30,000* words in their vocabulary for everyday conversation.

8 The average vocabulary of a foreign student starting an advanced English class is a) *2,000* b) *5,000* words.

b) Check your guesses on page 179. Is there anything that surprises you in the answers?

Listening **2** You are going to listen to extracts from an interview with Professor David Crystal, author of *English as a Global Language.*

a) Do you think these statements are True or False?
1 English has become a world language because it is an easy language to learn.
2 English has borrowed from over 150 languages.
3 There are many different varieties of written English around the world.
4 There are many different varieties of spoken English around the world.
5 The main reason other languages are dying is the growth of English.

b) [7.1] Listen and check your guesses.

c) How does David Crystal think we should help preserve our sense of identity?

3 Listen again and answer the questions. According to Professor Crystal:

1 Why are language and power closely linked?
2 Why are there many drawbacks in English being a global language?
3 Why does English sometimes seem familiar to foreign learners?
4 What are the 'new Englishes' and what characterises them?
5 What does Brazil illustrate about the death of native languages?

4 Do you disagree with any of Professor Crystal's views?

Speaking **5** In groups, discuss answers to either A or B.

A Has English influenced your language? If so, what English words have entered your language? In your opinion, is it a good or bad thing? What do other people in your country think?

B In northern Spain the regional languages of Catalan and Basque are very important in the autonomous regions of Catalonia and the Basque Provinces.

– What does your language mean to you (e.g. Is it simply personal and communicative or does it have cultural, political and historical meaning for you)?

– At what cost should we preserve 'minority' native languages? Should there be political and financial support and should the languages be made compulsory in local schools and in the local media?

6 Is it a good idea to learn a foreign language? Which foreign language other than English would you most like to learn? Why?

SECTION 2 | GRAMMAR: Perfect and continuous aspects

The perfect aspect

1 Read these sentences and decide on the correct form for the context. Why is the other form wrong?

① I'm a successful athlete but one of the most difficult problems I *have had/had* to deal with in my career is my asthma.

② I only started writing in my seventies. At school I *have always been/had always been* very lazy.

③ I *'ll retire/'ll have retired* from football by the time my son's old enough to turn professional.

④ Do you know why I *'ve come/came/had come* to this country in the first place? Because of the job opportunities – and now there are none.

⑤ When this interview is printed, I *have been/'ll be/'ll have been* at the university for about a year.

When do we use perfect forms? What do they have in common? Check in the section 'The perfect aspect' in the Language Reference on page 101.

2 Continue what each person says in different ways using the cues. Use only the Simple Past, the *'ll* future or any perfect form (but not the Perfect Continuous). In some cases there is more than one possibility.

1 Why are you asking me?
   a) I/already/tell/you! Example: *I've already told you*.
   b) I/tell/you last night!

2 They started going out together ages ago.
   a) Suzie/never/have a boyfriend before she/meet/Ben.
   b) My guess is they/split up sometime in the next couple of months.

3 I could tell from his face that he ...
   a) already/know the truth.
   b) find out/what/happen to his father.

4 Ah! There you are!
   a) Where/you/be/recently?
   b) When we/get/to the hotel last week you/already/leave.
   c) By the end of the evening you/dance/with everyone except me!

Perfect Continuous

3a) Why is the Present Perfect Simple used in the sentences in a) and the Present Perfect Continuous used in the sentences in b)? Ask yourself these questions:
– Is the action/situation completed or unfinished?
– Is the action/situation temporary?
– Does the action recently in progress have a present effect?

1   a)   No, I'm not hungry. *I've had* breakfast.
     b)   Where were you? *I've been waiting* for you.
2   a)   *I've written* a letter to my accountant this morning about his fees.
     b)   *I've been writing* a letter to my accountant this morning. I'm exhausted.
3   a)   *She has lived* in that house for years.
     b)   *She's been living* with me recently.

b)   Can you say when the continuous form is usually used? Check in the Language Reference on page 101.

c)   These sentences use other Perfect and Perfect Continuous forms. Explain why one is Perfect Simple and the other Continuous.
     1   a)   The house was empty but obviously *someone had been staying* there.
          b)   The house was empty but obviously *someone had broken in.*
     2   a)   Up to that point *I'd had* a rather boring life.
          b)   Up to that point *I'd been living* in Tunisia.
     3   a)   Jo *will have gone* to her mother's by the time you finish that ironing.
          b)   Jo *will have been cooking* for about half an hour by the time you finish that ironing.

4   Work in pairs and take it in turns to be A and B. B makes responses in the Perfect Simple or the Perfect Continuous using the cues.

1   A: What's the matter?
     B: (sprain my ankle)

2   A: Aren't you hungry?
     B: (No/eat biscuits/all day)

3   A: Who's this Tania woman?
     B: (you/read/my private correspondence?)

4   A: Don't men ever help around the house?
     B: (What do you mean? I/iron/all the socks –
          I deserve a rest)

5 A: Is it cold in Moscow now?
   B: (Yes/snow/here for days)

6 A: You look fit!
   B: (Yes/this time next year/I/go to yoga classes/twenty years!)

7 A: Why are you so cheerful?
   B: (When we finish this course next week/I feel I/achieve/a lot!)

8 A: Why did you send them to bed?
   B: (I found out they/watch TV all evening and they/not/do their homework)

5a) Write your name in the middle of a piece of paper. Write the names of three or four friends and acquaintances around your name to show how close you are to that person. If the friends know each other, draw a line between their names. Think about some things these friends have done/are doing in their life and make some guesses about their future lives (relationships, career etc.).

b) Ask another student about his/her friends. Start with some of these phrases:
Has (X) ever ... ?
How long ... ?
When ... ?
What happened before ... ?
Had (X) ever ... ?
What will (X) ... ?
What do you think (X)'ll have ... ?

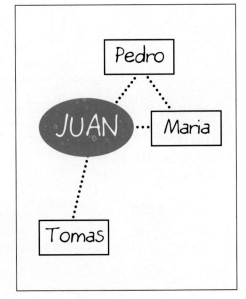

SECTION 3   READING: *Lost in translation*

Before reading   **1**   Read the opening part of the autobiography *Lost in Translation* by the Polish writer Ewa Hoffman.

a)   Why does she feel her life is ending?

It is April 1959, I'm standing at the railing of the Batory's upper deck, and I feel that my life is ending.

I'm looking out at the crowd that has
5 gathered on the shore to see the ship's departure from Gdynia – a crowd that, all of a sudden, is irrevocably on the other side – and I want to break out, run back, run towards the familiar
10 excitement, the waving hands, the exclamations. We can't be leaving all this behind – but we are. I am thirteen years old, and we are emigrating.

b)   What do these phrases tell you about her feelings?
1   a crowd that ... is irrevocably on the other side (line 6)
2   the familiar excitement (line 9)

Reading   **2**   Ewa's family emigrated to Canada when she was thirteen. Work in groups of three. Each person will read a different extract.

Read your extract and find out how well she integrates into her new life. Use a dictionary to help you with any new words.

STUDENT A: Ewa's new social life:

The car is full of my new friends, or at least the crowd that has more or less accepted me as one of their own, the odd 'greener' tag-along. They're as lively as a group of puppies, jostling each other
5 with sharp elbows, crawling over each other to change seats, and expressing their well-being and amiability by trying to outshout each other. It's Saturday night, or rather Saturday Night, and party spirits are obligatory. We're on our way to the local
10 White Spot, an early Canadian version of McDonald's, where we'll engage in the barbarous – as far as I'm concerned – rite of the 'drive-in'. This activity of sitting in your car in a large parking lot, and having sloppy, big hamburgers brought to you 15 on a tray, accompanied by greasy french fries bounding out of their cardboard containers, mustard, spilly catsup, and sickly smelling relish, seems to fill these peers of mine with warm, monkeyish, groupy comfort. It fills me with a
20 finicky distaste. I feel my lips tighten into an unaccustomed thinness – which, in turn, fills me with a small dislike for myself.

'Come on, foreign student, cheer up,' one of the boys sporting a flowery Hawaiian shirt and crew
25 cut tells me, poking me in the ribs good-naturedly. 'What's the matter, don't you like it here?'

'greener': a foreigner recently arrived in a country
crew cut: a very short haircut

a)   1   What are her new friends like?
2   What do they do on Saturday nights?
3   Why does she hate the 'drive-in' hamburger restaurant?
4   What does it make her feel?
5   How do we know she has mixed feelings?

b)   What do these phrases tell you about the writer's attitude/feelings?
1   at least the crowd that has more or less accepted me (line 1)
2   I feel my lips tighten into an unaccustomed thinness (line 20)

STUDENT B: How Ewa's behaviour changed:

My mother says I'm becoming 'English'. This hurts me, because I know she means I'm becoming cold. I'm no colder than I've ever been, but I'm learning to be less demonstrative. I learn this from a teacher 5 who, after contemplating the gesticulations with which I help myself describe the digestive system of a frog, tells me to 'sit on my hands and then try talking'. I learn my new reserve from people who take a step back when we talk, because I'm standing 10 too close, crowding them. Cultural distances are different, I later learn in a sociology class, but I know it already. I learn restraint from Penny, who looks offended when I shake her by the arm in excitement, as if my gesture had been one of 15 aggression instead of friendliness. I learn it from a girl who pulls away when I hook my arm through hers as we walk down the street – this movement of friendly intimacy is an embarrassment to her. I learn also that certain kinds of truth are impolite. 20 One shouldn't criticise the person one is with, at least not directly. You shouldn't say, 'You are wrong about that' – though you may say, 'On the other hand, there is that to consider.' You shouldn't say, 'This doesn't look good on you,' though you may 25 say, 'I like you better in that other outfit.' I learn to tone down my sharpness, to do a more careful conversational minuet.

Perhaps my mother is right, after all; perhaps I'm becoming colder. After a while, emotion follows 30 action, response grows warmer or cooler according to gesture. I'm more careful about what I say, how loud I laugh, whether I give vent to grief. The storminess of emotion prevailing in our family is in excess of the normal here ...

c) 1 Why does her mother think she is becoming a colder person?
2 On what occasions did she learn to be less demonstrative?
3 How was her behaviour different when she first arrived in Canada?
4 What other things did she learn?
5 How is her own family life different to those around her?

d) What do these phrases tell you about her attitude/feelings?
1 My mother says I'm becoming 'English'. (line 1)
2 a more careful conversational minuet. (line 26)

STUDENT C: The first house Ewa lived in:

The garden itself is of such pruned and trimmed neatness that I'm half afraid to walk in it. Its lawn is improbably smooth and velvety (Ah, the time and worry spent on the shaving of these lawns!) ...
5 Still, I much prefer sitting out here in the sun to being inside. The house is larger than any apartment I have seen in Poland, with enormous 'picture' windows, a separate room for every member of the family and soft-pastel-colored rugs 10 covering all the floors. These are all features that, I know, are intended to signify good taste and wealth – but there's an incongruity between the message I'm supposed to get and my secret perceptions of these surroundings. To me, these interiors seem oddly flat, devoid of imagination, ingenuous. The 15 spaces are so plain, low-ceilinged, obvious; there are no curves, niches, odd angles, nooks or crannies – nothing that gathers a house into itself, giving it a sense of privacy or depth – of interiority. There's no solid wood here, no accretion either of age or 20 dust. There is only the open sincerity of simple spaces, open right out to the street. (No peering out the window here, to catch glimpses of exchanges on the street; the picture windows are designed to give everyone a full view of everyone 25 else, to declare there's no mystery, nothing to hide. Not true, of course, but that's the statement.)

e) 1 Why does she feel uncomfortable in the garden?
2 How do Canadians seem to like their houses?
3 What do their houses try to show?
4 What would she prefer the house to be like?
5 What do you imagine her apartment in Poland was like?

f) What do these phrases tell you about her attitude/feelings?
1 I'm half afraid to walk in it. (line 2)
2 No peering out of the window here (line 22)

3 All three extracts are about Ewa's early life in Canada.

Extract A is about going to a hamburger 'drive-in' with some young Canadians; B is about how her behaviour started to change when she was with people; C is about the first house she lived in and how it was different from apartments in Poland. Tell the other two students about your extract and ask them some questions about their extracts.

Speaking **4** Discuss answers to some of these questions:

1 How was Canada different from Poland? How is Ewa's life different in Canada? How is she different from other people?

2 What are your overall impressions of:
  – Canada in the early 1960s? Do you know if it was similar to your country?
  – Her life abroad? Was she happy?

3 Ewa later became an editor of the *New York Times Book Review.* She wrote this autobiography in English and it was first published in 1989. What do you think about the way she writes? What are the advantages/disadvantages of writing in a second language?

4 Could you imagine leaving your country forever or for a very long period? If so, where would you prefer to go if you had a choice? Why? How would it differ from going abroad to work or for a holiday? What would you miss most about your country?

VOCABULARY: American English

1   There are far fewer differences between standard American and standard British English than many people think and even these seem to be disappearing. The main difference is in pronunciation and idiomatic language. There are some small differences in grammar, spelling and vocabulary.

Can you answer these questions about American English?

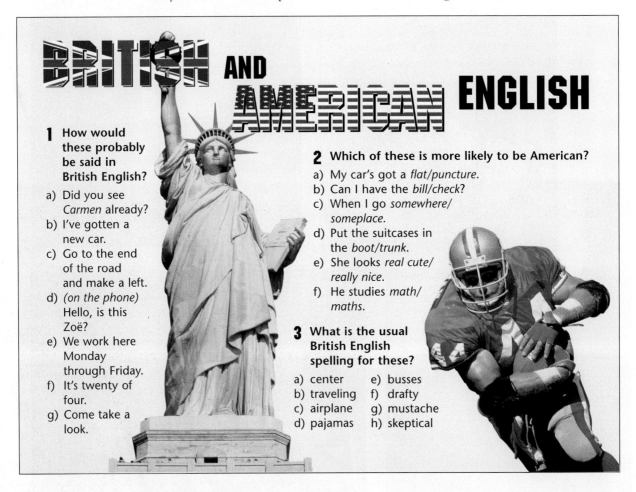

BRITISH AND AMERICAN ENGLISH

1 How would these probably be said in British English?

a) Did you see *Carmen* already?

b) I've gotten a new car.

c) Go to the end of the road and make a left.

d) *(on the phone)* Hello, is this Zoë?

e) We work here Monday through Friday.

f) It's twenty of four.

g) Come take a look.

2 Which of these is more likely to be American?

a) My car's got a *flat/puncture*.

b) Can I have the *bill/check*?

c) When I go *somewhere/ someplace*.

d) Put the suitcases in the *boot/trunk*.

e) She looks *real cute/ really nice*.

f) He studies *math/ maths*.

3 What is the usual British English spelling for these?

a) center   e) busses
b) traveling   f) drafty
c) airplane   g) mustache
d) pajamas   h) skeptical

2   [🔲 7.2]   Listen to this anecdote by an American who lived in Britain for a short time.

a)   How did his friend's joke fail?

b)   The actor pronounces words a little differently from the British. Which words strike you in particular?

3a) How would Americans say the words in the box?

duty	fertile	tomatoes	bananas	progress	route
marathon	anti	leisure			

b)   How do you think they would be pronounced in standard British English?

c)   [🔲 7.3]   Listen and compare.

4   [🔲 7.4]   There are also some habits of conversation that are different. Listen to the American talking about a trip to Britain. Why could the use of the word 'right' be confusing?

5   Discuss answers to one or both of these questions.

1   Have you ever been confused in understanding what a native speaker of your language says because of variations in accent, habits of conversation etc? If so, when? Which variations in your language do you particularly like/dislike? If there are students from other countries in your class tell them what variations there are in your language (e.g. pronunciation, vocabulary, grammar and conversational habits). These may link to country, region, social status, educational background and age of the person talking.

2   In Britain there is no Academy controlling or regulating the language. Do you think such control of a language is a good thing? Do you think control is necessary to maintain standards or does it inhibit creativity?

SPEAKING AND WRITING: Comparing and contrasting

1   Work in pairs.

STUDENT A: Look at this photograph.
STUDENT B: Look at the photograph on page 179.

a)   Take one minute to describe your photograph to your partner. Try to agree on some similarities and differences.

b)   Look at each other's photographs. What mood is suggested by each? Which place would you prefer to be in and why?

c)   Use some of the expressions in the box to write a paragraph:
   1   comparing what you can see in the photographs.
   2   talking about any feelings or attitudes you have about the different situations.

> whereas   while   on the other hand
> by contrast   conversely   similarly

Example: *In your picture it sounds as if ... whereas in my picture ...*

d)   Compare your paragraph with your partner's. What do they have in common? How do they differ?

2a) Underline the comparative constructions in these car advertisements.

Example:

The very happiest car owners in the UK consider their Subaru to be as good as gold.

It's built along the same lines as our big estates. But without all the straight lines.

Our new model — sleeker than ever.

THE JEEP that looks as if it's made to last.

THE ALFA GTV.
IT DRIVES LIKE THE WIND.
IT LOOKS AS THOUGH
WE'VE REACHED
PERFECTION.

b) Make sentences of comparison using these cues.

1 A: This flat/look/considerably/small/your old flat.
   B: Yes. big/room/is the kitchen!

2 A: What/far/you ever (fly) in your balloon?
   B: I went from Morocco to Switzerland once.
   A: That/much far/than me. I've never been out of the country.

3 A: You look/you (be) up all night!
   B: No, I was a bit late to bed. Unfortunately, I/(not) young/I used to be.

4 A: Will I get/same size audience/last week?
   B: Twice/many/that, I hope!

5 A: (be)/quite a lot/people here.
   B: The more/merry! I want to have a good time.

3   In American English, and informal British English, *like* is often used instead of *as/as if*.

Example: *It looks like it's going to rain.* (*It looks as if ...*)
She's a good swimmer, like her brother used to be. (*She's as good a swimmer as ...*)

This substitution is often not acceptable in more formal written English. In which of these sentences is *like* correct/acceptable in informal British English? Which sentence would not be acceptable? Which one is completely incorrect?

1 You look like my friend.
2 On Monday, like on Thursday, the shops will be closed.
3 Like I told you, it's an offer you can't refuse.
4 He's worked like a waiter in McDonald's for the last two years.
5 He spends money like there's no tomorrow.

▶ **Language Bank page 144: Comparatives and superlatives**

1 TENSE AND ASPECT

In English we talk about the present **tense** (Present Simple) and the past **tense** (Past Simple). They are called 'tenses' because they show whether the forms are referring to the present or the past. (We show future time through a variety of forms – see Unit 5.)

We also talk about the perfect **aspect** and the continuous **aspect**. An aspect describes how we see an action or state in terms of the passing of time.

The perfect aspect

Most perfect verb forms show that an event comes before another time (the past, present or future):
*I'll **have visited** Dublin before the end of the year.*
*She'**d finished** all the work by lunchtime.*

In some cases the event is complete – and the exact time of the action may be not important or not known:
*I've **read** the paper. Here you are.* (The action of reading is complete. The fact that it was completed in the past is relevant to us now because I can give the paper to you. It doesn't matter when I read it in the past.)

Sometimes the event is incomplete:
*I've **lived** here for three years.* (and I'm still living here.)

Sometimes the verb form refers to general experience:
*We've **had** some wonderful holidays in Greece.*

The continuous aspect

The continuous (or 'progressive') aspect may show the event is ongoing and temporary rather than completed or permanent:
*He **was** still **speaking** to her at half past three.* (The action was still in progress at that time.)

NOTE:
State verbs (e.g. *be, seem, know, believe, like*) are not normally used in the continuous. However, some (e.g. *look, hear, want*) can be used to emphasise a situation in progress:
*I've **been hearing** a lot about you!*

The Perfect Continuous

The perfect and continuous aspects may be combined:
*I've **been playing tennis** all day. I'm exhausted.*
*When I got home **he had been waiting** for an hour.*
*When they finally got there, **they'd been travelling** for fourteen hours.*

2 THE PRESENT PERFECT SIMPLE AND THE PRESENT PERFECT CONTINUOUS

1 The Present Perfect (= before now) connects the present to the past. It is used to show:
  a) past experiences/events with relevance to now:
     *I've **broken** my leg. I'm sorry I can't go skiing.* (past action with a present result)
     *I've **just seen** him. If you hurry, you'll catch him up.*
     *I've **seen** lots of ghosts. Have you?* (general experience)

  b) an unfinished state/habitual action:
     *She'**s worked** here all her life. It's time she got a different job.*
     *I've **been** to see him every weekend. I'm getting a bit tired of it.*

2 The Past Simple (= then) is used for completed actions/states which took place at a specific time in the past:
   *I **broke** my leg when I was on holiday.*
   *I **saw** him in hospital last night.*

3 The Present Perfect Continuous is used to focus on an ongoing, temporary action or situation. It can refer to:
  a) temporary unfinished actions/situations:
     *You'**ve been watching** TV for over an hour. Turn it off!* (The action started in the past and it is still in progress.)

  b) temporary actions/situations recently in progress:
     *You'**ve been crying**. Your eyes are red.* (present effect)
     *A: What'**ve you been doing** all day?*
     *B: I'**ve been reading**.* (focus on the activity – the activity has finished but the day hasn't)

NOTE:
1 We use the Present Perfect Simple not the Present Perfect Continuous with *ever, never* and *yet.*

2 For short, completed actions we use the Present Perfect Simple not the Present Perfect Continuous.
  *I'**ve broken** my leg.* (NOT *I've ~~been breaking~~ ...*)

3 THE PAST PERFECT SIMPLE AND THE PAST PERFECT CONTINUOUS

The Past Perfect (= before then in the past) connects a past event/state to an earlier past event/state:
When I got home (i.e. then) *I realised that **she'd packed** her bags and left.*

The Past Perfect Continuous focuses on something in progress at a particular time in the past:
*When the war broke out, we **had been living** in the city for about ten years.*

▶ Language Reference page 31

4 THE FUTURE PERFECT AND THE FUTURE PERFECT CONTINUOUS

The Future Perfect (= before a specific time in the future) connects a time in the future with an earlier event/state. We use it to say that by a certain time in the future things will be completed or achieved:
*When you get there tomorrow he'**ll already have left**.* (completed action)
*Next year we'**ll have been** in this house for ten years.* (ongoing state)
*Do you realise that by the time I hand in this thesis I'**ll have been working** on it for about a year?* (temporary action in progress)

▶ Language Reference page 73

GOOD OLD DAYS?

LISTENING: Relative values

1 Sharron Davies was an Olympic swimmer and now has a career in TV. When she went to the Montreal Olympics at thirteen she was the youngest British competitor ever.

a) What effect do you think her 'drive for gold' (her attempt to win a gold medal) might have had on the family she grew up in?

b) What qualities do you think you need to have to be successful so young? What kind of support do you need?

2 [📼 8.1] Work in pairs. Listen to these extracts from a radio programme called *Relative Values*, where Sharron and her younger brother Mark talk about their lives.

STUDENT A: Listen particularly to Mark.
STUDENT B: Listen particularly to Sharron.

a) Make notes under these headings according to what 'your' person says.

Family activities	How he/she was treated	Effect of Sharron's 'drive for gold'	His/her attitude to father

b) Compare the notes you made in Exercise 2a). Are there any differences in the way Mark and Sharron see the past?

3   Who says these and what do they refer to? If necessary, listen again or check with the tapescript on page 188.

1   It was more of a shadow life
2   He was without doubt a better coach than he was a father
3   I think the price was the family
4   that was the start of my life
5   I have a good life

4a) How would you describe Sharron, Mark and their father? You may choose words from the box (or their opposites) but give reasons for your choice.

Example: *To be successful Sharron had to be very determined, which she admits she was.*

obsessive	determined	selfish	stubborn	equable
fair-minded	self-deprecatory	resentful	spoilt	compulsive
egotistical	lacking in self-esteem	placid		

b)   Very little is said about their mother in these extracts. There is just one clue. Which word in the box describes her most closely?

Speaking   **5a)** Were your own family relationships in any way similar to Mark or Sharron's? If you have brothers and sisters, was one given more encouragement to develop than another?

b)   How do you feel about the following?
1   Sacrificing a 'normal' family life to develop a child with an obvious talent. Would you do it?
2   Making young children very competitive.
3   Giving 'gifted' children a specialist education.
4   Making young children perform in public.

Tiger Woods

Mozart

Drew Barrymore

SPEAKING: Talking personally

1a) Work in groups. What do you think is meant by each of these quotations? Which opinion do you most agree with? Which do you least agree with?

b) Modify any you don't agree with.

> *(On parents)*
> They fill you with the faults they had. And add some extra, just for you.

> Children begin by loving their parents. After a time they judge them. Rarely, if ever, do they forgive them.

OSCAR WILDE
(English author born in Ireland 1854–1900)

PHILIP LARKIN
(English poet 1922–1985)

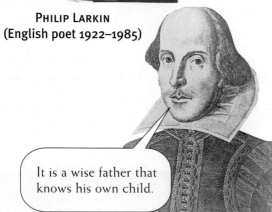

> If you strike a child, take care that you strike it in anger, even at the risk of maiming it for life. A blow in cold blood neither can nor should be forgiven.

> It is a wise father that knows his own child.

WILLIAM SHAKESPEARE
(English dramatist and poet 1564–1616)

GEORGE BERNARD SHAW
(Irish dramatist 1856–1950)

2 If possible, work in four groups according to your position in the family.

GROUP A: Eldest children   GROUP C: Youngest children
GROUP B: Middle children   GROUP D: Only children

a) Compare your experiences. What was it like being the eldest, middle, youngest, 'only' child? Do you wish the situation had been different (e.g. if you were a 'middle' child, do you wish you had been an 'only' child)? Think of things like:
   – what your parents expected of you (e.g. in terms of domestic duties; how you should behave in relation to brothers and sisters)
   – what you were not allowed to have or wear
   – discipline and punishments
   – how far you could talk openly as a family
   – going out with friends or the opposite sex

b) Re-group so that you work with one person from each of the other groups. How are your experiences similar/different?

SECTION 2 GRAMMAR: Complex sentences

1a) Read paragraph A. What creature is the writer talking about?

A It is the first night of your holiday. You go to bed happy. You are intoxicated by the scent of orange blossom. You are drifting contentedly into unconsciousness. The buzzing begins. It is a hideous whining noise. It is full of resentment. It is the buzzing of a creature. This creature is preparing to feast on your blood. It first does a ritual war dance to intimidate you. The buzzing rises and falls. Then it stops. This causes you a moment of pure panic.

B It is the first night of your holiday and you go to bed happy. Intoxicated by the scent of orange blossom, you are drifting contentedly into unconsciousness when the buzzing begins. This hideous whining noise, full of resentment, is the buzzing of a creature preparing to feast on your blood but only after a ritual war dance to intimidate you. The buzzing rises and falls and then it stops, which causes you a moment of pure panic.

b) Paragraph B creates a different effect. Which paragraph (A or B) sounds:
- smoother and more fluent?
- more dramatic and tense?

c) What differences can you see in the way the sentences are constructed? Example: *In A there are no connecting expressions.*

d) Match the extracts in A below with the definitions in B.

   A 1 It is the first night of your holiday and you go to bed happy.
      2 Intoxicated by the scent of orange blossom, you are drifting contentedly into unconsciousness when the buzzing begins.
      3 It is a hideous whining noise.

   B a) In *simple sentences* there are no connecting expressions (*and, but* etc.).
      b) In *compound sentences* the clauses are joined by a connecting expression. They can be broken up and written as separate sentences.
      c) In *complex sentences* there are clauses which are dependent on (or 'subordinate' to) other clauses in the sentence. They cannot be written as separate sentences.

2   The sentences below are all complex sentences. The clauses in italics are called 'dependent' (or 'subordinate') clauses.

a)   Find dependent clauses in B which have a similar form to the dependent clauses in A. Use the description in brackets to help you. Example: *1* and *g)* (they are both *wh-* noun clauses).

A   1   It's a mystery *why he did it*. (*wh-* noun clause)
2   We didn't meet *until after the war was over*. (time adverbial)
3   The idea is *to get the ball in the back of the net*. (infinitive)
4   *If you feel ill*, go to bed. (condition)
5   A car (*which was*) *full of joyriders* crashed into a wall. (relative)
6   I love you *more than I can say*. (comparative)
7   *Having given him his head*, I'm sure he'll make a success of it. (participle)

B   a)   You sing *much better than I do*.
b)   *Being an honest person*, he decided to hand in the wallet.
c)   I'll go in, *provided you come with me*.
d)   Give him my love *when you see him*.
e)   Is there a plan *to get an early flight?*
f)   The man *hurt in the accident* was taken to hospital.
g)   *Where he goes at nights* is not at all clear to me.

There are explanations of these clauses in the Language Reference on page 113.

b)   Think of other phrases you can substitute for the clauses in italics in A, using a similar form. Example 1: It's a mystery *what he does for a living*.

▶ **Language Bank page 149:** *It/there*

3   Change the sentences below into simple sentences. Add any words you think are necessary to help the sentence stand on its own (e.g. words like *it, there, then, however* and *they* to refer to a previous sentence). Example:

At least 500 people have been killed in floods which have submerged a large part of the country.
At least 500 have been killed in floods. These floods have submerged a large part of the country.

1   After being sacked by the football club he went back to Amsterdam.
2   When I went to London I had a cup of coffee in the new Philosophy Café and discussed the meaning of life.
3   Teenagers nowadays lead healthy lives, at least more so than their counterparts of a decade ago, but a minority are couch potatoes who drink, smoke and eat chips with everything. The survey, conducted last year, paints a picture of a health-conscious generation, with more teenagers visiting their doctors regularly and more brushing their teeth and having fewer fillings.

4 Now do the reverse process and make these simple sentences into one compound and/or complex sentence. Decide on your punctuation and connecting expressions. Add or change as many words as you need but keep the ideas of each sentence.

1 Heavy drinkers may lose their friends. Heavy drinkers always have a good head of hair. Dr Hugh Rushton claims this. (*Dr Hugh Rushton ...*)

2 His father was a builder. His father, his mother, and six brothers and sisters lived in just three rooms. His youngest sister was three months old. (*His father ...*)

3 The massive Place Djemaa is at the physical and spiritual heart of Marrakech. It lies in the centre of the Medina. The Medina was the ancient city. (*At* or *The ...*)

4 The results of a survey appeared in a newspaper. One of the results was about Norwegians. Norwegians are strong on saying thank you. They are sometimes offended by foreigners. Some foreigners hardly ever say thank you. (*One of the results ...*)

5 Veruschka is a German aristocrat. She had her heyday in the 1960s. She achieved notoriety for covering herself in psychedelic body paint. (*Veruschka ...*)

6 We were in Rome last year. Rome is the most beautiful city in Europe. I once taught English there. We stayed in an incredible hotel. The hotel looked absolutely gorgeous. However, every room had something wrong with it. For example, the light switches and the showers. The showers didn't work. The showers only gave you cold water. (*When ...*)

SECTION 3 READING AND SPEAKING: Getting older

Before reading **1a)** How old do you think these people are? Choose four of the things below which you think are the most important for people of their age. You can use the same word more than once and ignore any words that you feel are not appropriate.

friends	health	education	work	family	love	travel
money	appearance	social life	possessions			

b) Are there things in the box which are not important for people of their age?

2 Which age would you associate with the following expressions?

set in his/her ways	footloose and fancy free	putting down roots
has seen it all before	having a whale of a time	not having ties
being stuck in a rut	spreading his/her wings	settled down

Reading **3** Read this poem by the American poet, Maya Angelou.

a) Choose the best summary of her attitude.
1 Because I'm old it doesn't mean I'm finished. I'm glad to be alive.
2 When I'm old, I'll be no different from the younger me.
3 I may look old one day but I'll be the same person inside and I won't need any favours.

> **NOTE:**
> Both poems in this exercise are on the recording.

On Aging

When you see me sitting quietly,
Like a sack left on the shelf,
Don't think I need your chattering,
I'm listening to myself.
Hold! Stop! Don't pity me!
Hold! Stop your sympathy!
Understanding if you got it,
Otherwise I'll do without it!

When my bones are stiff and aching
And my feet won't climb the stair,
I will only ask one favor;
Don't bring me no rocking chair.

When you see me walking, stumbling,
Don't study and get it wrong.
'Cause tired don't mean lazy
And every goodbye ain't gone.
I'm the same person I was back then,
A little less hair, a little less chin,
A lot less lungs and much less wind,
But ain't I lucky I can still breathe in.

b) Find as many examples in the poem as you can of where younger people can misinterpret the old.

c) Which of these would she prefer?
- People to talk to or to be left alone?
- Pity or understanding?
- To struggle on physically or to rest?

d) Now read this poem by Jim Burns. In what way is the poem's view of old age similar/different to the poem in a)?

Note for the Future

When I get old
don't dress me in
frayed jackets
and too-short-trousers,
and send me out
to sit around bowling greens
in summer.
Don't give me just enough
to exist on, and expect me
to like passing
the winter days
in the reading room
of the local library, waiting
my turn to read
last night's local paper.
Shoot me!
Find a reason, any reason,
say I'm a troublemaker,
or can't take care of myself
and live in a dirty room.
If you're afraid
of justifying my execution
on those terms,
tell everyone I leer
at little girls, and then
shoot me!
I don't care why you do it,
but do it,
and don't leave me
to walk to corner-shops,
counting my coppers,
or give me a pass to travel cheap
at certain times, like a leper.

coppers: small change (money)

e) Which of these do you most agree with and why?
- He's frightened and angry.
- He's trying to shock us.
- He wants to be with young people when he gets old.
- He's being very sensible.

Speaking **4a)** When you are old and unable to live by yourself how would you like to be treated? Which of the two poets' views are most similar to yours?

b) Would you like to live with your family or live in special accommodation for the elderly? What are the advantages/disadvantages of each?

c) The proportion of people over 65 is increasing in many parts of the world due to declining birth rate and better medicine. The young can benefit from the experience and support of older people but what problems are caused (e.g. the cost of pensions)?

WRITING: Articles

▶ Before doing this section you might wish to review some of the
techniques for writing articles on page 164 of the Writing Bank.

1　You have been asked to write an article for a magazine, journal or
newspaper.

a) Analyse these article topics. Does the topic have one or more parts?

    1 A feature on the problems caused by an ageing population. Examine the issue for either a 'human-interest' magazine or a political journal.

    2 The position of 'minority groups' (people of a different race, culture, religion, set of political beliefs etc.) in your country. Examine one particular group as an example, for a magazine sold worldwide. In your view what are the main problems and possible solutions?

    3 A 'Saints and Sinners' page for a newspaper – i.e. write about a famous person you love or hate.

    4 A light-hearted article for a weekly magazine for women on the topic, 'If you could have your life again, would you rather be a man or a woman and why?'

b) Are you being asked:
– for your opinion about something?
– to describe a situation, process, a set of facts etc?
– to state the pros and cons of an argument (for and against)?

c) How would the type of magazine etc. affect the way you presented your information (e.g. in a 'human interest' magazine you would probably start with some real-life examples; in a political magazine you might start with a controversial statement.)?

2 This is a possible structure for at least one of the articles in Exercise 1.

STAGE 1 Introduction/purpose of the article + background information

STAGE 2 Arguments 'for'
(Each argument → development/extra information → example)

STAGE 3 Arguments 'against'
(Each argument → development/extra information → example)

STAGE 4 State your opinion

There are many other possibilities. Example: *2 – Analyse the current situation; 3 – Give your views; 4 – Suggested solution (+ justification and practical example)*

a) You are going to write one of the articles in Exercise 1. Form groups according to the topic you prefer to write about.

b) Decide where you will submit your article and brainstorm as many ideas as you can on the chosen topic, keeping your target audience in mind.

c) Make some notes for the article that you intend to write and select the most interesting ideas.

d) Find ideas which go together and divide the article into sections. Try to make a logical sequence in your notes that will show development from one point to another.

e) One of the group should be a 'scribe'. Help the scribe write a first draft of your article quickly (about 250 words).

f) Imagine you are submitting your article to a magazine. Go back over the draft and check it. Make changes if necessary and give the article a title.

g) Each member of the group should rewrite part of the article.

h) Submit your article to another group, who will act as editor. Ask them for their views. Is it interesting? Are there things they don't agree with?

VOCABULARY: Choosing the right words

1a) Words with the same basic meaning as other words can suggest different feelings, ideas or attitudes. Read these sentences. Why might b) be used instead of a)?

Example: 1b) *to lose someone* is often used to soften for the speaker/hearer the news of someone close to you dying.

1   a) My husband died last week b) I lost my husband last week.
2   Let me introduce you to our new a) chairman b) chairperson.
3   A a) noisy crowd b) howling mob descended on the city centre.
4   How a) thin b) slim you are!
5   Cambridge has a lot of a) foreign tourists b) overseas visitors.

b)   These sentences all contain euphemisms (attempts to make the language pleasanter through being less direct). How could you express the phrases in italics in a more direct way?

1   I'm afraid I've been *rather economical with the truth.*
2   Tell me, *have you got a drink problem?*
3   *The company is being downsized* so that we can *emerge leaner and fitter.*
4   Discounts are available for *senior citizens.*
5   Could you tell me where the *ladies' room* is?
6   I can't pay you right now – I'm somewhat *financially embarrassed.*
7   Unfortunately we had to have the cat *put to sleep* last night.

c)   Say what the following mean and whether you think they sound offensive or humorous.

1   Some of your staff seem not only intellectually challenged but past their sell-by date.
2   I'm sorry but you're interfering with my personal space.
3   The prime minister is tired and emotional and will probably have a hangover in the morning.
4   It seems we are in a non-profit situation and may have to withdraw our services.

2   'Politically correct' language attempts to make language less socially offensive. Some generally used common examples include: 'native Americans' (instead of 'American Indians') and 'headteacher' (instead of 'headmaster'/'headmistress'). Some less generally used examples include: 'visually impaired' (for 'blind') and 'follicly challenged' (for 'bald'). What do you think of these kinds of changes to language? Necessary? Absurd? Some are necessary, some aren't? Give your reasons.

1 CLAUSES

1 A clause usually consists of a subject + verb phrase. These are some examples of clauses:
   a) subject + verb phrase (*I'm leaving.*)
   b) subject + verb phrase + object (*She speaks Russian.*)
   c) subject + verb phrase + indirect object + direct object (*She gave me a kiss.*)
   d) subject + verb phrase + complement (*He's nice.*)
   e) subject + verb phrase + direct object + complement (*You make me happy.*)
   f) subject + verb phrase + adverbial (*They live in London.*)
   g) subject + verb phrase + direct object + adverbial (*He took me home.*)

2 There are also verbless clauses which have the meaning and some of the elements of a clause (e.g. subject, object and adverbial):
   a) *What a mess!/How about a lift?/Sorry about that.*
   b) **An excellent cook**, *he was always experimenting with new dishes.*
      With everyone off work, *the company was in serious trouble.*

2 COMPOUND SENTENCES

A compound sentence is a sentence consisting of two or more independent clauses (i.e. they can stand on their own). When we want to link the clauses in a compound sentence we can use a semi-colon (*She speaks Polish; she doesn't speak Hungarian.*) or, in informal writing, we can use a dash (*She speaks Polish – she doesn't speak Hungarian.*). More commonly, however, a conjunction is used such as *and, and then, but, yet, so, or/nor, either/or, neither/nor*:
She speaks Polish **but** *(she) doesn't speak Hungarian.*
   When we use a co-ordinating conjunction and the subject is the same in both parts of the sentence it is possible not to repeat the subject: *She speaks Polish but doesn't ...*

3 COMPLEX SENTENCES

A complex sentence is a sentence consisting of a main clause and one or more dependent (or 'subordinate') clauses (i.e. they cannot stand on their own away from the main clause). When we want to develop some aspect of what we are saying we can add the dependent clauses to the main clause:
When you see him (dependent clause), *give him my regards* (main clause).

We can do this for example by:
a) joining the dependent clause to the main clause with a conjunction (*if, when, since* etc.):
   I read it **while** *you were having a bath.*

b) using an infinitive construction:
   To make the world a safer place, *we have to get rid of landmines.*

c) using a participle construction:
   Having been a politician, *she never likes to admit she's wrong.*

The main types of dependent clause are:

1 Noun clause:
   He swears **(that)** *he didn't take it.* (*that* clause, as in a reported clause)
   What I think *is no concern of yours.*
   It is no concern of yours **what I think.** (*wh-* clause)
   Where he gets the money from *I haven't a clue.*
   I haven't a clue **where he gets the money from.**
   His idea is **to get government backing.** (infinitive clause)
   There is no chance of him **getting government backing.** (participle clause)

   Noun clauses, like nouns, can have a different role in the sentence:
   Whether or not you agree *isn't important.* (subject)
   The question is **whether or not you agree.** (complement)
   I want to know **whether or not you agree.** (object)

2 Relative (or adjectival) clauses:
   I never met him, **which was a pity.** (I never met him. It was a pity.)

3 Adverbial clauses:
   When you leave, *turn out the light.* (time)
   I'd come with you **if I could afford it.** (condition)
   We bought some paper cups **so that we could have a picnic.** (purpose)
   He failed a drug test **so the race had to be rerun.** (result)
   I couldn't leave her **because I loved her too much.** (reason)
   Although I did well at maths, *my overall result was poor.* (concession)
   He left it **where it was.** (place)
   I feel **as if I have a cold coming.** (manner)
   If possible, *can you come early?* (verbless clause of condition)

4 Comparative clauses:
   You are more understanding **than you used to be.**

NOTE:
1 When we refer to the subject of the main clause in a dependent clause we avoid repetition of the subject by using (for example) a pronoun:
   Ben is more understanding than **he** *used to be.*

2 Some types of dependent clause can change their place in a sentence:
   If you want, *I'll take it round.*/*I'll take it round* **if you want.** (without a comma)
   To prove their guilt *would be difficult.*/*It would be difficult* **to prove their guilt.** (+ *it* as an introductory subject)

3 A sentence can consist of both co-ordinate clauses (as in compound sentences) and dependent clauses (as in complex sentences) and be as long as you like. However, the average sentence in written English is said to be about 17 words and very long sentences can often be heavy and difficult to understand.

WHAT DO YOU THINK?

READING: *Flight* (1)

Before reading **1** You are going to read a story called *Flight* by the novelist and short story writer, Doris Lessing. The story is about an old man, his pigeons and his granddaughter.

a) Why do you think someone might want to keep homing pigeons?

b) What do you think the story might be about? (The title is a clue.)

Vocabulary **2a)** The words in the box below are all associated with pigeons (doves). Use a dictionary to help you and say which word means:

1 to make a low soft noise
2 their home
3 to clean their feathers with their beaks
4 a way of walking, with the chest pushed out
5 the nails on a bird or animal's foot

| to strut | to preen | to coo/croon | a dovecote | claws |

b) Look at the verbs in the box below. Some are from the story.

glimpse	mutter	gaze	spot	growl
gape	glance	stammer	mumble	murmur

1 Divide them into ways of *speaking* and ways of *seeing/looking*.

2 What is the difference in meaning between the words of *speaking*? Example: *mutter* is to speak in a low voice (usually when somebody is complaining).

3 Write sentences to show the meaning of the words of *seeing/looking*. Example: *I just glimpsed her yellow dress before she disappeared.*

3a) Read these extracts from the first part of the story and check the words in italics with the dictionary definitions below.

1 in a sudden access of troubled *spite* he shut the bird into a small box
2 He moved *warily* along the hedge, *stalking* his granddaughter
3 He *confronted* her
4 Think you're old enough to go *courting*?
5 He would be left, *uncherished*

spite /spaɪt/ *n* [U] a feeling of wanting to hurt or upset people

wary /weəri/ *adj* careful because something or someone might be dangerous or harmful

stalk /stɔːk/ *v* [T] to follow a person quietly in order to catch them

confront /kən'frʌnt/ *v* [T] to behave in a threatening way towards someone

court /kɔːt/ *v* [T] (old-fashioned) if a man and a woman are courting, they are having a romantic relationship, and may get married

cherish /'tʃerɪʃ/ *v* [T] (usually passive) to love someone/thing very much and take good care of them/it

From the *Longman Dictionary of Contemporary English*.

b) The extracts above are all about the old man.
1 What do you learn about him?
2 What do you think his feelings are towards his pigeons and his granddaughter? Why?

Reading **4a)** Read the first part of the story quickly.

> 1 Were the guesses you made in Exercise 3b) right?
> 2 What other people are mentioned in the extract?

Above the old man's head was the dovecote, a tall wire-netted shelf on stilts, full of strutting, preening birds. The sunlight broke on their grey breasts into small rainbows. His ears were lulled by their crooning, his hands stretched up towards his favourite, a homing pigeon, a young plump-bodied bird which stood still when it saw him and cocked a shrewd bright eye.

'Pretty, pretty, pretty,' he said, as he grasped the bird and drew it down, feeling the cold coral claws tighten around his finger. Content, he rested the bird lightly on his chest, and leaned against a tree, gazing out beyond the dovecote into the landscape of a late afternoon. In folds and hollows of sunlight and shade, the dark red soil, which was broken into great dusty clods, stretched wide to a tall horizon. Trees marked the course of the valley; a stream of rich green grass the road.

His eyes travelled homewards along this road until he saw his granddaughter swinging on the gate underneath a frangipani tree. Her hair fell down her back in a wave of sunlight, and her long bare legs repeated the angles of the frangipani stems, bare, shining-brown stems among patterns of pale blossoms.

She was gazing past the pink flowers, past the railway cottage where they lived, along the road to the village.

His mood shifted. He deliberately held out his wrist for the bird to take flight, and caught it again at the moment it spread its wings. He felt the plump shape strive and strain under his fingers; and, in a sudden access of troubled spite, shut the bird into a small box and fastened the bolt. 'Now you stay there,' he muttered; and turned his back on the shelf of birds. He moved warily along the hedge, stalking his granddaughter, who was now looped over the gate, her head loose on her arms, singing. The light happy sound mingled with the crooning of the birds, and his anger mounted.

'Hey!' he shouted; saw her jump, look back, and abandon the gate. Her eyes veiled themselves, and she said in a pert neutral voice: 'Hullo, Granddad.' Politely she moved towards him, after a lingering backward glance at the road.

'Waiting for Steven, hey?' he said, his fingers curling like claws into his palm.

'Any objection?' She asked lightly, refusing to look at him.

He confronted her, his eyes narrowed, shoulders hunched tight in a hard knot of pain which included the preening birds, the sunlight, the flowers. He said: 'Think you're old enough to go courting, hey?'

The girl tossed her head at the old-fashioned phrase and sulked, 'Oh Granddad!'

'Think you want to leave home, hey? Think you can go running round the fields at night?'

Her smile made him see her, as he had every evening of this warm end-of-summer month, swinging hand in hand along the road to the village with that red-handed, red-throated, violent-bodied youth, the son of the postmaster. Misery went to his head and he shouted angrily: 'I'll tell your mother!'

'Tell away!' she said, laughing, and went back to the gate. He heard her singing, for him to hear:

'I've got you under my skin,
I've got you deep in the heart of ...'

'Rubbish,' he shouted. 'Rubbish. Impudent little bit of rubbish!'

Growling under his breath he turned towards the dovecote, which was his refuge from the house he shared with his daughter and her husband and their children.

But now the house would be empty. Gone all the young girls with their laughter and their squabbling and their teasing. He would be left, uncherished and alone, with that square-fronted, calm-eyed woman, his daughter.

He stooped, muttering, before the dovecote, resenting the absorbed cooing birds.

From the gate the girl shouted: 'Go and tell! Go on, what are you waiting for?'

b) Read the story again more carefully and answer the following questions. Find words from the text to support your opinions.

1 What is the old man's mood at the beginning of the story and why does it change?
2 Why does he lock his favourite pigeon up?
3 What is his granddaughter's mood at the beginning of the story? How do you know?
4 How does she react when she sees her grandfather?
5 How does her grandfather feel when he speaks to her?
6 How do you think the old man and his daughter get on?

c) What are the following things compared to:

1 the rich green grass?
2 the girl's hair?
3 the girl's legs?

d) Why do you think the grandfather is so unhappy? Have you ever felt like him?

e) What do you think will happen next?

INTEGRATED SKILLS: *Flight* (2)

Listening **1** [🔊 9.1] Read the statements below, then listen to the second part of the story.

a) As you listen, underline the correct alternative in each statement.

1 His granddaughter *watched/didn't watch* him walk to the house.
2 The old man felt *guilty for how he had spoken to his granddaughter/ angry with his granddaughter.*
3 Steven *had a present for her/had something with him.*
4 The old man *watched them from the house/ignored them.*
5 His daughter *got angry with him/was tolerant to him.*
6 The old man's granddaughter is *seventeen/eighteen.*
7 The old man's daughter has *four/five* daughters.
8 The granddaughter is called *Alice/Lucy.*
9 The grandfather thinks that when she gets married *he will never see her/she will change.*
10 The old man feels *happy/unhappy* after speaking to his daughter.

b) What is the attitude of the old man's daughter to her father? Look at the tapescript on page 189 and find words or expressions to describe it.

c) What does this sentence convey about the old man's attitude to marriage? *They were caught and finished, both of them, but the girl was still running free.*

Reading and speaking

2 You are going to read the last part of the story.

a) First read only the first and last paragraphs.
1 What do you think happens in the last part of the story?
2 How is the end of the story very different from the beginning?

b) Read the whole of the last part of the story and then finish these sentences, according to your interpretation.
1 The young couple brought the old man a pigeon because ....
2 The old man lets his favourite bird go because ....
3 He 'smiled proudly' at the end because ....
4 The girl is crying because ....
5 The end of the story is different to the beginning because ....

c) Discuss your answers with someone else.

d) In pairs, give your opinions in answer to the following questions.
1 What impression do you get of the girl in the last part of the story?
2 In what way does the old man's attitude change? Why?
3 Which of the characters do you have most sympathy with? The grandfather? Lucy? Alice? Steven? Why?

3 What do you think the theme of this story is? You may want to choose more than one answer. Give reasons for your choice(s). These are some ideas:

– power
– loneliness
– a man's relationship with birds

– youth and age
– loss
– possessiveness

Writing

4 Write one of the following:

1 A conversation between Alice and her mother about the grandfather.
2 A letter from Alice to Steven, saying how she had felt on the day in the story.
3 Alice's or the old man's diary for the day described in the story.

From around the corner came the young couple; but their faces were no longer set against him. On the wrist of the postmaster's son balanced a young pigeon, the light gleaming on its breast. 'For me?' said the old man, letting the drops shake off his chin. 'For me?'

'Do you like it?' The girl grabbed his hand and swung on it. 'It's for you, Granddad. Steven brought it for you.'

They hung about him, affectionate, concerned, trying to charm away his wet eyes and his misery. They took his arms and directed him to the shelf of birds, one on each side, enclosing him, petting him, saying wordlessly that nothing would be changed, nothing could change, and that they would be with him always. The bird was proof of it, they said, from their lying happy eyes, as they thrust it on him. 'There, Granddad, it's yours. It's for you.'

They watched him as he held it on his wrist, stroking its soft, sun-warmed back, watching the wings lift and balance.

'You must shut it up for a bit,' said the girl intimately. 'Until it knows this is its home.'

'Teach your grandmother to suck eggs,' growled the old man. Released by his half-deliberate anger, they fell back, laughing at him. 'We're glad you like it.' They moved off, now serious and full of purpose, to the gate, where they hung, backs to him, talking quietly. More than anything could, their grown-up seriousness shut him out, making him alone; also, it quietened him, took the sting out of their tumbling like puppies on the grass. They had forgotten him again. Well, so they should, the old man reassured himself, feeling his throat clotted with tears, his lips trembling. He held the new bird to his face, for the caress of its silken feathers. Then he shut it in a box and took out his favourite. 'Now you can go,' he said aloud. He held it poised, ready for flight, while he looked down the garden towards the boy and the girl. Then, clenched in the pain of loss, he lifted the bird on his wrist, and watched it soar. A whirr and a spatter of wings, and a cloud of birds rose into the evening from the dovecote.

At the gate Alice and Steven forgot their talk and watched the birds.

On the veranda, that woman, his daughter, stood gazing, her eyes shaded with a hand that still held her sewing.

It seemed to the old man that the whole afternoon had stilled to watch his gesture of self-command, that even the leaves of the trees had stopped shaking.

Dry-eyed and calm, he let his hands fall to his sides and stood erect, staring up into the sky.

The cloud of shining silver birds flew up and up, with a shrill cleaving of wings, over the dark ploughed land and the darker belts of trees and the bright folds of grass, until they floated high in the sunlight, like a cloud of motes of dust.

They wheeled in a wide circle, tilting their wings so there was flash after flash of light, and one after another they dropped from the sunshine of the upper sky to shadow, one after another, returning to the shadowed earth over trees and grass and field, returning to the valley and shelter of night.

The garden was all a fluster and a flurry of returning birds. Then silence, and the sky was empty.

The old man turned, slowly, taking his time; he lifted his eyes to smile proudly down the garden at his granddaughter. She was staring at him. She did not smile. She was wide-eyed, and pale in the cold shadow, and he saw the tears run shivering off her face.

SECTION 2   GRAMMAR: Modals

Revision of modals: Present and future

1   Answer these questions about modals:

How much do you remember about modals?

Verbs like *can, could, shall, should, must, will, would, may, might* are called modal auxiliary verbs.

1   Are these statements about the modal verbs above True or False?

     a)   They don't take *-s* in the third person singular.
     b)   They have no *-ing* or *-ed* form.
     c)   They cannot be followed by another verb.
     d)   Questions and negatives are not formed with *do*.
     e)   After the modals we use the *to*-infinitive.
     f)   It is not possible to use the continuous (*be eating*), perfect (*have eaten*) and passive infinitives (*be eaten*) with the modals.

2   *Ought* is a modal, but different in form to the other modals. In what way? What other modal is often used instead?

3   *Dare* and *need* are often called 'marginal modals'. In what way are they different from the others?

4   Look at the sentences below. What is the difference in meaning between the pairs of sentences (a and b)? In general, why do we use modals?

     1   a)   That's Mary at the door.
        b)   That will be Mary at the door.

     2   a)   She's German, I'm sure.
        b)   She must be German.

     3   a)   It's raining.
        b)   It can't be raining again.

     4   a)   Phone him. I expect he's home by now.
        b)   Phone him. He should be home by now.

5   What do the following sentences mean? Express them in another way, without using a modal.

     1   You don't have to eat that.
     2   You mustn't eat that.
     3   You should really phone him and apologise.
     4   You have to wear a tie at that club.
     5   You must try that new restaurant.

Now check your answers on page 179.

▶ **Language Bank page 152: Modals in the present and future**

Using modals to refer to the past: the perfect infinitive

2   Modal verbs can be used with *have* and the past participle (the perfect infinitive) to express certainty, possibility etc. about the past. Example: *It's pouring down outside. He* **can't have gone** *out in this!* (I don't believe he's gone out in this weather. He's mad!)

a)   Read the dialogue below and fill in the gaps so that the sentences refer to the past. Use the modal and verb in brackets. The first one is done for you.

    A: I'm beginning to get worried about Simon. It's nearly seven and the train *should have got* in by six thirty. (*should/get*)

    B: Well, he .... it. (*may/miss*)

    A: No, he .... (*can't*) He phoned me from the station – he had plenty of time to catch it.

    B: Well then, it .... (*must/be/delay*) for some reason otherwise we .... something. (*would/hear*)

b)   [🖭 9.2]   Listen and then practise reading the dialogue. Make sure you use contracted forms such as /ˈʃʊdəv/ and /ˈmeɪjəv/ when you are speaking.

3a)   Make sentences using the cues. The first is done for you.

1   I *could/go* to university if I'd worked harder.
    I **could have gone** *to university if I'd worked harder.*

2   Did the person who phoned have a northern accent? Ah, in that case it *will/be* Tim.

3   What beautiful flowers! But you really *should not/bother.*

4   You *might/tell* me you'd be this late!

5   He *can't/fail.* He was the cleverest in his class!

b)   [🖭 9.3]   Listen and check your answers.

c)   In which of the sentences above is the person:
    a) expressing regret?
    b) disbelieving?
    c) complaining/being angry?
    d) making an assumption?
    e) reacting to being given something?

d)   Practise reading the sentences, trying to sound disbelieving, angry etc. as appropriate.

4   Reword B's answers to these statements or questions, using a modal verb with the Perfect Infinitive.

Example:

A: What on earth has happened to Susan's hair? It's gone curly.

B: Well, presumably, she had a perm. There's no other explanation.
*She **must have had** a perm.*

1   A: I heard Steve left his car unlocked and it was stolen.

   B: Serves him right. It's his own fault for not locking it.

2   A: The phone has been engaged for an hour. Mum never talks for that long!

   B: It's possible you dialled the wrong number.

3   A: I saw Laura in town. She's looking extremely sun-tanned.

   B: Well I haven't seen her for a while and there's been no sun here, so I'm sure she's been on holiday.

4   A: I wonder who that delightful young man with Alex was.

   B: Did he look like him? I expect it was his son.

5   A: Yes, I know I'm three hours late. You must be starving.

   B: I am. You've got a mobile phone. Why didn't you phone me?

5   [🔊 9.4]   Listen to these sentences read aloud and say what the meaning is, a) or b). There could be two different meanings so it will depend on the intonation you hear.

1   He might have phoned me.
   a)   it's possible
   b)   he didn't but I wish he had

2   You shouldn't have done that.
   a)   because it's dangerous
   b)   but it's very kind of you

3   I could have hugged him.
   a)   but I decided not to
   b)   because I was so happy

4   She should have finished by now.
   a)   so why hasn't she?
   b)   and I expect she has

Modals: Other ways of referring to the past

6 *Could* and *would* have different meanings depending on whether or not the Perfect Infinitive is used.

a) Match the first part of the sentences to the endings.
1 I could walk ...
2 I could have walked here ...
3 He would sit up talking all night ...
4 He would have sat up talking all night ...

a) ... when he was younger.
b) ... if I'd let him.
c) ... when I was ten months old.
d) ... but I got a taxi instead.

b) Which of the sentences refer to situations which didn't actually take place?

7 Underline the best alternative in the sentences below. Explain why you chose them.

1 I *didn't need to go/needn't have gone* to the shops after all. Tom had already gone. I read the paper instead.
2 Luckily, Kate's father *could/managed to* find her before it got dark.
3 I *could/managed to* talk when I was eleven months old.
4 *Could/Were you able to* finish that report last night?
5 He *must/had to* finish the report before he went out.
6 Michael was *allowed to/could* buy a new CD as long as he used his own money.
7 I *didn't need to go/needn't have gone* to the meeting after all. They didn't tell me anything I didn't know already.
8 When I was young children *mustn't/weren't allowed to* stay up as late as they do these days.

8 Work in groups and exchange experiences. Talk about things in your past that you:
– should/shouldn't have done or said.
– could have done/would have done or may have done or said in different circumstances.

Examples:
I shouldn't have gone out with Charlie for so long. I could have travelled more or met more interesting people.
I might have kept my job if I hadn't been so rude to my boss the other day. In fact I think I would have been promoted by now!

SECTION 3 | LISTENING: Do you agree?

1 Read this extract from an article in a weekly news magazine.

> Eat what you like, drink what you like, smoke if you want to and be merry! Don't let the doctors get you down – we're all going to die anyway!

a) What do you think of the view expressed? Which of the expressions below would you use in response?

I suppose so.

You must be joking!

Exactly!

Come off it!

Fair enough.

Quite!

They may have a point there.

That may well be true, but ...

I can see what they're getting at, but ...

Yes, but it depends,

b) [9.5] Listen to some people reacting to the article and mark where the main stress falls in the expressions above.

c) Divide the expressions into the three categories in the table below. Add any others you know.

DEFINITE AGREEMENT	DEFINITE DISAGREEMENT	TENTATIVE
Exactly!	*You must be joking!*	*I suppose so.*

2 You are going to listen to three people having a discussion about whether university students should have to pay for their own tuition and living expenses.

a) Can you think of arguments for and against paying for your own education?

b) [9.6] Listen and make notes of all the points made *for* the argument and all the points made *against*.

c) Listen again and/or read the tapescript on page 190. As you read or listen, make a note of any expressions not in Exercise 1 used to agree and disagree with another person and then put them in the appropriate category in the table above.

d) Which point(s) of view do you agree with? Discuss in groups, using some of the language of agreeing and disagreeing if possible.

SPEAKING AND WRITING: Contentious issues

1 Read this letter printed in a British newspaper. Readers of this newspaper were encouraged to contribute any strong opinions they had to *Letters to the Editor.*

a) Summarise the argument in one sentence.

Dear Editor,

Mrs Jenkins, in Friday's edition of the Mail, asked why NHS hospital waiting lists were so long.

In my opinion one of the reasons is that hospitals are full of people who don't deserve to get treated by the state.

Too many people are treated for illnesses which are caused by drinking or smoking or taking drugs.

One result of this is that deserving people do not get a bed and have to wait for up to a year, or even longer in some cases, to be treated. My mother – waiting for a hip replacement operation – is one such case.

I think I am speaking for many when I say that people who have illnesses brought on by themselves should be made to pay for the treatment themselves!

I know they pay taxes like we do but the NHS will still protect them from illnesses which are NOT self-induced. After all, if they can afford to drink and smoke they can surely afford to pay for their own medical care.

Yours,

Sidney Laws

NHS: National Health Service

b) Work in groups and choose one of the topics in the letters below. If you are not interested in any of them, choose another topic that people feel strongly about and have different opinions on.

All surviving monarchies should be made into republics.

I personally think marriage should be banned before the age of 35. These days people are not prepared to put in what it takes for a marriage to survive.

Lying is necessary in all walks of life. We often lie to our friends so as not to hurt them. Politicians have to lie because most people cannot accept the truth.

c) Decide on a 'chairperson'. The 'chairperson' will:
- allow each person to give their views first without interruption (for a maximum of one minute)
- allow time for discussion. The 'chairperson's' job is to keep the peace and change the subject when necessary
- bring the discussion to a conclusion and try to summarise what was said

d) Give your views on the issue. Use a variety of expressions to agree, disagree, clarify, change the subject etc. (See the box below).

ASKING FOR CLARIFICATION

Do you mean ... (you'd refuse to give treatment?)
Is what you're saying ... (that you'd refuse them a bed?)
Sorry, I'm not quite with you.
I think I've lost you there!
I didn't quite understand what you meant by ... (refusing them treatment.)

GIVING CLARIFICATION

What I mean is ... (they shouldn't automatically be entitled to free treatment.)
The point I'm trying to make is ... (they shouldn't ...)
Let me put it another way. (The more undeserving people get treated, the more deserving people have to wait.)
In other words ... (the more ...)
What I'm trying to say ... (is that the more ...)

CHANGING THE SUBJECT

Anyway, ... (have you got any ideas for what we could do to help them?)
Right. (Let's move on to the next point.)
We'll come back to that later.
Shall we leave that issue for the moment?

---

2 Write a reply to the letter on page 125. Alternatively, choose an issue which is in the news at the moment, or another of the issues you discussed above that you feel strongly about.

a) Think about who you might be likely to be writing to. For example, it could be to:
- the editor of a local or national newspaper
- a local politician
- a national political organisation
- the regional government

b) Check the advice in the Writing Bank on page 173 about laying out a formal letter.

c) Decide what you will include in each paragraph, and make sure that the issue and your opinion is clearly stated in the opening paragraph.

d) Decide how you will end the letter (with a threat? a warning? a suggestion?).

3 Give your letter to someone else and see if they feel strongly enough to want to write a reply to it.

1 MODALS: TALKING ABOUT THE PAST

Modal auxiliary verbs express the speaker's attitude or emotions to an event or situation and are therefore a very subtle area of language.

Many modals can be used with the perfect infinitive (*have* + past participle) to express attitudes about the past.

Will have/won't/would(n't) have

Will have, *won't have* and *would(n't) have* express certainty about the past based on our knowledge (of people, routines etc.):
Oh, that **will/would have** been Fred you spoke to. He is very boring! (= I'm sure it was him.)
She **won't/wouldn't have** arrived yet. She never gets home before six. (= I'm sure she hasn't arrived.)

NOTE:
In some contexts *would* and *wouldn't* sound more tentative and polite than *will/won't*.

Must/can't/couldn't have

Must/can't/couldn't have can also express certainty about the past, often based on deduction.

The use of *couldn't* makes one's opinion a little less certain:
The burglar **must have** got in through the window. It's broken. (= I'm sure he did.)
You **can't have** lost them. I saw them a minute ago. (= I'm sure you haven't.)
He got to you very quickly. He **couldn't have** left here before 7.00, I don't think.

We often use *can't have* to express disbelief about something which has happened:
He **can't have** forgotten! (but he has.)

Should/shouldn't have

We use *should(n't) have* (or *ought(n't) to have*) when we expect something to have happened (or not happened) because it is logical or normal. It is sometimes used as a politer, more tentative form of *must have* or *can't have*:
She **should have** got up by now. Let's phone her.
The car **shouldn't have** broken down. I've just had it serviced.

Should(n't) have can also be used to talk about unreal situations – situations which are different from what actually happened. This can imply regret or criticism:
I **shouldn't have become** a doctor. (but I did!) It's too much work.
I **should have phoned** her. (but I didn't!)
You **ought to have brought** a spare set of keys. (but you didn't!)

NOTE:
We also use **You shouldn't have**! to express thanks.

May/might/could have

May have, *might have* and *could have* all refer to possibility in the past.
We **may have missed** the bus. There's no one waiting.
They **might have changed** their minds about meeting us. I'd better phone.

Might have and *could/couldn't have* can also be used to talk about unreal situations – things that were possible or impossible in the past but which didn't happen. This can imply criticism:
You **could/might have phoned** me! (It was possible, but you didn't and I'm annoyed!)
She **could have won** the race. (but she didn't!)
I **could have come** if I'd been invited. (I would have been allowed.)
She **couldn't have met** us, anyway. She's away on holiday. (= It would have been impossible.)
You **might/could have hurt** yourself. (= It was possible but you didn't.)

NOTE:
The perfect infinitive is also used with *would/wouldn't* and *needn't* to talk about other unreal situations:
I **would have told** you if I'd remembered. (but I didn't.)
I **needn't have** finished it today, but I did. (It wasn't necessary, but I did.)
Compare this with I **didn't need** to do it. (It wasn't necessary and I didn't do it.)

Can/could have

Can and *could have* both express possibility. Note that *can have* is not used in the affirmative:
Can he have escaped, do you think? (= Is it possible?)
Well, he **could have**. (= It's possible, but not very likely.)

2 OTHER MODALS IN THE PAST

Modals do not always take the perfect form when referring to the past.

Would/wouldn't

He **would drink** like a fish whenever he was invited out. (characteristic behaviour. Both *used to* and *would* can be used to talk about habit in the past, but *would* can only be used for discontinued actions, not states.)
She **wouldn't talk** about it. (refusal to do something)

Could/was able to/managed to/was allowed to

I **could** drive when I was 17 or I **was able** to drive when I was 17. (general ability)
BUT:
I **was able to/managed to** contact him at his office. (ability on a specific occasion. Note that *was able* (not I *could ...*) can be used in both contexts.)

Must/mustn't

Must(n't) changes its form when referring to obligation in the past:
You **must** drive more carefully.
He **had to** drive more carefully.
You **mustn't** speak to me like that.
He **wasn't allowed to** speak to me like that.

A REASON TO BELIEVE

READING AND WRITING: How sceptical are you?

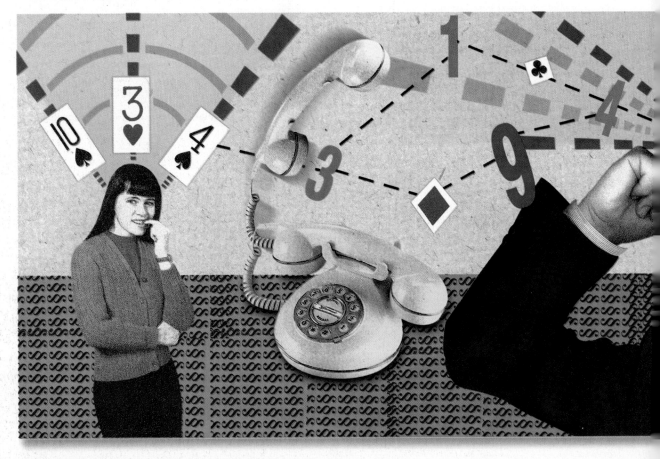

Before reading **1a)** Do you believe that ...

1   the planets influence your life?
2   you can tell someone's personality from their handwriting?
3   complete strangers can give you accurate information about your present and future life?
4   your success or physical energy depends on which day of the month it is, as determined by the three 'cycles' (emotional, physical and intellectual) fixed when you were born?
5   people can communicate without using any of the five senses?
6   you return to earth after you die?

b)   Match the name below with the belief above.

| biorhythms | reincarnation | astrology | telepathy |
| cold readings | graphology | | |

c)   Work in groups.
1   What do you know about any of the beliefs above? Do you have any personal experience of them? Do you think they are based on science or superstition?
2   Do you disbelieve any or all of them? Explain why.

Reading **2** Work in two groups. Group A read Text A below and Group B read Text B on page 130.

a) Read the text and make notes. Include answers to the following questions.
1 Which of the beliefs in Exercise 1 is the text about?
2 What's the writer's attitude to this belief? Find examples of language which show this.
3 Compare your notes with the rest of your group.

b) What is your opinion of what the writer says? Can you think of any arguments for or against their opinion?

Text A

This is the technique used by innumerable charlatans, including fortune-tellers, palmists, astrologers, and spiritualists – anyone who wants to appear to have a unique, paranormal method of finding out about complete strangers. It is not too difficult to learn, but it does require hard work, cunning and acute observation, plus a certain amount of sheer fraud. Luckily there are plenty of how-to-do-it books available. The techniques are many, but they all rely on the suspension of scepticism by the customer, who, after all, has paid the money in the hope of receiving reassurance, or to get a message from a departed loved one and who is anxious for the cold reader to succeed.

One standard technique is to use general statements which people think refer uniquely to them, but which could apply to almost all of us: 'You are sometimes too sensitive ... you occasionally let your good nature get the better of you ... now and again you are aggressive and regret it later.' The customer's reply often provides further information which can be cleverly turned into more surprising knowledge.

The late Mrs Doris Stokes, the 'spirit medium' who did both individual sessions and mass gatherings in concert halls, was a remarkably skilled cold reader. She would produce a stream of guesses, a few of which were inevitably correct. Mistakes were either ignored or turned to her advantage. Her warm cosy manner made it impossible that such a delightful old lady could be a fraud.

Sometimes distressed people phoned her home, and were encouraged to tell their story by her husband, who then offered free tickets to her next show. When the people appeared she seemed to have a miraculous knowledge of their circumstances. Either they had forgotten the chat with Mr Stokes or else were too polite to say 'I told *you* that'. Other listeners were mightily impressed. Mistakes were blamed on the fact that many dead people were trying to talk to her at once and their 'lines' were crossed.

(From *The Observer*)

3 Work with someone who read the other text (i.e. if you read Text A, work with someone who read Text B).

a) Say what your article was about. Give your opinion of the article and the opinions of the group you discussed it with.

b) Answer any questions your partner wants to ask.

c) Listen to your partner talking about his/her article and ask him/her questions about it if you want.

Text B

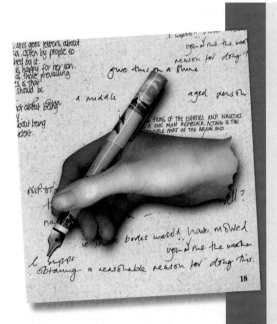

The pseudo-science of being able to determine personality from handwriting has gained quite a worrying level of acceptance. Estimates suggest 85 per cent of firms in Europe use graphological analysis in making at least some of their hiring decisions – which is why application forms often ask you to complete them in your own handwriting. Yet a moment's thought should make anyone sceptical. Is there really some immutable law of the universe which compels everyone with a particular set of characteristics to dot their 'i's' cross their 't's' or slope their letters in the same way?

What is true, of course, is that your mental state can affect your writing. And you can make some informed guesses from handwriting: in the past, at least, the upper and professional classes were said to have scruffier scripts than the lower or clerical classes; handwriting can often deteriorate with over-use, as in the infamous scrawl of doctors.

These generalisations are dangerous enough without going further. Texts which graphologists examine are often taken from autobiographical sketches that contain clues. Without such help, graphologists tend to perform less well. One study showed graphologists unable to distinguish between the scripts of mental hospital patients and undergraduates.

A few years ago a BBC science programme asked four graphologists to do three tests, including distinguishing a group of actors from a group of monks. The graphologists didn't do badly, averaging a success rate of 65 per cent. The programme then asked ordinary people to play amateur graphologists and they did almost as well, getting the right answer 59 per cent of the time.

If careers are to be decided on our penmanship, shouldn't we be looking for success rates among professional graphologists of nearer 100 per cent?

(From *The Observer*)

Writing **4** Below is a jumbled paragraph from an article entitled *Biorhythms*.

a) Unjumble the lines to form a coherent paragraph. There are five sentences. The first sentence begins with the line numbered 1.

..... by citing specific examples.
..... such as the circadian rhythm,
..... and the menstrual cycle.
..... although, sadly, almost none of their work survives.
..... These acknowledged phenomena are cited as support for the pseudo-science of biorhythms.
..1.. Biorhythm 'science' was allegedly invented and tested by three European researchers,
..... Advocates also like to 'prove' their case
..... Proponents often cash in on the fact that humans are, indeed, subject to certain rhythms,
..... Marilyn Monroe, for example, killed herself on a bad day for both her emotional and intellectual cycles.
..... which helps cause jet lag,

b) Underline the words which help to create links within the paragraph above. Example: *although*

5 Write two paragraphs on *Coincidence*, using the notes below.

> **coincidence** /kəʊˈɪnsɪdəns/ *n* a surprising and unexpected situation in which two things that are connected happen at the same time, in the same place, or to the same people

a) Try to have a maximum of three sentences in each paragraph. Keeping the notes in sequence, link sentences together using conjunctions such as *and* and *but* and words such as *which* and *this*. Begin each paragraph with the phrase in italics.

Paragraph 1

This was a subject which fascinated Carl Jung, who collected ...

- a subject which fascinated Carl Jung
- he collected a number of examples
- the examples were extraordinary
- he felt that there must be an explanation
- he felt it couldn't just be chance
- he called this phenomenon 'synchronicity'
- synchronicity means 'the simultaneous occurrence of two meaningful but not causally related events'
- he argued that clusters of events must indicate the presence of some greater force

Paragraph 2

Every day literally thousands of events happen to us. We meet people, ...

- every day thousands of events happen to us
- we meet people
- we see people
- we talk to people
- we think about people
- we observe thousands of objects
- we read thousands of words
- we read books, newspapers and magazines
- there are about five billion people in the world
- incredible if chance did *not* throw up an astonishing number of coincidences

b) Compare your paragraphs with other people's and try to improve on them. See page 180 for the original text.

GRAMMAR: Written discourse

Grammatical reference words

1   The text below shows how grammatical words operate in a piece of writing, to refer backwards and forwards, and to avoid repetition of a word or phrase.

Example: *This* in line 1 is a demonstrative pronoun which refers back to the title *Astrology*.

ASTROLOGY

(This) is the oldest and best known of the pseudo-sciences. Ancient peoples must have noticed that important times
5   in (their) lives – harvests, domestic animals giving birth – coincided with certain positions of heavenly bodies. It's not surprising that (they)
10   might have thought (the latter) caused (the former).
And perhaps there is nobody in the country today who has not, at some time, read (their)
15   horoscope and wondered whether there might not be something in (it) – *though* one should bear in mind the Punch

cartoon of a radio announcer
20   saying: 'In a major breakthrough for the science of astrology, all people born under Scorpio were yesterday run over by egg lorries.'

25   You would imagine that few people put any serious store by newspaper horoscopes. The kind of astrologers consulted by the likes of Nancy Reagan
30   are, *however*, somewhat swankier. *As well as* offering humble sun signs, (they) concern themselves with arcana *such as* cusps.
35   *Regrettably*, few astrologers agree with (each other) on what (these impressive mysteries)

mean.
Most astrologers ignore that
40   there is a slight wobble of the earth on (its) axis. (This) means that the vernal equinox moves through the constellations 1.4. degrees east every century, *so*
45   *that* in the 2,000 years since the signs were codified (they) have moved 30 degrees and we are now one full sign out of kilter. Classical astrology *also* ignores
50   all the planets (which) were discovered recently.

(From *The Observer*)

---

arcana: (lit.) secret and mysterious things
cusp: the time when one star sign ends and another begins
vernal equinox: in the spring when all places in the world have a day and a night of equal length
out of kilter: not working as well as usual

a)   Draw an arrow to connect the circled word(s) to the word or group of words it refers to.

b)   Compare your work with somebody else's. Look at the section 'Grammatical reference words' in the Language Reference on page 139.

2   Improve the sentences below by changing the words in italics to avoid repetition.

Example: *Tim earns more than we earn.* → *Tim earns more than we **do**.*

1   I didn't go to the meeting, but Jill *went*. Apparently, Vanessa just got up and walked out. *Walking out* was a very silly thing to do, if you ask me.

2   My parents are thinking of going to Florida. Have you ever been *to Florida?* I'd love to go on holiday but I can't afford *to go on holiday.*

3   I decided to buy some locks for the windows. I thought that *the locks* would make the house more secure.

4   A: Did you see that film on TV last night? I didn't see it *last night*, but I've seen it before. I really enjoyed it.
    B: *I enjoyed it, too.*

5   I last saw her in 1969. *1969* was just after her son was born. I realised *in 1969* that I would never see her again.

Linking expressions: Conjunctions and adverbs

3   Look at some examples of linking expressions in the text opposite. They are the words in italics.

a)   What function do these words have? Example:
***And** perhaps there is nobody in the country today ...* (line 12) *And* is adding information to the text.

b)   Work in pairs and together finish these sentences in any logical way that you can think of.
1   Considering you're not supposed to be hungry ....
2   The house is lovely, whereas ....
3   You can pay the bill, given that ....
4   Provided you are nice to me ....
5   We should have a break shortly. Otherwise, ...

4a)   Choose the most appropriate linking expression for each of the sentences below.

1   I didn't really like the play at all. .... , I thought it was dreadful.
    a) Apparently   b) Actually   c) Ironically   d) Anyway

2   .... I go to college or not depends on my exam results.
    a) If   b) Unless   c) Whether   d) Provided

3   Yes, I think that's a fair point. .... , to go back to what I was saying earlier, I think we should contact the parents and ask their opinions.
    a) Personally   b) Anyway   c) Presumably   d) Obviously

4   We could wait for her another five minutes. .... , we could leave now.
    a) Or   b) Alternatively   c) Either   d) Instead

5   I'm late, as usual! .... , could I have a lift tomorrow?
    a) Ideally   b) Surely   c) By the way   d) Apparently

6   I haven't seen Susan this week but, ... , according to Roger, she's out of hospital.
    a) personally   b) apparently   c) basically   d) honestly

b)   Use five expressions which you didn't choose in Exercise 4a). Write sentences to show them in context. Compare your sentences with a partner.

   ▶ **Language Bank page 150: Linking expressions**

SECTION 2   VOCABULARY: Idioms

Proverbs

1a) Match the two halves of the proverbs. Example: *1 = d*

1 One man's meat ...	a) the mice will play.
2 It's no use crying ...	b) than the one you don't know.
3 There's no smoke ...	c) flock together.
4 While the cat's away ...	d) is another man's poison.
5 One good turn ...	e) catches the worm.
6 The early bird ...	f) deserves another.
7 Never judge a book ...	g) over spilt milk.
8 Birds of a feather ...	h) without fire.
9 Better the devil you know ...	i) shouldn't throw stones.
10 People in glass houses ...	j) by its cover.

b)   What do the proverbs mean? Explain them to a partner.

c)   Practise reading them aloud, trying to achieve a natural rhythm.
Example: *Birds of a 'feather flock to'gether.*

d)   Do you have any proverbs in your own language with a similar message to those in 1a)? How would they be translated into English?

2   Which proverb from Exercise 1 do you think is appropriate for each of these contexts? Note that we often only say the first half of these proverbs.

1   The boss is on holiday. You see someone going home early, looking guilty. What do you say?
2   Your next door neighbour has just moved in and your husband says he looks a bit unfriendly. What do you say?
3   You don't believe the rumours in the paper about your local politician, but your friend is not so sure.
4   You deeply regret what you said at the party last night. Your friend tells you to forget about it.
5   You really enjoyed a video that your husband found very boring.
6   You advise a friend that it would be risky to sell her car and buy another.

3   Write a dialogue and/or a short anecdote in which other proverbs (choose from those above, or one of your own) would be appropriate.

Derivation of idiomatic expressions and customs

4 This is an example of a question that a reader recently sent in to a regular column in the British newspaper, the *Daily Express*.

a) Here are some other idiomatic expressions taken from other letters to the newspaper. First match them with their definitions a)–e).
1 *the be-all and end-all*
2 to *hoodwink* (someone)
3 *run of the mill*
4 to *take the flak*
5 it *gives you grief*

a) to deceive
b) something annoys you
c) the most important thing
d) ordinary, normal
e) to receive strong criticism

Why is it?

Q. Why is it that if you are very surprised you are flabbergasted?
M E Dyson, Pluckley, Kent

A. The word flabbergasted, meaning shocked or surprised, probably comes from 'flabby', meaning lacking resilience or firmness and 'aghast', meaning taken aback.

b) Now match the expressions with the answers to *'Why is it?'*
Example: *1 = D*

A It is an acronym for *FlugAbwehrKanone*, the German name for anti-aircraft guns, and originally used in English to describe the bursting of gun shells. It later became a colloquialism for any criticism or hostility.

B It came into the language in the 16th century and comes from the practice of covering the eyes with a hood as a blindfold.

C It comes from the Latin *gravis*, meaning heavy, and since the 13th century has been applied to all manner of bad experiences.

D It has been a commonly used cliché since the 19th century, and was used by Shakespeare in *Macbeth*.

E This was coined because a steady stream of water flowing from the millpond meant the mill would run smoothly.

5 Look at other questions that readers sent in. Do you know any of the answers yourself?

Why is it ...

1 we say 'white rabbits' on the first day of the month?
2 hit films are called 'blockbusters'?
3 there are thirteen in a 'baker's dozen'?
4 toilets are sometimes called 'loos'?
5 a long 'a' is spoken in the south of England and a short 'a' in the north?
6 there are twelve members of a jury?
7 that press photographers are sometimes known as the paparazzi?
8 we use the phrase 'You can't teach your grandmother to suck eggs'?
9 that we touch wood for good luck?
10 that our funny bone (the bone on the elbow that sticks out slightly) is so-called?

Look on page 180 for the answers.

(From the *Daily Express*)

SECTION 3   LISTENING: What do you believe in?

Before listening   **1a)** Read the newspaper extract below. From what you read do you think the following conclusions are True or False about Britain today?

1   Most people don't believe in any kind of a God.
2   Traditional worship has declined in popularity.
3   Belief in the paranormal is widespread.
4   The desire to believe in something or someone is still very strong.

In late 20th-century Britain, historically a Christian country, church going is now a minority activity; less than 10 per cent of Britons now enter a religious building at weekends. This statistic suggests a secular, atheistic nation in which the majority have come to believe that organised religion is no longer relevant to them.

And yet this retreat from traditional worship has not led to an age of rationalism and scepticism. Between two thirds and a half of respondents in most opinion polls still profess to believe in some kind of a God. Other religions such as Islam and Buddhism have become much more important. At the same time, superstition and acceptance of the paranormal seem – if the television and movie listings, and best selling book charts are any guide – to be on the increase. If a study conducted by the University of Leeds is to be believed, 55 per cent of people believe in second sight, 67 per cent believe there is some truth in astrology and 15 per cent believe that abduction by aliens is possible.

Others worship a dead celebrity. After the death of Princess Diana, for example, there was a massive outpouring of grief and most churches and cathedrals reported their highest attendance for decades.

There's a well-known quote attributed to the English writer GK Chesterton: 'When people stop believing in God they don't start to believe in nothing, they start to believe in anything.'

(From *The Times*)

b)   Discuss answers to the questions below.

1   Is traditional religion strong in your country, or is it changing and diversifying, as in Britain?
2   Do different generations have very different beliefs? Give examples.
3   Do you agree with the quote by GK Chesterton? Give examples of the 'anything' that young people and older people in your country believe in these days.

Listening **2** [📼 10.1] We interviewed three people about their beliefs. Listen and answer the questions.

a) Richard:
What does he say about God, piety and the humanist approach?

b) Gillie:
What does she say about her attitudes to astrology, western medicine and its alternatives?

c) Ruth:
Why did she start to explore religion? How does she justify her existence?

3 Listen again and discuss answers to these questions.

a) Listen to Richard again.
1 What does he say is the answer to life? Do you agree with him? Give examples if you can.
2 What does he think is essential to a religion? Do you agree?

b) Listen to Gillie again.
1 How does she summarise a typical Capricorn? Do you know what the typical summary of your own star sign is? Are you like this?
2 Do you believe in star signs?
3 What do you think she means when she says she 'flirts with' astrology. Look at the dictionary extract below to help you.

> **flirt with** sth *phr v* [T not in passive] **1** to consider doing something, but not be very serious about it **2** to take an unnecessary risk and not be worried about it

From the *Longman Dictionary of Contemporary English*.

4 Give examples of things that Gillie does to help cure her arthritic hip.
5 Do you believe in or practise any alternative forms of medicine (for example, homeopathy or aromatherapy)? Give other examples that you know of or have experienced.

c) Listen to Ruth again.
1 Do you agree with her that it's important to set yourself goals in life? Do you do/have you ever done this?
2 Do you agree that it's important for people to remember you for doing certain things? What would you like to be remembered for?

4 [📼 10.2] Listen to these people talking about the practical things that motivate them in life.

a) Listen and make a note of what is important to the following people.

ROSIE	KATE	CLIFF

b) Are any of the things mentioned by the speakers important to *you*? Are any of these things not important at all?

5 What is important to you in life? What motivates you to go on?

1 Try to think of at least five things and put them in order of importance.
2 Work in groups and talk to other people about their priorities.

SPEAKING: Revision of connected speech

1   Read the song lyrics below.

a)   Complete the gaps with one of the words from the box. Each pair of lines rhymes. Some words are used more than once.

more	hand	you	do	door	true	then
planned	again					

We used to go out walking hand in ....
You told me all the big things you had ....
It wasn't long till all your dreams came ....
Success put me in second place with ....
You have no time to love me any ....
Since fame and fortune knocked upon our ....
I spend my evenings all alone
Success has made a failure of our home
If we could spend an evening now and ....
Perhaps we'd find true happiness ....
You never hold me like you used to ....
It's funny what success has done for ....
You have no time to love me any ....
Since fame and fortune knocked upon our ....
I spend my evenings all alone
Success has made a failure of our home

b)   [🔊 10.3]   Listen and check your answers.

c)   How would you summarise what the song is about? What do you think the title is? Check in the tapescript on page 191.

2   Work in pairs and discuss how the text might be read.

1   Circle the word/s which you think is/are the main focus in each line (e.g. *hand* at the end of line 1).
2   Underline the words which are weak (unstressed) (e.g. *to* in line 1).
3   Find five words which link to the following one (e.g. *hand͜ in*). Put a symbol between the words which link together. If there is a linking sound (/j/, /w/, /r/), write it in (e.g. *go͜ out* in line 1 /gəʊwaʊt/).

3   [🔊 10.4]   Listen to the song read aloud and see to what extent it followed your predictions.

4a) Who do you think is the *you* in the song? Why do you think he became famous?

b)   Do you think it's possible to be successful and/or famous and have a 'normal' home life? Or is the situation described in the song inevitable?

1 FEATURES OF WRITTEN DISCOURSE

Grammatical reference words

Grammatical words (e.g. *he, which* etc.) are often used to avoid repetition of words and phrases:

Tony's brother drove to work. Tony's brother was at work by six. → *Tony's brother drove to work. **He** was **there** by six. **He*** (personal pronoun) avoids repetition of the noun phrase *Tony's brother* and ***there*** (adverb) avoids repetition of the adverbial of place *to work.*

In the example above *he* and *there* are 'reference words' because they refer to other words and phrases. Here are some of the most common grammatical 'reference words':

1 Words which replace noun phrases:
   Personal pronouns (*he*), impersonal pronouns (*one*), possessives (*theirs*), relatives (*which*), demonstratives (*this, those*), reflexives (*myself*), quantifying words (*one, some, none, all*), determiners (*each, neither, such*), (demonstrative) adjectives (*the former, the latter, this, that*):
   *Which is your car? The **one** over there.* (the car over there)
   *Bruce prepared a lovely meal and everyone ate it except **himself**.* (everyone except Bruce)

2 Words which replace verb phrases:
   Auxiliaries (*do/does, did, is, can*):
   I love pizza and my children love pizza, too.
   *I love pizza and my children **do**, too.*

3 Words which replace adverbials of time and place:
   there, then, this:
   I went to Bali twenty years ago.
   *It was unspoilt **then**.* (twenty years ago)

4 Words which replace clauses and sentences:
   so, not, to, it, that, this:
   She advised me to phone and complain.
   *Are you going **to**?* (phone and complain)

Linking expressions

Linking words and expressions (conjunctions, adverbs or prepositions) connect ideas within a sentence, ideas between sentences and ideas between paragraphs. They help to make a stretch of language coherent.

There are many different types of connectors. Here are some examples:

addition (*and, besides*)
contrast and concession (*although, whereas*)
comparison (*similarly, conversely*)
condition (*unless, provided that*)
reason and purpose (*because, since*)
cause and result (*therefore, so*)
time (*meanwhile, after*)
enumeration and summary (*first, in summary*)
exemplification (*such as, for instance*)

2 SOME FEATURES OF CONNECTED SPEECH

Linking consonants to vowels

As we saw in Unit 6, a feature of connected speech is that a word that ends in a consonant often links to the next word when it begins with a vowel:
/kʌpəv/ = cup‿of (tea)
When a word ends in a vowel and the next word begins with a vowel the sounds are often linked by an extra sound which helps maintain the flow and the rhythm of the speaking. There are three main 'extra' sounds of this kind:
a /j/ sound as in *pay‿attention* /peɪjətenʃən/
a /w/ sound as in *Here you‿are* /hɪəjuːwɑː/
a /r/ sound as in *saw‿a film* /sɔːrəfɪlm/

Linking consonants: Elision

As we saw in Unit 6, elision is when the /t/ and /d/ sounds disappear (are elided) at the end of the word. This can occur when there is a consonant sound before and after the /t/ or /d/ sound:
eas(t) wind

Weak forms

As we saw in Unit 1, 'non-content' or grammatical words are usually, but not always, weak or unstressed. There are about 40 of them and they include:
– auxiliary forms (*be/have*)
– modals (*can/should*)
– prepositions (*to/for*)
– articles (*a/the*)
– pronouns (*he/she*)
– conjunctions (*and/but*)

However, they also have a strong form which we use when we want to emphasise them. There is a list of weak forms and their strong forms on page 192.

'Content' words such as nouns, verbs, adjectives and adverbs, on the other hand, are usually stressed.

Grammar review

1 Read the text below quickly.

a) Answer the questions. Ignore the gaps at this stage.
1 In what way has Italy changed in recent years?
2 What reason is given for the situation?
3 Is the same true in your country?

Baby? I'd rather have a mobile phone

Italy is going through a population crisis of extraordinary proportions. It (1) .... be a country (2) .... babies, (3) .... there are almost no babies around any more. In truth, many Italians are more interested (4) .... a mobile phone (5) .... a son and heir.

When I (6) .... a well-known maternity hospital in Rome to see some friends with their new-born baby, there were 130 cots in the place, but only two (7) .... That's nothing unusual. My wife went to a clinic widely (8) .... to be the best in the city to have our baby. There is room for only five babies at a time, but (9) .... we were there we had the place virtually to ourselves.

In an industrialised world that (10) .... a decline in birth rates, Italy has the lowest rate of all – 1.17 children per couple, (11) .... one study, (12) .... 1.7 in France and 2.1 in the United States.

(13) .... is extraordinary is that in terms of abstract statistical projection, by the year 2150 Italy (14) .... millions of new cars, buildings, refrigerators, computers, mobile phones and video recorders – but no people.

(From the *Independent on Sunday*)

b) Now choose one of the words or phrases below to complete each gap.
1 a) can   b) may   c) could   d) can't
2 a) who'll love   b) that's loving   c) who love   d) that loves
3 a) but   b) and   c) although   d) however
4 a) to acquire   b) acquiring   c) in acquiring   d) acquire
5 a) that   b) to   c) than   d) having
6 a) visit   b) visited   c) have visited   d) 'm visiting
7 a) have been occupied   b) occupied   c) were occupied   d) occupying
8 a) reputing   b) which reputed   c) reputed   d) which reputing
9 a) while   b) during   c) as   d) for
10 a) was seen   b) has seen   c) see   d) sees
11 a) depending on   b) according to   c) providing that   d) accordingly
12 a) comparing to   b) compared with   c) different to   d) different from
13 a) It   b) What   c) There   d) Whatever
14 a) will have   b) has   c) is having   d) will be

2a) Which areas of grammar cause you the most problems (e.g. tenses and verb forms, linking expressions, complex sentences)?

b) Which answers in Exercise 1 did you get wrong? These are the pages in *Advanced Matters* where you will find them practised.

Active or passive? (no 7) on page 154
Comparatives (no 5) on page 144
Complex sentences (nos 2, 11, 12) on page 105
Linking expressions (nos 3, 9) on page 150
Emphasis (no 13) on page 46 and 146
Modals (no 1) on page 120 and 152
Noun clauses (no 4) on page 105

Participles (no 8) on page 80
Relative clauses (nos 2, 8, 10) on page 159
Verb forms
- narrative forms (no 6) on page 22 and 153
- Present Perfect (no 10) on page 92
- Present Simple (no 2) on page 158
- the future (no 14) on page 65 and 148

1 Adjective word order

1a) There are mistakes in the word order of the adjectives in these sentences. Try to correct them according to what sounds right to you.

1 There's an abundance of cycling good flat country.
2 Locals fill the wooden old tiny two churches every Sunday.
3 You pass by small terraced green fields in open broad areas where the river branches off.
4 Sheer cliffs and pointed steep mountains rise on either side of the black huge river.

b) Put each of the adjectives in Exercise 1a) under one of these headings.

NUMBER	OPINION	SIZE	AGE	SHAPE	COLOUR	MATERIAL	COMPOUND

c) Check Exercise 1a) against this language summary.

ADJECTIVE WORD ORDER

When adjectives come together they normally follow this order. However, it is unnatural to use more than two or three together in any one phrase.

DETERMINER	OPINION	SIZE/ CONDITION	AGE	SHAPE	COLOUR	PATTERN	ORIGIN	MATERIAL	COMPOUND	NOUN
two	nice		young				French			men
a		large			grey			woollen		jumper
his				round		spotty				face
Pete's		tatty	old						walking	shoes

---

2 Find three adjectives in the box below which could collocate with each of the nouns in these sentences and put them in the sentence in the order which sounds natural to you.

1 I like your shoes.
2 Can you see a rug?
3 I've got some software.
4 Have you read this novel?
5 Look at that tree.
6 It's an armchair.

rectangular	Russian	old	beautiful	large	oak	19th century
striped	weird	Italian	scruffy	new	Internet	blue
suede	running	lovely	leather	exquisite	antique	brilliant

3 Describe something you can see in the room or out of the window. See if other students can guess what you are describing.

2 Adverb position

> Most adverbs occur more often in one place in a sentence than another.
> Examples:
> - **Front** (before the subject)
>   *I like French.* **However**, *I don't like the book we're using.* (linking)
>   **Arguably**, *it is not a very serious crime.* (opinion/attitude/viewpoint)
> - **Middle** (after the first auxiliary, or before a main verb form like *went*)
>   *He is* **quite** *nice.* (degree)
>   *He has* **always** *seemed so rude.* (frequency)
>   *She'll* **probably** *turn up.* (certainty)
> - **End** (after the verb phrase)
>   *She cleaned her teeth* **quickly**. (manner)
>   *I live* **abroad**. (place)
>   *See you* **soon**. (time)
>
> For a few of these the position is optional and linked to style. (*She cleaned her teeth* **quickly** or *She* **quickly** *cleaned her teeth*.)

Some adverbs have more than one function and have to be positioned (and/or stressed) appropriately. What's the difference in meaning in sentences 1–8 below? Use the sentence stress marks to help you.

Example:
a) *Even the 'children enjoyed the concert.*
b) *The children even enjoyed the 'concert.*

In a) it is surprising that the children, as well as everybody else, enjoyed the concert.

In b) it is surprising that the children enjoyed the concert as well as everything else.

1 a) 'Frankly, I told him what I 'thought.
   b) I told him 'frankly what I thought.
2 a) 'Really, I don't 'like her.
   b) I don't really 'like her.
   c) I don't like her 'really.
3 a) Tom 'eventually worked so hard he made himself 'ill.
   b) Tom worked so 'hard he eventually made himself 'ill.
4 a) Kate's 'quite happy.
   b) Kate's quite 'happy.
5 a) 'Actually, he told her he 'loved her.
   b) He 'actually told her he 'loved her.
   c) He told her he actually 'loved her.
6 a) Sue 'only went to the restaurant.
   b) Only 'Sue went to the restaurant.
7 a) I thought he was personally 'offended.
   b) 'Personally, I thought he was 'offended.
8 a) He stupidly 'talked.
   b) He talked 'stupidly.

3 Articles

1a) Do you have articles in your language? How would you translate these sentences into your language?

1 I don't like cats.
2 He joined the army.
3 She speaks very good English.
4 Petrol's very expensive.
5 I'm a doctor.
6 It's on her head.
7 A kilo and a half of tomatoes.
8 Mary's bag.

b) Are these True or False about the use of the article in English?

1 When we refer back to something just mentioned (*Have you taken ... aspirin I bought you this morning?*) we use the definite article (*the*).
2 When we mention something for the first time (*We went to ... good restaurant last night.*) we do not use an article.
3 We use the indefinite article (*a/an*) when there is only one of something (*What do you think of ... government?*).

c) If you have articles, what differences are there in the way they are used in English and in your language?

2 One of the problems with articles is that the basic rules don't always seem to work!

Put *a/an/the* or x (no article) into these sentences and make extra 'rules' using the cues in brackets to help you.

1 She passed her exams and went to .... university. (the institution not a building)
2 He works at .... night. (prepositional phrases of place, time, movement)
3 He plays .... piano very well. (a generalisation about a category, genre, type)
4 .... cheetah can run faster than .... tiger. (talking about a species)
5 This is .... very strong cheese. (uncountable – a type of)
6 This painting is .... Picasso. (a work by)
7 Do you speak .... French? (languages, most countries, continents, towns, cities, counties)
8 I have no sympathy for .... rich. (a group of people, places, things.)

3a) Complete the newspaper article with *a/an/the* or no article. In some cases there is more than one possibility.

'What is (1) .... modern world coming to when (2) .... gang of (3) .... thieves arrives at (4) .... place they are going to rob in (5) .... taxi?' (6) .... Justice Morris asked (7) .... defendants in (8) .... robbery case at (9) .... Auckland High Court. 'I despair for (10) .... future of our country when (11) .... group of (12) .... louts like you lack (13) .... intelligence to take even (14) .... basic precautions to avoid (15) .... detection. It has been put to me that (16) .... reason you were so easily apprehended after (17) .... robbery was that you had no (18)......... getaway car. That is because you forgot to ask (19) .... taxi to wait for you while you committed (20) .... crime. Why couldn't you steal (21) .... car beforehand like everybody else? You tell me it's because you don't have (22) .... licences, but I preside daily over (23) .... cases involving (24) .... professional criminals who don't care about such (25) .... trivial matters. You are (26) .... imbeciles. I hereby sentence you both to five years in (27) .... jail.'

(From *The Southland Times*)

b) Say why you think each answer is correct.

4 Imagine you are telling somebody about these newspaper ads. Expand them using articles where appropriate.

① **Nanny required for foreign family recently arrived from USA. Elegant house in Cambridge area. Knowledge of Russian and ability to play piano essential. Advantage to be able to drive. Eldest child (15) at well-known drama school; youngest (7) studies music at home. Salary and working conditions excellent.**

② **For sale.** Excellent 3 bedroom detached house in Park Street close to town centre. Two bathrooms with separate WC, detached garage, superb good-sized gardens at rear and gravelled drive at front. Double glazing and central heating throughout. Excellent view of mountains of North Wales. House of immense character. Viewing essential. **Offers over £200,000.**

③ German millionaire with large house in UK, friend of Royal Family, seeks intelligent girl for champagne dinners and share with him expenses-paid trip to China. Photograph not necessary. Will take writer of best letter.

4 Comparatives and superlatives

1 Recently, a survey entitled *Europeans: Citizens of the World* questioned people about 'A Day in the Life of a European'. We often tend to stereotype people from other countries. But do these stereotypes live up to scrutiny?

a) Work in pairs.
STUDENT A: Look at page 181.
STUDENT B: Read the text. Underline which nationalities (in italics) you think the article might be about and try to guess which comparative structure completes gaps 12–21. Then ask Student A questions to check your answers.
Examples: *Who are the earliest risers? Is it 'Almost **as many** Swiss'?*

A day in the life of a European

EARLY BIRDS

The earliest risers are the *Czechs/Italians* although almost the same number of *Hungarians/Austrians* get up before 6.00. The people who stay in bed the latest are the *French/Spanish* together with the other lie-in-beds, the *Irish/Portuguese*.

NIGHT OWLS

Despite their early rising, many *Eastern Europeans/Western Europeans* stay up late but not nearly as late as the *Poles/Italians*, more than half of whom stay up beyond midnight.

NAPPING

Interestingly, the industrious *Belgians/Dutch* are unveiled as Europe's most avid nappers, considerably more than the allegedly siesta-loving *Spanish/Croatians*, whereas the *Romanians/Irish* are the people in Europe least prone to napping.

NEWSHOUNDS

A few more of the *French/Swiss* will have read a newspaper than the *Poles/Norwegians* but less than a third of *Germans/Greeks* will have read a newspaper. The *British/Danes* were easily the most avid radio listeners.

ON THE BUS

Almost (12) *as many* Swiss as Czechs are likely to go to work by bus but nowhere near (13) .... Finns – only 6.6% do so. Indeed the results seem to show that these days (14) .... and .... Scandinavians are travelling by public transport.

EATING OUT

The Swiss are by far (15) .... assiduous restaurant patrons, closely followed by the Czechs. (16) .... likely to be found in a restaurant are the Ukrainians and Russians.

BAD TEMPER

(17) .... tempers were found in Turkey but the researchers were (18) .... surprised to find that it was almost (19) .... number .... the allegedly phlegmatic British!

HAPPINESS

Another surprise was that supposedly gloomy Scandinavians felt a great deal (20) .... the Greeks and Russians, and quite (21) .... nations in Europe were the Italians and British!

(From *The European Magazine*)

b) Was there anything you found surprising, predictable, interesting?

2 Find examples in the completed text above of words/phrases which modify or intensify the comparative form. Example: ***almost** the same number*. Can you think of another word or phrase you could use instead of each one? Example: ***nearly** the same number*.

3 Correct the mistakes in these sentences.
1 We are most serious nation of the world.
2 Obviously the Irish go to church much more that the secular Swedes.
3 The Swedes are almost same than the Russians in this.
4 Bigger bath fans in Europe are the British.
5 The most keen showerers are the Danes.

4 How would the results in the article compare with any non-European nationalities you know? Compare your country with other countries you know.

MODIFYING/INTENSIFYING EXPRESSIONS

1 *Just/Almost/(Not) nearly/Twice/Three times/(Not) quite/Hardly/Nowhere near/(Not) half as many* Poles go shopping as ...

2 *Slightly/(Quite) a few/A lot/Lots/(A great) many/Far/ Considerably/Half as many/Twice as many/Three times as many* more (French people) read magazines than ...
NOTE: *A great deal more/less* likely is that ....

3 *All the more remarkable was that .../Easily the most (remarkable) .../By far the most .../Quite the best ...*

OTHER STRUCTURES

• **Continuing process**
More and more people use computers to do their shopping.
Fewer and fewer people go to the shops.
People are going to the shops *less and less*.

• **Extreme**
The researchers were *more than/less than* (surprised) *that ...*
(= extremely surprised/not at all surprised)

• **Cause and effect**
the ... the
The harder we work, *the happier* we are.
We like to go to bed late – *the later the better*.

---

5 Conditionals

1 Describe the difference in meaning between these pairs of sentences. What different verb forms are used?

1 a) You'll be exhausted if you work like that all day.
 b) You'd be exhausted if you worked like that all day.
2 a) If I were to ask you your age, would you tell me?
 b) If I ask you your age, will you tell me?
3 a) We would never have gone out if we had listened to the weather forecast.
 b) We would never go out if we listened to the weather forecast.
4 a) Let me know if she won't help.
 b) Let me know if she doesn't help.
5 a) If we hadn't got lost, we would be home by 10.00.
 b) If we hadn't got lost, we would have been home by 10.00.

2a) Match the sentences in Exercise 1 with these four basic conditional types. Which don't fit exactly?

• **Type 0:** *If I work late, I always get tired.* (situations which are always true)

• **Type 1:** *If I see Carol, I'll (=I will) give her the tickets.* (situations which are likely to happen)

• **Type 2:** *If I knew your address, I'd (= I would) send you a photo.* (imaginary situations in the present or future)

• **Type 3:** *If you'd (= you had) listened more carefully, you'd (= you would) have understood.* (imaginary situations in the past)

b) In which sentence in Exercise 1 is *will* used to express (lack of) willingness? In which sentence is the Type 2 conditional used to be polite? In which sentence is the speaker talking about an imaginary situation in the past with a present result?

c) How are these sentences similar/different to Types 0, 1, 2, 3 ? Look at the meaning, the verb forms and the words used to express a condition (e.g. *if*).

1 If you've finished, then let's go.
2 We won't know whether the invasion's actually started unless we listen to the news.
3 If you happen to be passing, could you bring me the CDs?
4 I could tell you what to do if I knew how it worked.
5 Had you listened a bit more carefully, you'd understand.
6 Why did he go that way if he really was going home?
7 If you wouldn't mind helping, we'd get finished by lunch.
8 But for his bad health, he'd have made a good president.
9 Thanks for lending me your car. I wouldn't have been able to get home otherwise.
10 It might be cheaper if you went to France by train.

3 Put an appropriate word or phrase in the gaps. Think of at least one alternative. Include modals (e.g. *might, could*) where appropriate.

Type 1

1 If you *touch* that hot pan, you *'ll/might/could burn yourself*!
2 Tell me the truth or I .... you.
3 As long as .... , I don't mind lending you my computer.
4 Unless you .... other plans, why .... this evening?
5 Should anyone call when I'm out, ... phone back.

Type 2

6 If by any chance we .... , we wouldn't get there until lunchtime.
7 We .... go out for a meal if you ....
8 Even if .... , I .... tell you!
9 If the TV .... , what would you do?
10 Were we to reduce the price, ...

Type 3

11 If I'd known you were coming, I .... something to eat.
12 Poor Hannah might still be waiting on the corner of the street if ....
13 Had you listened, you .... understood what I'm trying to say.
14 But for your help, ... succeeded.
15 That striker's great! England .... last night if it hadn't been for his last goal.

4 Paragraphs A and B contain a mix of conditionals. Put the verbs in the most appropriate form. In cases where there is more than one possibility, explain the reason for your choice.

A I'm a soldier but I've never killed anyone. But in a future war I (1) .... (*have*) no choice. Obviously if I (2) .... (*be*) one of those unfortunate men in the trenches in the First World War, I (3) .... (*have to*) have killed or been killed. It (4) .... (*not be*) easy even then but in any war situation if you (5) .... (*not fight*), you (6) .... (*put*) the lives of your colleagues at risk.

B It wasn't a very good performance. It (1) .... (*not be*) so bad if his voice (2) .... (*be*) in good shape but he was obviously tired. Actually I'm fed up with opera. Unless there (3) .... (*be*) something special on, I (4) .... (*not go*). Having said that, if you (5) .... (*happen to be*) near Covent Garden next week, you

(6) .... (*get*) tickets for *Don Giovanni*. It might be cheaper if we (7) .... (*buy*) them directly rather than through an agency.

5 Talk about yourself in some of these situations and give reasons for your choices.

1 You are shopping in London. What would you do if you saw:
   – a fire on the floor below you in a large store?
   – someone next to you stealing a wallet?
   – a bomb in a carrier bag in the changing room of a department store?
   – a large group of teenagers attacking an old lady in the street?

2 Last night you went to a very expensive restaurant with a close friend. What would you have done if:
   – you had seen a rat running across the floor?
   – another old friend you hadn't seen for ages had come across to your table?
   – the waiter had spilt wine on your friend's clothes?
   – your close friend had had bad breath?

6 Emphasis: inversion

1 Look at paragraphs A and B below. They are slightly exaggerated ways of writing or speaking.

a) Where do you think each extract comes from (a report? a letter? a speech? an article? a story?)?

A

Hardly had I taken my place when I saw him. *Directly opposite me sat* the man I had seen leaving the house. *Not until later did I realise* what had happened there that fateful January day. *Had I known* at the time, I would probably have panicked and got off the train. *It was only because I was* determined to find out what had really happened that I stayed.

B

Never has the economy of this country been at such a low ebb. *Little did we realise* what effect this new government would have. *What we have realised is* that promises made only six months ago are unlikely to be kept. *In our country exist* people who have little hope of making even a modest living.

b) What do you notice about the order of the words in italics? Check your answer below.

c) Work in pairs and say or write the sentences again, using 'normal' word order.
Example: *I had hardly taken my place when I saw him.*

2a) Divide the phrases in italics in paragraphs A and B into those which:

1 put the main verb before the subject
2 start the clause with *what* or *it is/was* (cleft sentences)
3 put an auxiliary verb in front of the main verb

b) Check your answers below.

We often change the 'normal' order of a sentence for emphasis or dramatic effect. One of the ways we do this is by starting the sentence with *what* or *it is/was* to focus on different parts of the sentence. Another way is by using inversion. There are two main ways of doing this:

INVERSION (1)

The auxiliary verb *have* or *be* can go before the subject (i.e. as in question forms). If there is no auxiliary verb we use *do/does/did*.
This pattern is commonly used after negative or restrictive adverbs and in conditional sentences for dramatic effect and emphasis, for example in speech-making.
Never *in the field of human conflict* **has** *so much been owed by so many to so few.* (negative adverb)
No sooner did *this government get into power than ...* (restrictive adverb)
Had *I your money I would ...* (conditional)

- **Negative or restrictive adverbs/expressions**
  At no time
  Barely
  Hardly ... when/than
  Little
  Never (before/again)
  No sooner ... than
  Not since/until
  Nowhere
  On no account
  Scarcely ... when/than
  Seldom/rarely
  Under no circumstances

- **Conditional clauses**
  If can be replaced by an auxiliary verb in formal or literary conditional clauses. The subject and the auxiliary verb then have to be inverted:
  Were I *in your shoes I would resign.*
  Should *it rain it won't take place.*

- **Other ways of making similar patterns**

1 **After so and such**
  So + adjective + be:
  So awful was *the situation that we left.*
  Such + be + noun:
  Such was *the impact that the top flew off.*

2 **After as**
  I was exhausted, **as was** *Tony.*

3 **After expressions with only**
  Only then/after/in:
  Only after *he had left home* **did** *he realise how much he would miss it.*

INVERSION (2)

The second type of inversion usually comes after prepositional phrases. This is common in speaking and in descriptive or literary writing and involves the main verb being placed in front of the subject in order to put the focus on the subject:

Right in front of me **stood** *a huge cockroach.*
Across the room **appeared** *a familiar face.*
In the house next door **lived** *a fearsome monster.*
Down **came** *the rain.*
There **goes** *John.*

NOTE:
1 A different verb form may be required after inversion:
The bus is **coming**.
Here **comes** *the bus*.
2 Subject-verb inversion cannot happen when the subject is a pronoun:
Here **comes** *the bus.*
Here it **comes.**

3 Rewrite the sentences, using the words in italics so that the meaning stays the same.

1 The match had hardly begun when it started to rain.
  Hardly ....
2 The impressive building towered above me.
  Above me ....
3 A week hardly ever goes by without us having to pay some bill or other.
  Rarely ....
4 I really enjoy curling up with a good book and a glass of wine.
  What I really enjoy ....
5 A group of protesters came round the corner.
  Around the corner ....

6　It's far too expensive and we don't need a
house that big, anyway.
Not only ....

7　You won't find a better restaurant than that
in the country.
Nowhere ....

8　Look, James is coming!
Here .... !

9　We solved the problem eventually but only
after a struggle.
Only after ....

10　If you have any problems, just bring it
back.
Should ....

11　I enjoy the atmosphere there, rather than
the food itself.
It's ....

12　I haven't had such a good laugh since
your party.
Not since ....

13　I'll never lend him a book again if that's
how he treats them.
Never again ....

14　She had no idea at all that she might win.
Not for one minute ....

15　I didn't realise how strongly she felt.
Little ....

4a) Make this politician's speech more
dramatic by putting the underlined words at
the front of the sentence. Make any other
changes necessary.

Ladies and Gentlemen,
Thank you for allowing me to address you
on the issue of our financial policy. I
would like to assess the record of the
present government and then go on to
outline the measures we intend to take
to improve the country's economy.
The present government had <u>scarcely</u> got
into power when it revoked the promises
it made to the taxpayers of this
country. A government can <u>seldom</u> have
made such a mess of the nation's
economy. We have <u>not only</u> high inflation
but also high unemployment, with no
outlook on the horizon for an
improvement in the employment figures.
I think it is true to say that we have
<u>never before</u> had such bleak prospects
before us.
If we <u>were</u> to be elected, we would not
hesitate to take the necessary steps to
reduce inflation while maintaining
acceptable interest rates. We will not
shrink from our task of restoring jobs
to our workforce <u>either</u>.
Our determination is <u>such</u> that we feel
the economy will have turned the corner
by the end of our first year in office.

b)　In pairs, practise reading the sentences,
trying to sound as emphatic and dramatic
as possible.

c)　Think of a couple of other complaints or
promises a politician might make, using
expressions from page 147.
Examples: **So awful is** the state of the
*Health Service that this will be our number
one priority.*
Under no circumstances *will we allow
the government to drain our resources in
this way.*

7　Future forms

1　Which is the best way of continuing the
sentences?

1　a)　I'm buying a new house ...
b)　I'm going to buy a new house ...
when I can afford it.
It's much bigger than this one.

2　a)　I'll meet you after college ...
b)　I'm going to meet you after college ...
Is that OK?
Remember?

3　a)　I retire ...
b)　I'm going to retire ...
early if I get any more of this hassle.
in three years.

4　a)　Her plane gets in at six ...
b)　Her plane is getting in at six ...
Unfortunately it's been delayed.
assuming it's on time.

5　a)　Will you get me a newspaper ...
b)　Are you getting me a newspaper ...
please? Here's some money.
Have you got it on your list?

2　Correct the verb forms which are incorrect.

1　It's hot in here. Will I open the window?
2　I'm sure everything'll be OK.
3　When you will come round, we'll watch a
video.
4　I'm hungry. I think I get a sandwich.
5　The bus leaves in half an hour. Get a move
on!
6　I promise I'm phoning you tonight.
7　Look at those clouds. It's going to snow.
8　If you hurry, you get there in time.

3 When we talk about the future, when do we use:

a) *will* and *shall*? b) *going to*?
c) Present Continuous?

4 What would you say in these situations? Use a future form.

1 You are a hotel receptionist and a guest is booking in. Ask politely about his/her length of stay.
2 An old friend wants you to come to London and have dinner with him/her. You don't want to. Refuse and make an excuse.
3 Your sister is going to a pop concert for the first time. Warn her of the dangers.
4 You are at the airport but have missed your plane. Ask about the next flight.
5 You planned to go to the beach today but have just seen a bad weather forecast on TV. Tell your friend.
6 You are late for a meeting with your boss. Phone and tell him/her.

8 It/there

IT

1 *It is obvious that he isn't telling the truth.*
2 *That he isn't telling the truth is obvious.*

In sentence 1 *it* is used as an introductory subject before a *that* clause. In English this construction is usually preferred to the construction in sentence 2.

It can also be used as an introductory subject (combined with a verb, adjective or noun) before:
• -ing clauses (*It's fun just **lying here**.*)
• infinitive clauses (*It's great **to see you**.*)
• noun clauses (*It doesn't matter **what you say.***)
• verb + clause (*It **seems** that he's left.*)
• passive verb + clause (*It's not **known** at what speed the train was travelling.*)

NOTE: *It* is used to talk about time, weather, distance: (***It**'s 8 o'clock.*)

THERE

There is used to say something exists. (***There**'s a burglar in the house.*)
There is used:
• with verbs like *seem, appear, happen, tend* to describe states before *to be* (*There **seems** to be something wrong.*)
• with modals and *sure, certain* etc. (*There **must** be/There's **sure** to be something wrong.*)
• with words like *some, any, no* (*There's **nothing** I can say.*)
• with a noun + present participle, infinitive or *that* clause (*There's **a woman watching TV**.*)
• with *to be/being* in some structures (*I don't want there **to be** any music playing when she walks in that door. There's no chance of there **being** an election this year.*)
• with some (formal/literary) inversions (*Suddenly **there came into the room a tall man** and ...*)

---

1 Look at the uses of *it* in these sentences. Say whether each example:
– is used as a subject (not for a person)
– is used as an introductory subject
– is not used as a subject

1 The cat's hungry because it hasn't been fed.
2 I don't know why it's thought to be such a good movie.
3 Don't you find it funny?
4 It would be interesting to see him do it by himself.

2a) Re-express these sentences using an introductory *it* construction. Make any grammatical changes necessary.

1 That he feels depressed is not surprising.
2 People fear the pound will fall shortly.
3 Working from home is much more fun.
4 They've decided to impose a smoking ban.
5 Giving a good performance must be very exhilarating.
6 What you say isn't important but what you do is important.
7 At the time he was thought to have had too much to drink.
8 Cancelling the concert would be disastrous.

b) Choose from these nouns, adjectives and verbs to make some sentences with the introductory *it* that are true for yourself. Think of things like work, education, family, where/how you live, interests and hobbies. Example: *I think it's unlikely that we'll ever move house.*

Adjectives: unlikely
inevitable
terribly sad
more entertaining
really unfair
easy for me

Nouns: a pity
a shame
not much use
my ambition
no use
my idea

Verbs: doesn't matter
seem
decide
suit
feel
occur to

c) Find a student whose choice of topics is similar to yours. Compare your sentences and see if you share similar attitudes.

3 Put *It* or *There* at the beginning of these sentences.

1 .... 's been a terrible accident.
2 .... 's very thoughtful of you.
3 .... won't matter what you think.
4 .... must have been a fire here.
5 .... doesn't seem to be any reason for the disaster.
6 .... 's a long way to town. Get a taxi.
7 .... 's a wonderful day. Let's go for a ride.
8 .... 's not much petrol in the car.
9 .... seems that Tim's already left.
10 .... 's likely to be a big row when he finds out.

9 Linking expressions (1)

Linking within the sentence: conjunctions and prepositions

1 Conjunctions (and sometimes prepositions) are used in both speaking and writing to link parts of the same sentence together.

Mixed linkers

a) Look below for examples under the different categories (e.g. Addition, Condition etc.). Then rewrite each of the sentences below so that the meaning stays the same. Make any grammatical changes necessary. Start with the words given.

CONJUNCTIONS AND PREPOSITIONS

- **Addition**
  as well as; in addition to; besides; not only ... but also; and

- **Cause (reason) and result**
  as; because (of); since; given/seeing that; so; owing to; due to; such/so ... that; as a result of

- **Condition**
  if; provided that; providing; unless; as/so long as; in case

---

- **Comparing and contrasting**
  while/whilst; whereas; but; both ... and; like; as ... as; instead of; although; much as; even though; despite; in spite of; (and) yet

- **Purpose**
  so as (not) to; so that; (in order) to

- **Time**
  as; while; after; but not before; before; the moment; when; as soon as; until; since; once; on; no sooner; hardly; immediately

---

1 I went to Mexico as well as Chile on my trip to Latin America.
   a) Besides ....
   b) Not only ....

2 Given that the weather was so awful we decided to get a taxi.
   a) Owing to ....
   b) As the weather ....
   c) The weather was awful ....

3 Although the food was wonderful I couldn't eat very much of it.
   a) In spite of ....
   b) Much as ....

4 If I have any money left, I'll get some wine.
   a) Unless ....
   b) Provided ....

5 She was very helpful so I finished early.
   a) She was so ....
   b) She was such ....

b) Which of the categories in the box do 1–5 above belong to (e.g. The sentences in 1 contain linkers of addition.)?

2 Correct the sentences below. Replace the linkers in italics with one (or more) that is/are appropriate.

1 I'm dying to get home. *While* I get there I'm going to have a cold drink.
2 *Immediately* had I left the house when it started to snow.
3 *Although* she can't drive, I gave her a lift.
4 Take an umbrella *provided* it rains. The weather man said it would.
5 I've changed my mind. I'll have the fish *whereas* the lamb.
6 *When* arriving at the airport I immediately checked in.
7 *Besides* the bad weather the flight has been cancelled.
8 *If* you come now, we'll be late. Hurry up.

Comparing and contrasting

3a) Which of the linking expressions in the category *Comparing and contrasting* in the box on page 150 emphasise similarities and which emphasise differences?

b) Link the ideas in these sentences using the word(s) in brackets. Make any changes to the sentence(s) that are necessary.

1 Running can strengthen your heart. It can damage your spine. (*while*)
2 Running on hard roads can damage your feet. It can damage your knee joints. (*both*)
3 Greg's so kind and thoughtful when he's relaxed. In arguments he's very thick-skinned. (*whereas*)
4 In the restaurant men must be appropriately dressed. Women must be appropriately dressed, too. (*both*)
5 Pat spends hours getting ready to go out. She still looks awful. (*even though*)
6 The house in the country was airy and spacious. The house in London was cramped and musty. (*and yet*)

10 Linking expressions (2)

Linking across sentences: adverbs and adverbial expressions

Adverbs (e.g. *then*) and adverbial expressions (e.g. *on the contrary*) are used, mainly in writing, to link ideas across sentences.
Example: *I didn't really want to go.* **However***, I felt I should.*
Look below for examples of these adverbs under different categories.

ADVERBS/ADVERBIAL EXPRESSIONS

- **Addition**
  also; as well; too; in addition; furthermore; moreover; besides; what's more; at the same time; on top of that

- **Cause (reason) and result**
  therefore; consequently; because of this; as a result; that's why; for this reason; thus; hence; accordingly

- **Comparing and contrasting**
  on the other hand; in/by contrast; on the contrary; conversely; in the same way; otherwise; similarly; likewise; nevertheless; nonetheless; however; yet; even so; still; instead; equally; alternatively

- **Organisation**
  first(ly); secondly; lastly; to begin with; next; all in all; to sum up; in conclusion; at the beginning; at the end; finally

---

- **Time**
  then; later; eventually; afterwards; in the end; finally; meanwhile; beforehand; after that; immediately; at last

NOTE:
Inevitably, there is an overlap between the categories of Organisation and Time.

Position of adverbs

1 Look at these two sentences:

She failed her first driving test. She failed her second one.

a) Which of these linkers of addition would always come at the end of the second sentence?

furthermore   too   in addition
as well   also

b) Which of these linkers could go in the middle of the second sentence (i.e. after the subject *she*)?

on top of that   also   what's more

c) Which of these linkers of addition are not so common in informal speech?

moreover   besides   furthermore
what's more

2a) In the sentence below, which of these linkers of time could go after the subject (*she*)?

She managed to finish the pile of work on her desk.

finally   afterwards   eventually
beforehand   at last

b) Where would the others go?

3 In the sentence below, which of these linkers of result can go after the subject in the second sentence?

I hate loud music. I didn't go to the party.

therefore   as a result   so   that's why
consequently

Mixed adverbs

4   Add an appropriate adverb/adverbial expression to link the ideas in the sentences below. Example: *I have always hated the winter months. So we decided to go to California for some sunshine.*

1   A: The present you bought me was wonderful. Thank you!
     B: I loved the one you bought me.
2   I tried everything to get the car started. Jim was phoning the breakdown services.
3   Stephen's very easy-going and sociable. His sister is quite diffident in company.
4   I'm going to begin by talking about the background to modern medicine. I'm going to examine alternative approaches to conventional medicine in this country. I want to assess the pros and cons of both approaches. I will share with you some exciting new developments for the future.
5   I was late for work again. I forgot the notes for my presentation.

Conjunctions and adverbs

5   Complete the gaps below with either a conjunction or an adverb/adverbial expression.

(1) .... I got to my mother's house I noticed there was no light on in the hall. This was strange (2) .... she never goes out at night. (3) .... I thought I would have to go home again (4) .... I didn't have my key with me. (5) .... , fortunately, I remembered that she kept a spare one in the garage. (6) .... I parked the car and opened the garage door. (7) .... had I got into the garage than I hit my head on a metal bar (8) .... it was so dark in there. (9) .... a few minutes I (10) .... managed to find the key and went up to the front door. (11) .... I got into the house I heard loud barking (12) .... a small dog hurled itself at my legs. (13) .... I was very surprised but (14) .... I remembered that my mother was looking after her friend's dog (15) .... she was on holiday. (16) .... I tried speaking to the dog it was absolutely convinced I was a burglar (17) .... would not stop yapping. (18) .... I tried stroking it (19) .... try and stop it making so much noise. (20) .... I put down the presents that I had come to deliver. (21) .... did the little beast bite my leg (22) .... it (23) .... ripped up the presents I had wrapped so carefully. (24) .... I decided to take my leave, (25) .... aiming a kick at the now furious animal.

11 Modals in the present and future

1   Match each sentence in A with its meaning in B. Example: *1 = b.* The meanings in B may relate to more than one sentence.

Can/could

A
1   Can you ski?
2   You can't smoke in here!
3   Can you tell me the way to the bank?
4   She can't be that young! She's got a child of four.
5   Could you give me a ring later?
6   It can often rain here in July.
7   Can I go?
8   We could go by bus instead.
9   Can I give you a lift?
10 It could be true, I suppose.

B

a)	impossibility/ certainty	e)	permission
		f)	prohibition
b)	ability	g)	offer
c)	request	h)	suggestion
d)	possibility		

May/might

A
1   May I open a window?
2   You may go when you've finished.
3   Might I have another drink?
4   He might be late home tonight.

B

a)	permission	b) possibility

Will/shall

A
1   I'll carry that for you.
2   Will you open the window?
3   I'll scream if you do that again.
4   Shall we meet at 6.00?
5   She *will* leave her keys around.
6   That'll be Sam at the door.
7   I'll have the fish, I think.
8   I'll pay you back soon.
9   Be careful. He'll bite you.

B

a)	promise	f)	assumption
b)	sudden decision	g)	request
c)	offer	h)	threat
d)	warning	i)	suggestion
e)	criticism		

Would

A

1 Would you come here, please?
2 We'd eat out every evening on holiday.
3 Would you like to meet for a coffee?
4 I didn't know you would be here.
5 That would be Tim you met.
6 You would say something like that.

B

a)	future in the past	d)	invitation
b)	request	e)	criticism
c)	past habit	f)	assumption

2 A variety of modals are used to talk about how sure you are about something.

a) Match the sentences in A to the most likely continuation in B.

A 1 He may be in.
   2 He can't be in.
   3 He won't be in.
   4 He must be in.
   5 He should be in.

B a) The curtains are still drawn.
   b) He sometimes gets home early.
   c) The car's not there.
   d) He's usually back by now.
   e) He never is at this time.

b) Which two other modals can be used to replace *may* with more or less the same meaning.

3 Look at these sentences which express obligation. What, if anything, are the differences in meaning between the following?

1 You *should/must/will/have to/need to* write that out again.
2 You *should/must/have to* try the pizza at that new restaurant.
3 You *mustn't/shouldn't/don't have to* eat that!
4 I *must/have to* go.

4 *Should* has a variety of other meanings apart from obligation. Express these sentences in any way you can, without using *should* or *ought to*.

1 Should we get the 10.40 train?
2 I should think he's there by now.
3 It should be really good.
4 Should it rain we'll put it off.
5 They shouldn't smoke so much.

5 Work in pairs. Use modals to invent short dialogues for the situations below. Take turns to be A and B.

1 A: You can't reach a book from a high shelf in the library. Ask a stranger to help you.
  B: Agree with enthusiasm.
2 A: Strongly recommend a film you have seen to a friend.
  B: Ask for more information about it, where it's on, who's in it etc.
3 A: Offer to go to the shops for your mother.
  B: Say it's not necessary, and explain why.

12 Narrative forms

1 Read this extract from a true account of a successful emergency landing. When the account begins the plane is only seconds into the air.

I (1) .... (*sit*) with my friend, we (2) .... (*strap*) in and we (3) .... (*take off*). The weather in London (4) .... (*be*) terrible, the heavens (5) .... (*open*), but I (6) .... (*not/think*) anything of it.

Five minutes later there (7) .... (*be*) an explosion and a gigantic flash of white light. The plane (8) .... (*shake*) so violently I (9) .... (*think*) we (10) .... (*hit*) by a missile.

The pilot (11) .... (*say*) we (12) .... (*strike*) by lightning but everything (13) .... (*be*) absolutely fine. Four hours later we (14) .... (*come*) in to land. We (15) .... (*see*) the lights of the airport and we (16) .... (*wait*) for touchdown. But suddenly we (17) .... (*zoom*) up again at top speed. The pilot (18) .... (*say*) that we had a slight problem – the lightning earlier (19) .... (*blow*) the light which (20) .... (*tell*) him whether the landing gear (21) .... (*work*) or not. He (22) .... (*say*) he (23) .... (*fly*) over the control tower so that they could see whether the gear (24) .... (*be*) actually in place. He then (25) .... (*announce*) that the control tower couldn't quite see so they (26) .... (*send*) a fighter plane to check it out. He was incredibly calm. Minutes later, however, things (27) .... (*change*). His voice (28) .... (*shake*).

He (29) .... (*say*) the fighter plane (30) .... (*see*) our wheels were in place, but they couldn't tell if they (31) .... (*lock*) and (32) .... (*stay*) there. He said, 'Ladies and gentlemen we are going to have to prepare you for an emergency landing.'

(Adapted from the *Independent on Sunday*)

a) Complete the gaps with a form of the verb in brackets. Use the Past Simple, Past Continuous, Past Perfect (Continuous) or a form of the Future in the Past (e.g. *was going to*). There may be more than one possibility.

b) Compare the verbs you chose in groups. Defend your choices if necessary.

c) Work in pairs and decide what the end of the story could be.

d) Compare your stories in groups.

Past habits: *used to* and *would*

2a) Decide which of the verb forms below are possible in the context.

1 When I was a child my town *didn't use to have/wouldn't have/didn't have* so many supermarkets. We *had/would have/used to have* lots of small family-run shops instead.
2 Once upon a time I *used to write/would write/wrote* everything by hand. Now I rely on my word processor.
3 The school *used to be run/would be run/was run* by the local government, but now it's run by central government.
4 I first *saw/used to see/would see* him on the station platform and I *would watch/used to watch/watched* him secretly over the top of my newspaper. I don't think he *noticed/would notice/used to notice*.
5 I *lived/used to live/would live* in the country – that's why I'm not used to traffic.
6 He *used to be/was/would be* so happy before he retired.
7 On our anniversary my husband *would buy/used to buy/bought* me red roses but this has stopped now.
8 We *didn't use to see/wouldn't see/didn't see* much traffic on these roads at one time, but now there are traffic jams everywhere.

Used to and **would**

A common way of talking about habit in the past is to use the Past Simple. However, habits which are no longer true and which are contrasted with present habits can also be described using *used to* and *would*:
*When I was working in London I **used to** get the train at 7.30 every morning.*
*I **would** arrive in London at twenty to nine, and get the Underground to work.*

However, *would* cannot be used to talk about discontinued *states*:
*He **used to live** in Paris when he was a student.*
(NOT *He would live* ...)

---

b) Talk about your experiences when you first started learning English. Use *used to* and *would* to talk about how you used to study and how you managed to learn enough English to reach advanced level.

13 The passive

1a) Read the first part of the newspaper article below.

Darts team takes flight after cakes are spiked with LSD

A darts match was abandoned as one team collapsed into laughter and hysteria after its pre-match buffet was spiked with hallucinogenic drugs. Most of the team from the Fortynine Club, aged between 21 and 62, were taken to hospital after they were either reduced to tears or uncontrollable fits of giggling during an away match.

---

darts: game in which special pointed objects are thrown at a round board with numbers
spike: add strong alcohol or drugs to something without people knowing

b) Complete the rest of the newspaper extract below with the appropriate passive form of the verb in brackets.

Three men (1) .... (*detain*) overnight because their heart rate (2) .... (*affect*) by the drug, which (3) .... (*believe*) to be LSD and which (4) ....(*add*) to their cakes. Despite the ill-effects, the Fortynine club was winning when the match had to (5) ....(*call off*).
The ten men who (6) .... (*take*) to hospital had all eaten at the Fortynine club before setting off for the match. South Wales Constabulary said yesterday a man and a woman (7) .... (*interview*) at Caerphilly police station.

(From The Times)

2   Look at the sentences in A below and match them with the different uses of the passive in B. There may be more than one possibility.

A

1   Income tax will be increased next year.
2   An old man was robbed yesterday in a horrific attack.
3   Do you like it? It was bought for us by my father.
4   More information can be obtained by calling this number.
5   After this the chocolates are sorted into boxes.
6   The plants have died because they weren't watered.

B

a)   The actions are more important than who did it (sometimes referred to as the 'agent').
b)   It is not known, not important or obvious who did it.
c)   We want to be impersonal and formal.
d)   We want to avoid blaming someone directly or putting the responsibility in a particular area.
e)   We want to focus on or emphasise 'who did it' by putting the agent at the end of the sentence.

> NOTE:
> With verbs such as *believe, think, expect* an alternative passive form with the introductory *it* is possible: ***It is expected that*** *the Prime Minister will give a press conference later today.*

3   Work in pairs.

a)   Which of the sentences below would:

- not sound appropriate in the passive?
- sound more appropriate in the passive?
- also sound appropriate in the passive but have a different emphasis?

Give reasons for your answers.

1   Someone has to stack the shelves before the shop opens.
2   Have you not put the baby to bed yet? It's way past her bedtime.
3   I strongly advise you to take a day or two off. You look exhausted.
4   I'm feeling much happier because the university authorities gave me an extra year to complete my course.
5   Excuse me, is that the operator? Somebody has just cut me off.
6   I love that film. The Taviani brothers directed it.

7   I'll phone you about the time of the film.
8   The painters are painting my spare room.
9   Jim won the prize this year, much to everyone's surprise.
10   They include vegetables in the price of the meal.
11   Unfortunately the office is going to have to make some of the staff redundant.
12   I've just baked a cake. Have a piece.
13   I love this symphony. The composer wrote it in 1912.
14   Sorry I'm late. Cars blocked the road as far as the roundabout so I was stuck in a jam.

b)   Rewrite the sentences which would sound more appropriate in the passive.

4   Work in pairs and prepare a short paragraph based on the news headline of your choice. Use both active and passive forms, as appropriate. Then exchange your work with someone else and try to improve their story.

OVER 80s TO MARCH IN PROTEST OVER PENSION CUTS

MORE VICTIMS FOUND IN AIR CRASH HORROR

7-YEAR-OLD ARRESTED IN CONNECTION WITH TIMOTHY'S DISAPPEARANCE

Lottery winner refuses million pound jackpot. 'I'm happy as I am,' he says

14 Phrasal verbs (grammar)

1a) Do the quiz below to see how much you know about the grammar of phrasal verbs.

1 A phrasal verb is made up of a verb and a particle. What is a particle:

- an adverb?
- a preposition?
- an adverb and a preposition?
- any or all of these?

2 Look at the phrasal verbs below.

1 Henry finally *turned up* late as usual.
2 Anna has *given up* smoking.
3 He *fell over* the cat.
4 He *gets on with* his brother.

3 Look at the dictionary entries.

a) How does the dictionary tell you where the particle can go in a sentence?
b) In which use of *take off*:
1 can the particle go before or after the noun?
2 can the particle only go after the noun?
3 does the verb have no object?

---

take off *phr v*
1 ▶ **REMOVE STH** ◀ [T **take** sth ↔ **off**] to remove something, especially a piece of clothing: *Take your coat off.* \ *I forgot to take off my make-up last night.*—opposite **put on**
2 ▶ **AIRCRAFT/SPACECRAFT** ◀ [I] to rise into the air at the beginning of a flight: *As the plane was taking off, I remembered I hadn't turned the iron off.*
3 ▶ **COPY SB** ◀ [T **take** sb ↔ **off**] *informal* to copy the way someone speaks or behaves, in order to entertain people
4 ▶ **HOLIDAY** ◀ [T **take** sth **off**] to have a holiday from work on a particular day, or for a particular length of time: *I'm taking Thursday off to do some Christmas shopping.*
5 ▶ **SUCCESS** ◀ [I] to suddenly start being successful: *I hear the business is really taking off.*
6 ▶ **LEAVE A PLACE** ◀ [I] *informal* to leave somewhere suddenly, especially without telling anyone: *Clare just took off without saying goodbye.*

---

a) What do you think the phrasal verbs mean?
b) In which sentence can you guess the meaning of the phrasal verb from the two parts? Is the particle an adverb or a preposition?
c) Which example cannot take an object (i.e. is intransitive)?
d) In which sentence(s) can the particle NOT be separated (by a noun or pronoun) from the verb?
e) In sentence 2, if smoking is replaced by the pronoun it, where does it go in the sentence?

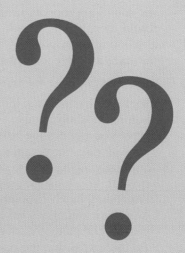

b) Check as many answers as you can in the box below.

PHRASAL VERBS: THE DIFFERENT TYPES

• Type 1

a) verb + adverb (intransitive)

These verbs cannot be followed by an object and cannot be made passive:
*The missing book finally **turned up**.*

b) verb + adverb + object (transitive)

The most common category of phrasal verbs:
*I **looked up** the word in the dictionary.*

NOTE:

1 Word order: The particle can be separated from the verb and can go after the noun/object:
*He **warmed** the milk **up**.*
If the object is very long, it goes after the adverb:
*She **warmed up** the milk which had been left in the fridge.*

2 However, in some verbs, the particle can only come *after* the object:
*I **answered** my mother **back**.*
*I **caught** her **out**.*
If the object is a pronoun, it always goes before the particle:
*I **warmed** it **up**.*

3 Some of the verbs in Type 1 (e.g. *turn up*) can also come into a different category, with a different meaning, or can change from intransitive to transitive:
*The dress was too long so I **turned it up**.*
*I **looked up** and saw him there.*

• Type 2

verb + preposition (transitive)

(sometimes more accurately called 'prepositional verbs') These are followed by a preposition, which takes an object. They are very often literal (e.g. **pay for** the meal, **listen to** the programme) but can sometimes be idiomatic (**pull through** an illness).

NOTE:

The preposition cannot be put after the object. It is inseparable (stays with the verb):
***talk about** your work* (not ~~talk your work about~~).
It goes before the pronoun (***talk about** it*).
A preposition can come at the end of the sentence:
*Tell me what it **consists of**.*

• Type 3

verb + adverb particle + preposition (transitive)

These are three-part phrasal verbs (sometimes called 'phrasal-prepositional verbs'). They can be literal (*run over to*) or idiomatic (*put up with*).
Some have an object before the adverb or preposition and object:
*He **took Sam up on** his offer.*
*I **put it down to** the weather.*

NOTE:

The particles cannot be separated (except that an adverb can sometimes come between the first and second particles):
*He took me **up**, *finally*, **on** my offer.*
The noun or pronoun must go after the second particle.

2a) Match the more formal word or phrase in italics below with one of the phrasal verbs in the box.

beat up	take on	take after	take off	get over	set up
look into	tell off	get round	come into		

1 It took her a long time to *recover from* her illness.
2 The business is so successful that they're having to *employ* more staff.
3 Lorna really enjoys *imitating* the teacher.
4 The police have begun to *investigate* the fraud.
5 The woman *reprimanded* Jack for walking over her garden.
6 Nick has just *inherited* a lot of money.
7 Do you think we'll be able to *persuade* him?
8 The thugs *assaulted* the old man.
9 It's amazing how much your son *resembles* you.
10 It takes a lot of work to *establish* a successful business.

b) Rewrite the sentences using the phrasal verb. Where possible, separate the verb from the particle. Use a dictionary to help you.

15 Present verb forms

1a) Which sentence, 1 or 2, refers to the Present Continuous and which to the Present Simple?

1 It refers to the general (more permanent) present including the present moment. (*I .... (work) at the university. I've been there for years.*)

2 It refers to temporary states/actions going on around now. (*We .... (have) a party. Come in.*)

b) When do we use the Present Simple and Present Continuous to talk about the future? Examples: *I'll phone you when I .... (get) home. / What .... (you/do) tomorrow morning?*

c) Can you think of any other situations when we use the Present Simple and the Present Continuous?

2 Look at the extracts below.

① " Perez gets the ball, Di Maggio's moving into a good position – Perez passes to Di Maggio who ...

③ Slim, fit male, 33, loves fine wine and jazz. Sadly this wealthy, non-smoking bachelor is leaving England for good at the end of the year. In the meantime a modest Mr Right is looking for attractive fun lover for final fling.

② I enclose two references and a full CV as requested and I look forward to hearing from you at your earliest convenience.

④ So I tell him not to eat the salad but he tells me not to interrupt him when he's eating – Sue's laughing her head off by this time – then he asks me what it was and ...

⑤ At the end of *Casablanca*, Ilsa flies off with her husband and leaves Rick ...

⑥ **TWA BOMB: SUSPICION INCREASES**

⑦
I always tell you what you want to hear
But you're always giving me sheer ...

⑧ OK. This is the plan. You get to the bank – I'm waiting inside cashing a cheque – and you come and ask to speak to the manager and then I ...

⑨ It starts at 9.00 – let's go for a drink first.

a) Underline the present verb forms.

b) Does each form refer to past time, present time or future time?

c) Why do we choose the present forms in the contexts above?

PRESENT SIMPLE

We can use the Present Simple:

1 when we write reviews and in summaries of plays, novels etc.:
Daniel Day-Lewis **plays** *the part of Mr Proctor.*
The author **says** *that genetics is getting out of hand.*

2 in TV and radio commentaries to talk about a series of events which are completed as we speak:
The Queen **gets** *out of her carriage and* **gives** *a wave to the crowd.*

3 when commenting on what we are doing (e.g. *promise, swear, agree, deny*):
I **admit** *I* **prefer** *them to family holidays.*
I **enclose** *a cheque.* (in formal correspondence)

4 to give directions:
You **go** *down the road.*

5 to talk about the past in stories, anecdotes, jokes (to make them more vivid):
She **comes** *into the pub and* **bops** *him on the nose.*

PRESENT CONTINUOUS

1 We use the Present Continuous in TV and radio commentaries to talk about background and situations in progress before the action described in the commentary:
The crowd **are waiting** *patiently. Here he comes now.*

2 We do not use the Present Continuous for repeated actions not closely linked to the present:
I **go** *to the dentist's twice a year.* NOT *I'm going...*

3 Because the Present Continuous suggests something temporary it can sound casual and less definite:
I'm hoping *you'll lend me your car* is more tentative and less definite than **I hope** *you'll lend me your car.*

4 Some verbs (sometimes called 'state' verbs) do not usually take the continuous form, e.g. verbs of the senses (*seem, look, sound, hear*), mental and emotional states (*love, believe, remember, want*), and others (*agree, deny, be, belong*).

NOTE:
In TV/radio commentaries we sometimes use 'state' verbs in the continuous: *Liverpool* **are looking** *a poor side tonight. I don't think they'll ever score.*

3 What verbs can you think of to fill the gaps in these extracts? Put them in either the Present Simple or Continuous.

1

BIG-SPENDING BUSINESSMAN .... HEMINGWAY'S CAFE IN PARIS.

2 Her parents live in Vancouver. They .... down to Malibu soon to be with her for the baby's birth.

3 I .... for the cafe to open. I .... here every day at this time but today it's shut!

4 I'm up at about 6.30 am – I .... people who can lie in and not feel guilty but I can't.

5 Well, this lady .... dinner in a very posh restaurant. Suddenly she .... the head-waiter over and .... him, 'What .... this fly .... in my soup?' The waiter .... out his spectacles and carefully .... into her soup bowl. 'I'm not absolutely certain,' he .... , 'but it .... to be drowning.'

6 I .... this book about the French Revolution at the moment. I .... it .... a very good idea of what it must have been like.

7 Then you .... the olive oil gently in a pan, ... the onion, garlic and tomatoes and .... for about ten minutes.

4 Tell each other something unusual that happened to you when you were young. Make the story more vivid by using present verb forms where possible.

16 Relative clauses

1a) Read the text, *Cat's eyes*, below and answer the following questions.

1 What are 'cat's eyes'?
2 Who invented them?
3 How do they work?

Cat's eyes, <u>which</u> is the popular name for reflecting road studs, have been on our roads since the 1930s.

Percy Shaw, whose brainwave it was, got the idea when trams were removed from the roads in Britain. The lines which trams ran along were in the middle of the road and drivers relied on the light which reflected off the rails to act as a guide.

The glass reflector, which is a bi-convex lens, is inserted in a rubber pad and then sealed in a copper container, which protects the surface of the reflector. The base, into which the pad is put, is then set deeply into the road.

Light which enters the reflector is made to converge by the convex lens and the light then reflects off an aluminium covering, which is on the back of the reflector. The light beams which are reflected do so in a straight line.

On the motorway, cat's eyes have coloured lenses, which is done by spraying the back of the reflector with coloured lacquer.

The company which Percy Shaw founded to make the cat's eyes now makes over 800,000 a year.

(Adapted from *The Guardian Education*)

b) Underline all the relative pronouns you can find in the text. The first one is done for you.

c) Find two examples of where prepositions are used in the relative clause.

2a) Answer the following questions about relative clauses.

1   Which of the relative clauses in the text are defining relative clauses (essential to the meaning) and which are non-defining (add extra information)? Which type is separated from the rest of the sentence by commas?

2   Which of the pronouns *which, who, that* are used for a) things and b) people in defining relative clauses? Fill in the gaps below with two possibilities for each sentence.
  – The man .... lives opposite complained about the noise.
  – Have you seen the film .... won all the Oscars?

3   Which pronouns do we use in non-defining relative clauses? Put one pronoun in each gap.
  – My best friend, ... lives in Zimbabwe, phoned me last night.
  – My new jumper, ... I spent a fortune on, has shrunk.

4   In defining relative clauses, can the relative pronoun be left out when it is defining a) the subject or b) the object? Look at the sentences below and say which one is correct.
  – The meal (that) we had last night was expensive.
  – I saw the boy (who) did all the damage.

5   *Where, whose* and *when* are used in both defining and non-defining relative clauses. Use the cues below to make sentences.
  – Are you the woman/son/won prize?
  – I set off at 6/traffic/not too bad.
  – That's the museum/we went last week.

6   Look at the two examples below. Which word in italics refers to a) the object of the sentence or b) the whole 'idea' of the sentence?
  – I don't know *what* you are talking about.
  – He's very quiet today, *which* is unusual.

b) Discuss your answers in pairs before doing Exercise 3.

3   Correct the sentences below.

1   My brother who is in Australia phoned last night. (I have only one brother.)
2   The meal, that was absolutely delicious, must have taken hours to prepare.
3   We decided to go to a place which we'd already been.
4   He lives next door to the teacher who's daughter is in my class.
5   I've got to phone the man which is coming to fit the carpet.
6   I know a really good beach, at where there are very few people.
7   That's the car which it reversed into mine.
8   I have to go for an injection next week which I'm terrified of.
9   I have a few ideas which I can use them in my essay.
10   She never speaks, what always surprises me.

4   Combine the sentences below with a relative pronoun. If the information is not essential to the sentence, add commas.

1   We're going to a ski resort next month. *The Sunday Times* recommended it.
2   Do you remember me talking about Kate? She's the curator at the museum.
3   I think I told you about Helen, too. Her brother used to come and play with Ben.
4   This is the house. Tolstoy used to live in it.
5   The rain came down heavily. It had started after lunch.
6   Her new book has had a lot of publicity. It comes out next month.
7   The new film. We were talking about it. It's on video from next week.
8   Tom told me a joke. It was very funny.
9   She was driving in the opposite direction. I thought this was very strange.
10   The boss wants to speak to me. This is a bit worrying.

5a) Complete these unfinished sentences in any way you like.

1   I bought a present last week which ....
2   She's never been on a plane before, which ....
3   I'd like a car ....
4   Have you heard of the person who .... ?
5   My mother, who ....
6   The driver that ....
7   She spoke to the boss, who ....
8   The Greek island, where ....
9   The new Greek restaurant where ....
10   The chair on which ....

b) Compare your sentences with other people's.

c) Practise reading them, remembering to pause when there are commas giving extra information.

17 Reported speech

1 When we report what people say the verbs which are reported are usually (but not always) in the past:
'Are you OK?' → *He wanted to know if I **was** OK. (is/are → was/were)*

a) Work in pairs. Take it in turns to be Student A and Student B.
STUDENT A: Write sentences using 1–7 below.
STUDENT B: Transform Student A's sentences as in the example above.

1 Present Simple
2 Present Perfect or Past Simple
3 *shall/will*
4 *can/may*
5 *now*
6 *tomorrow*
7 *ago*

b) Why is this example correct?
'I'm studying Russian.' → *He said he's studying Russian.*

c) STUDENT A: Write two sentences for 1–4 below.
STUDENT B: Transform Student A's sentences as in the example. Use two different reporting verbs for each.

1 statements (Example: *'It's a lovely day.'* → *She said (that) it was a lovely day.*)
2 questions
3 requests/commands
4 suggestions

2a) Think of two situations for each of the following (who is speaking and why) and answer the questions below.

1 'Go away! Leave me alone!'
2 'Please give me the letter. Please.'
3 'I'll call the police unless you go away.'
4 'You're a very cold-hearted person.'
5 'I know this is my fault.'
– What is the function of the utterance? (command? apology?)
– What is the speaker's mood/attitude?
– Describe the direct speech as creatively as you like.

Example:
'Go away! Leave me alone!'
'Go away! Leave me alone!' screamed Sarah as Matthew came closer.

b) Rewrite the sentences in indirect speech. Try to be creative. Example:
As Matthew came closer, Sarah, terrified of him, screamed at him to go away.

18 Verbs followed by *-ing* or infinitive (+/– *to*) or *that*

A few verbs can be followed by both the *-ing* form or the infinitive with *to* with a change of meaning. In these cases *-ing* forms are sometimes (but not always) used to talk about past events; *to*-infinitives are used for present or future events (if the main verb is in the past, the *to*-infinitive refers to the future from the point of view of the past).

1a) What is the difference in meaning between each pair of sentences? Can you think of a situation where each sentence might be used?

1 a) I remember putting in an application.
  b) I remembered to put in an application.
2 a) She went on talking about the same old problems.
  b) She went on to talk about the same old problems.
3 a) I regret to tell you that I have no money.
  b) I regret telling you that I have no money.
4 a) He stopped to talk to me after dinner.
  b) He stopped talking to me after dinner.
5 a) Have you forgotten to buy me a birthday present?
  b) Have you forgotten buying me a birthday present?
6 a) Try telling her what you think of her.
  b) Try to tell her what you think of her.
7 a) I saw him reading the fax.
  b) I saw him read the fax.
8 a) He went on praising our efforts.
  b) He went on to praise our efforts.
9 a) Love means never having to say you're sorry.
  b) Did you mean to get married?
10 a) The company requires you to have a sense of responsibility.
  b) Success in this job requires anticipating the boss's every need, I'm afraid.

1
go on + *-ing* = continue
go on + *to*-infinitive = change the activity

2
try + *-ing* = do something to see what happens (experiment)
try + *to*-infinitive (or *try* + *-ing*) = make an effort to do something

3
mean + *-ing* = involve
mean + *to*-infinitive = intend

4
require + *-ing* = involve
require + object + *to*-infinitive = officially demand

---

b) Look at sentence 1a) on page 161. To emphasise that the activity is completed we can say: *I remember **having put** in an application*. Which other sentences in Exercise 1a) can you change in the same way with *having* + past participle?

2a) Which of these are not grammatically possible?

1 I *promise/hope/resent/can't stand/plan* to get home early.
2 She *enjoys/wants/refuses/feels like/avoids* seeing new places.
3 He *asked/suggested/wanted/disliked/forgave/resented/dared/expected* me to hurry.
4 They *agreed/wished/considered/mentioned/hesitated/fancied* turning on the TV.

b) As quickly as possible make a list of verbs under these headings:

Verbs + *-ing*
Verbs + *to*-infinitive
Verbs + *-ing*/*to*-infinitive (little change of meaning)
Verbs + *-ing*/*to*-infinitive (change of meaning)

c) Compare your chart with another student's.

When choosing whether a verb following is an *-ing* form or a *to*-infinitive it is helpful to remember that *-ing* forms sometimes suggest a general statement and *to*-infinitives suggest a specific action in the future:

I like riding horses and cycling. (general)
I'd like to go out for a walk. I'm fed up. (specific)

However, some people do say *I like to ride* even when talking generally.
Indeed, some other verbs can be followed by either an *-ing* form or a *to*-infinitive with little change of meaning: *start/continue/begin; love, hate, can't bear, prefer; allow/permit/forbid.*
But there are many verbs where there are no 'rules'. You just have to remember which form follows.

NOTE:
dare can be used without *to*.
He didn't dare (to) say anything.

3a) Which of these can you change into *that* clauses with little change of meaning?

1 I saw him peeling an orange.
2 I watched him peeling an orange.
3 She's forgotten to give you the key.
4 She's forgotten giving you the key.
5 She refused to help me.
6 I enjoy meeting people.
7 Let's pretend not to see them.
8 Are you suggesting going out?
9 Do you want me to pick you up at the airport?
10 She can't stand anyone touching her.
11 He threatened to kidnap the boy.
12 She was chosen to be the new manager.
13 I always avoid driving on a Sunday.
14 Can you deny being wrong?
15 There seems to be something wrong.

b) Make sentences using these cues. In some cases you can only use a *that* clause, in some cases you can either use a *that* clause or verb +-*ing/to*, in some cases you cannot use a *that* clause.

1 appear/be/very angry
2 He/complain/be/something wrong with the food.
3 Avoid/go shopping/Saturdays! It's too crowded.
4 Do you still insist/do/nothing wrong? Why are you lying to me?
5 I/expect/be OK on the night! Don't worry!
6 He/warn me/not put up with any more of your nonsense! He'll give you the sack next time.
7 I hate/miss/the beginning of a film.
8 I promise/be/home by midnight.
9 I must point out/be/afraid of heights. I can't go up there.
10 Let's delay/decide about this/until next week.

WRITING CHECKLISTS

1 After writing a first draft use the General and Organisation checklists below to assess your own writing. Everything you write should be appropriate to why you are writing, who you are writing for and the kind of text it is.

General

- Is it clear *why* you are writing (i.e. what your purpose is)?
- Does your writing make sense?
- Is all the information there? Is there too much information for your reader? (e.g. Is there any unnecessary repetition? Can points be combined?)
- Is your style too wordy or too abrupt for the purpose?
- Is your text easy to read? Have you expressed yourself clearly?
- Is it organised clearly and logically? Is the text divided up appropriately?

Organisation

- Is the layout appropriate? (e.g. Is the address in a letter in the correct place?)
- Have you included an introduction and conclusion, if appropriate. Are they sufficiently 'eye-catching'?
- Is your writing divided into paragraphs appropriate to your purpose?
- Are the paragraphs themselves clearly organised? Do you need to rearrange them? Would it be useful to include a 'topic sentence' in each paragraph (a sentence which summarises what the paragraph is about)?
- Have you included linking expressions within and between sentences?

2 After the first or second draft it is a good idea to check your writing for specific details of language.

Language

Vocabulary
- Is the style of vocabulary appropriate? (e.g. Is it formal enough for the situation you are writing for?)
- Have you included a range of words and expressions, and included words with a specific, rather than just a general meaning when necessary? (e.g. *She* **crept** *upstairs*, rather than *went upstairs* if you want to make it clear that she was trying to be quiet).
- Is your choice of vocabulary appropriate to the purpose? (e.g. If you are writing a brochure, is it interesting and colourful enough?)
- Is your spelling accurate?

Grammar
- Have you included a range of verb forms and tenses? (e.g. If it is a narrative, have you included, for example, the Past Perfect and Future in the Past, as well as the Past Simple and Continuous?)
- Have you considered using a range of sentence structures (e.g. complex sentences, such as relative and participle clauses, as well as simple and compound sentences)? Obviously this will depend on what you are writing.
- Have you looked through your work to check areas of grammar that you find problematic (e.g. articles)?

Punctuation Check this carefully, especially if your writing includes much dialogue.

3 It may be helpful to exchange your work with someone else in the class and ask them for their advice before you write your final draft.

1 ARTICLE WRITING

1　Do you know the names of any species of birds that migrate? Do you know where they migrate to and at what time of the year?

2　Imagine you were asked to write a magazine article on bird migration. Think of techniques you could use to make it interesting for a general reader.

3　Read the extracts below and find examples of:
1　an attempt to capture the reader's imagination and put him/her into the situation
2　relating a specific example to a general situation
3　introducing interesting facts
4　giving concrete details
5　making dramatic comparisons

Title

Opening paragraphs

THE INCREDIBLE JOURNEY OUT OF AFRICA

Imagine having to meet someone on the banks of a remote stream in tropical South-East Africa. You have never been to Africa, and you have to get there in four days – on your own, without a compass or a map.

Every cuckoo faces such a prospect in its first autumn. It has never known its mother or father and has been brought up alone by its tireless foster parents. Despite these seemingly impossible odds, the young cuckoo will fly successfully to its African destination. The return journey is, perhaps, a little easier – and that is what approximately 2,000 million birds of more than 200 species are doing at the moment. The great spring migration is underway.

Closing paragraph

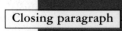

A willow warbler was singing in my garden this week. The previous night it had completed the last section of a journey that began thousands of kilometres away in the heat of Africa. The bird had survived all kinds of dangers, and yet this tiny creature, weighing little more than a spoonful of sugar, was just one of millions that made a similar journey – and in September it will fly all that way back again.

4 A topic sentence expresses what a paragraph is about. Read these paragraphs from the middle of the article on page 164. Underline the topic sentences in the paragraphs below and explain the purpose of each of the other sentences (e.g. to develop the argument in the topic sentence/to explain it/to provide extra information/to give an example).

1 Migrating uses up a lot of energy. Some birds, like the swallow and swift, can feed as they fly, but others have to store fat in preparation for the journey. Small birds like warblers have the added problem of heat loss and have to store up to double their mass before setting off.

2 The mechanisms involved in migration are still imperfectly understood. A bird's navigation system is instinctive and must comprise some sort of in-built map, together with a compass sense and navigational aids to help it cope with varying wind speeds and direction and to allow night flight. Studies have established a directional sense (homing pigeons orient themselves on to the correct bearing within 30 seconds of being released) and an ability to detect the earth's magnetic field.

5a) Put these sentences in the correct order to make a paragraph.

1 Others are partly the result of human interference, for instance desertification.
2 Some – the weather, disease and disability – are natural and claim the young and the weak.
3 The Sahara is moving south up to 20km a year, making it harder for birds like the whitethroat and sedge warbler to cross.
4 Birds on the wing face many hazards.

b) Why did you put the sentences in the order you did?

6 Read this information about a famous historical example of human migration. Rewrite the information to make it an interesting opening paragraph for a magazine article. Use some of the techniques from Exercise 3.

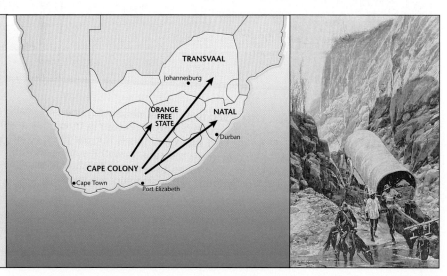

THE GREAT TREK (1835–1840s)

The Great Trek was a series of migrations by Afrikaner farmers (or 'Boers') in Southern Africa, from Cape Colony into the interior of the country. Between 12,000 and 14,000 Afrikaners took part in the Trek (an Afrikaans word meaning 'a journey by ox wagon').

7 Rewrite the notes in A and B to make the next two paragraphs of the article.

A

Migrants mostly from poorer eastern region of the Cape/took families, livestock, weapons, wagons/many ex-slaves and free blacks also took part.

B

Reasons: Afrikaners needed more land for farming/cheap land only available in the interior/political grievances against the British who had occupied the Cape in 1806/feared that the British, influenced by missionaries and humanitarians, were hostile to their interests and would not protect them from attack/also slavery abolished in 1833 – widely resented in the Cape.

8 Make some or all of these notes into an interesting concluding sentence or sentences:

Great hardships on route/migrants settled as far afield as Natal, the Orange Free State, and the Transvaal/milestone in building Afrikaner national consciousness.

2 BUSINESS FORMATS

1a) What is the general purpose of each of the documents on pages 166–168?

b) What differences of style and register are there? For example, which is the most/least informal?

c) Find examples of:
1 making an announcement
2 saying why the person is writing
3 giving information about:
    a) the company
    b) market research
    c) the product
    d) the customers

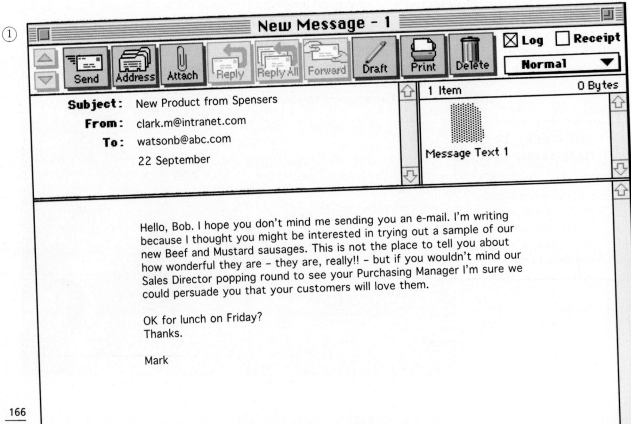

① New Message – 1

Subject: New Product from Spensers
From: clark.m@intranet.com
To: watsonb@abc.com
22 September

Hello, Bob. I hope you don't mind me sending you an e-mail. I'm writing because I thought you might be interested in trying out a sample of our new Beef and Mustard sausages. This is not the place to tell you about how wonderful they are – they are, really!! – but if you wouldn't mind our Sales Director popping round to see your Purchasing Manager I'm sure we could persuade you that your customers will love them.

OK for lunch on Friday?
Thanks.

Mark

②

barbecue bonanza

1221-K Pukkaville Pike
Bluemountain MD 21201-1432
Tel: (410) 55-9687
Fax: (410) 55-9632
E-mail: billc@barbecue.com

DATE:	1 July
TIME:	12:30
TO:	Charles Richards
	Vice President
	Atmo Ads
PHONE:	(718) 899-3486
FAX:	(718) 890-3486
FROM:	Bill Hollett
	Vice President
	Barbecue Bonanza
PHONE:	(410) 55-9687
FAX:	(410) 555-9632
RE:	Proposed advertising campaign
	1 page

Dear Mr. Richards

We are a small company recently set up to provide a range of barbecue accessories.

We are approaching you because we are about to launch a major nationwide advertising campaign and we are seeking an agency with a proven track record best suited to our needs to assist us.

Our customers are mainly ordinary families who like to light up their charcoal grill in the garden on warm summer evenings. We see our image as the one to beat in barbecue accessories, having the widest range at the most competitive prices. Among the products for which we are renowned are our lightweight, portable barbecues and our elegant terracotta barbecues. In addition, we offer the standard range of gas-powered grills and disposable charcoal trays suitable for picnics.

Obviously we would need to meet, discuss initial ideas for our campaign and tackle the thorny issue of costs. If you are interested in being considered for this project, please contact my assistant at one of the above numbers as soon as possible.

We look forward to hearing from you.

Sincerely

Bill Hollett

Bill Hollett
Vice President

③

Netsite: http://www.childroc/dev.html

PRESS RELEASE

CHILDREN 'N' US

New Leicester Rd, Coventry, CV9 8TS
(voice) 01203-663698 (fax) 01203-663699 (e-mail) childroc@intercom.co.uk

FOR IMMEDIATE RELEASE
Contact: Director of Marketing

CHILDREN 'N' US launches **Childrock**

Children 'n' Us announces the launch of Childrock, a new child pacifier.

Childrock was developed after intensive research found that the greatest need among parents of young children was for a safe and fun device that would get their children off to sleep while the parents got on with their busy lives.

Childrock consists of an electronic swing-cradle in the shape of an attractive cuddly bear. The child is put in the cradle, details of the desired programme are keyed in by the parent to the console on the sole of the bear's foot, and the swing-cradle rocks automatically for the desired amount of time.

Childrock incorporates the latest microchip technology and is designed to the highest industry standards. Constructed of long-lasting and damage-proof materials it can also be used to pacify restless pets such as cats and small dogs.

Childrock has a suggested retail price of £99.99 although there is a special offer price of £79.99 if purchased by mail order before 31st January.

Children 'n' Us is confident that Childrock fills an important market need and will rapidly achieve vigorous sales.

2 Read the small advertisement below about a new computer game. If you were asked to create a major advertising campaign for the product, what image would you try and create?

The company **Hardline Games** (126 Back Street, Lower Edmonton, Liverpool LR4 5DF Tel: 0151-8764321 Fax: 0151-8764322 e-mail: hline@abc.com Web page: http://www.hline.co.uk) has just produced a new computer game called 'Beastlie Bubbies' (price £29.99; introductory price of £19.99 before October 31st). Requires Windows or Apple Mac, 4Mb RAM, 256-colour, 12-inch monitor and 5Mb of free hard disk space.

The game was developed last year to appeal to grown adults with a child's sense of humour. The game incorporates the latest 3-D and video technology. The game is about a group of fluffy and cute but very dangerous bubbies, who throw fireballs and eat opponents and try and take over your world. There are 90 levels of difficulty.

3 Write one of the following about the game in Exercise 2:
  – A press release on the World Wide Web to announce the new game.
  – A fax asking a major computer store to stock the game.
  – An e-mail to a business colleague explaining you've just tried out this new game and suggesting they buy it.

3 DESCRIBING PLACES

1 What are the general aims of a guidebook in contrast to a personal letter to a friend describing a place?

a) In the extracts below find examples of:
1 phrases with adjectives
2 intensifying adverbs (e.g. *entirely*)
3 different sentence structures (e.g. passives, relative clauses, parenthetical statements – extra ideas added to the main sentence)
4 prepositional phrases (e.g. *in the heart of, close to*)

(A)

(B)

lbufeira, whose beautiful sandy beaches are among the best in Europe, is cooled in the hot summer months by refreshing Atlantic breezes. This favourite destination for the British remains the Algarve's most well-known resort, fashionable and utterly charming, and retains a unique fishing village atmosphere. You can stroll around the Old Town in the morning when it's quiet, take a leisurely walk past the whitewashed fishermen's cottages nearby, set in narrow twisted streets, or sit in the cafes in the evening, watching street musicians and buskers as the town comes alive.

We like Albufeira a lot. The beaches are fantastic. Very sandy. It's quite hot – I spend a lot of the day sleeping and drinking ice-cold milk-shakes – but you don't really notice the heat when you're on the beach because there's a lovely sea breeze.
Last night we went for a walk around the town. Very fashionable – everyone was out in their Gucci gear – but even so the town still manages to hang on to its oldy-worldy fishing-village atmosphere. We spent a bit of time in a cafe listening to some absolutely fantastic street musicians and generally watching the world go by. Nadia thought she was in heaven!

b) Compare the extracts. How do they differ in style? Which has more complex sentences?

2a) What do you expect a tourist-guide description of a place to include (e.g. where the place is, its history)?

b) Which adjectives in the box are most likely to describe 1–7 below. There are often several possibilities. Add others you know.

panoramic	historic	balmy	breathtaking	mouth-watering
exquisite	spacious	unrivalled	relaxing	beautifully-situated
stunning	rich	lively	quaint	

1 the weather
2 the views
3 the buildings and monuments
4 the people
5 the atmosphere
6 the food
7 the towns

c) How is a holiday brochure different from a tourist guide?

d) What tone do you think each should have when describing places? Why?
- positive-sounding?
- realistic (good and less good points)?
- neutral (factual without opinions)?

3 Read this extract from a brochure for a holiday in Buenos Aires.

a) Where is a positive-sounding 'flavour' of the city given? What kind of language is used (e.g. typical vocabulary, typical grammatical constructions)?

b) Where is detailed practical information given?

c) What other typical words/phrases might you find in a brochure?

ON SUNDAYS, tourists and locals alike flock to the flea market in San Telmo. Enjoy the cafes, small restaurants and old pubs surrounding this lively square frequented by interesting characters from Argentina's more bohemian circles. Where better to chat and find out more about life and the hustle and bustle in this great metropolis on the wide Rio de la Plata – a vast estuary more akin to a sea than a river.

On arrival at the airport you will be met by our well-trained staff and taken to your luxury hotel, approximately five minutes' walk from Plaza de Mayo, the ideal starting point for your explorations of this fascinating city.
Facilities include heated indoor swimming pool, health club, sauna and gym. Rooms are beautifully furnished and have air conditioning and satellite TV. Prices are for Bed and Breakfast with two persons sharing a twin room. Car hire, airport transfers, two city excursions and an exhilarating tango evening in La Boca, the old harbour district, are included in the price.

4 This is an extract from a draft of a brochure offering excursions in Iceland.

> There are many fjords (1) in the plateau (2) in North-West Iceland. They seem strange to foreigners. We arrive at Isafjordur after a flight (3) over fjords (4) and mountains (5). We board a bus (6) and go and see the fjord (7) from a high point. We'll visit the town (8) and harbour (9), drive along the shores (10) and look at the Djup (11), an ocean inlet (12), and the mountains (13).

a) Add the information below and rewrite the extract.
Begin: *There are many often very beautiful and very wide fjords that penetrate deep into the rugged plateau ...*

1 The fjords are often very wide and very beautiful.
   They penetrate deep into the plateau.
2 The plateau is high and rugged.
3 The flight lasts 45 minutes.
4 The fjords are alluring.
5 The mountains are craggy.
6 The bus is our tour bus.
7 The fjord is small.
   It has a long flat spit which protrudes into the sea.
   On this spit lies the principal town in the West Fjord.
8 Part of the town is old.
9 The harbour is bustling.
10 The shores are rugged.
11 The views of the Djup are fascinating.
12 The inlet is broad.
13 The mountains have snow-clad sides even in summer.

> *fjord:* long strip of sea between steep hills
> *inlet:* narrow strip of water that goes from the sea into the land
> *spit:* long, thin, flat beach which goes out into the sea

b) Can you improve your draft for a final version? Will it interest people? Are there enough adjectives? What verb forms should be used?

4 LETTERS: FORMAL

The language of formal letters

1a) Match the word or phrase in A (commonly found in formal letters) with the more informal one in B.

A

1 assistance	2 wish	3 stated	4 advise/inform	5 purchase
6 subsequently	7 concerns	8 currently	9 enable	10 were unable
11 many	12 assurance			

B

a) lots of	b) couldn't	c) buy	d) tell	e) said/wrote	f) let
g) promise	h) help	i) then	j) want	k) at the moment	l) worries

b) Rewrite the sentences below in a more formal style.
1 Thanks a lot for all the help you gave me last week!
2 I'm really sorry I haven't written back sooner.
3 I just wanted to tell you that your current account is overdrawn.
4 Please write back as soon as you can.
5 Sorry I couldn't make the meeting a couple of days ago.
6 I thought I'd drop you a line to let you know we've moved house.
7 It's great news about Meg being born.
8 I saw your ad – I'd love to buy one of your special spider catchers.

c) Read the letter and fill in the gaps with the most suitable alternative below.

Dear Mr Rowe,

I am writing (1) .... an incident that occurred in Cardiff market square (2) .... , when your car was observed to be parked without (3) .... the (4) .... ticket. We would like to point out that, (5) .... about non-payment of the relevant fine, (6) .... (7) .... we will feel obliged to (8) .... ; as you will appreciate we are reluctant to (9) .... so we would be grateful (10) .... (11) .... further information, please do not hesitate to (12) .... on the number above. (13) .... the relevant documentation regarding payment. (14) .... to hearing from you (15) ....

1 a) regarding   b) about   c) with reference to
2 a) this January   b) in January of this year   c) a few months ago
3 a) displaying   b) showing   c) demonstrating purchase of
4 a) right   b) relevant   c) necessary
5 a) despite previous correspondence   b) though we've written before
   c) although we've contacted you before
6 a) you haven't paid yet   b) the fine has remained unpaid
   c) we have not yet received the aforesaid remuneration
7 a) If you don't pay soon   b) Should no steps be taken to rectify the
   situation   c) Unless we receive payment within seven days
8 a) put the matter in the hands of our solicitors   b) tell our solicitors to
   sort it out   c) resort to legal action
9 a) go this far   b) take this measure   c) do this
10 a) if you'd settle up soon   b) for prompt settlement of the account
   c) for your speedy cooperation in this matter

11   a) If you need   b) Should you require   c) In the event of needing

12   a) contact us   b) give us a ring   c) get in touch with us

13   a) Please find enclosed   b) We've enclosed   c) Enclosed is

14   a) We look forward   b) Looking forward   c) We are looking forward

15   a) as soon as possible   b) at your earliest convenience   c) asap

The organisation and layout of formal letters

2a) Divide the letter in Exercise 1c) into paragraphs and say what the purpose of each paragraph is.

b) Rewrite the letter appropriately, adding the conventional layout for a formal letter. Put the following in the correct place and check with the box below:

Mr S Rowe
26, Chapel Street
Swansea
SA4 4DT
19 July 1999

Jonire Collection Agency
Drayton Industrial Park
Cardiff
CS2 2OP
Yours sincerely,
R S Pratt
Assistant Manager

LAYOUT CONVENTIONS

Put your address either on the right-hand side or in the centre of the page. (Do not write your name.)	23 Park Row Bristol BS8 1QT
Put the date here. In British English it must be day, month, year. (It can also be written 20.2.99.)	20th February 1999
Write the name (and/or position if you know it) of the person you are writing to, followed by their address.	Chris Smith Orwells plc Britannia Warehouse The Docks Gloucester GL1 2EH
Write the name (if you know it) of the person you are writing to. (If you don't know it, write *Dear Sir or Madam*.)	Dear Mr Smith
Begin with an introductory sentence, saying why you are writing.	Re your letter of 9 February, I am writing to let you know …
Divide the rest of the letter into paragraphs, being as concise as possible.	
End with a sentence like this.	I look forward to hearing from you.
If you began the letter with the person's name, end like this. (If you began *Sir/Madam*, end *Yours faithfully*.)	Yours sincerely, *Joan Kidman*
Print your name under the signature.	JOAN KIDMAN

c) Read the e-mail below that Stephen Rowe left for his PA, and use it to help you write a reply to the letter he received from the Jonire Collection Agency. Lay out the letter appropriately.

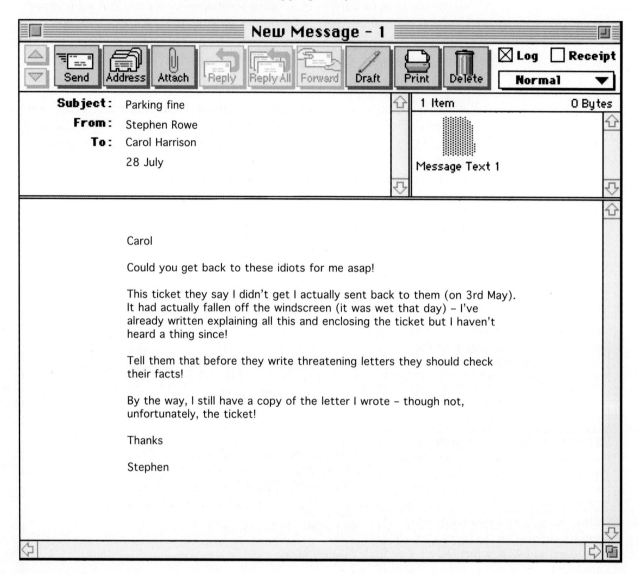

Subject: Parking fine

From: Stephen Rowe

To: Carol Harrison

28 July

Carol

Could you get back to these idiots for me asap!

This ticket they say I didn't get I actually sent back to them (on 3rd May). It had actually fallen off the windscreen (it was wet that day) – I've already written explaining all this and enclosing the ticket but I haven't heard a thing since!

Tell them that before they write threatening letters they should check their facts!

By the way, I still have a copy of the letter I wrote – though not, unfortunately, the ticket!

Thanks

Stephen

5 REPORT WRITING

1 A report is a piece of factual or impersonal writing, often to be given to an official body. It usually incorporates recommendations.

a) When are reports written? Here are some examples:
- an account of an accident (Example: a police report)
- a progress report (Example: an end of year achievement report from a teacher to a child's parents)
- an investigative report (Example: a company wants to expand its business)

b) Work in pairs and choose one of the examples above or one you thought of. Say how you might organise the report. Which of these would you include?
- main title
- aim and scope of the report (or 'terms of reference')
- introduction
- how you proceeded
- the facts of the situation (or 'findings')
- what you discovered
- your evaluation of individual aspects
- an overall evaluation
- conclusion
- recommendation
- a summary of the main points

2 Read the report on page 176.

a) Which of the following points does it include?
- a clear introduction, including background
- a 'neutral', fairly formal style
- a lot of precise and detailed information
- logical organisation
- a balanced view but negative where necessary
- clear headings with ideas grouped according to topic
- clearly organised paragraphs, possibly including a topic sentence
- a succinct summary, incorporating personal recommendations

b) Look at the language features in the report.

1 Which verb forms are used:
- to give the purpose of the report?
- to give the facts of the situation?
- to make a recommendation?
2 Why is the passive used?
3 Which adverbs and adjectives give personal opinions?
4 Find examples of linking expressions.
5 Find examples of the language of generalisation (e.g. *all in all, in general*).

3 In what ways would this report be different if you were writing to a friend?

4 Write a report on one of the following:

1 facilities for tourists in your town
2 a language course you have attended
3 ideas for a new business initiative in your area

BRITISH COUNCIL COURSE ON INDIVIDUALISED LEARNING

Introduction

This report describes a course on individualised learning which I attended between 26th June and 11th July 1999. It took place at University College, Cardiff, and 26 people attended from British Council institutions in six different countries. Most participants seem to have had very little previous experience of individualised approaches. Surprisingly, some participants had also had very little teaching experience.

Course programme

The course was run by two tutors from the university itself. As a result we were able to use the full range of facilities at the university. The working day was from 9 a.m. until 5 p.m. with an hour for lunch and two short breaks. In addition there were optional seminars two evenings a week.

Accommodation

Accommodation was in single study-bedrooms, with shared bathrooms. Breakfast and lunch were provided but not an evening meal. Participants were expected to find restaurants locally. However, there were many of them and they tended to be reasonably priced.

Course content

The course consisted of three sessions a day. The first session was given by the main course tutor and focused on theories of learning and individualisation. The second session looked at practical examples of methodology in a number of different contexts where individualisation was desirable. Sometimes this session was given by guest speakers from different institutions. Finally, the third session focused on the participants' own teaching situations and was given over to the development of individualised materials.

Conclusion

All things considered the course was excellent. I enjoyed it enormously and felt I learnt a lot. The tutors were very approachable and down-to-earth, giving us a lot of practical guidance. Furthermore, what was particularly pleasing was that they were very sensitive to the fact that our teaching situations were very different and so gave us a lot of opportunities in the sessions to give our individual perspective.

On the whole accommodation was perfectly adequate. However, oddly enough, the food was rather stodgy and not very suitable for a summer course when the temperature reached over 30°C every day! Perhaps the course organisers could consider providing more salads and fruit.

Recommendation

On balance, I would certainly recommend that our university sends someone on the course again next year.

6 SUMMARY WRITING

1 Many people suffer from insomnia and there are a variety of techniques people use to try to get to sleep.

a) Read this newspaper summary of a long article in a scientific journal.

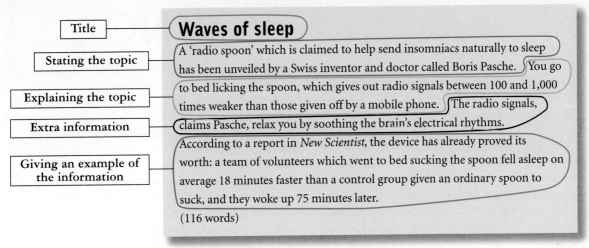

Title

Stating the topic

Explaining the topic

Extra information

Giving an example of the information

Waves of sleep

A 'radio spoon' which is claimed to help send insomniacs naturally to sleep has been unveiled by a Swiss inventor and doctor called Boris Pasche. You go to bed licking the spoon, which gives out radio signals between 100 and 1,000 times weaker than those given off by a mobile phone. The radio signals, claims Pasche, relax you by soothing the brain's electrical rhythms. According to a report in *New Scientist*, the device has already proved its worth: a team of volunteers which went to bed sucking the spoon fell asleep on average 18 minutes faster than a control group given an ordinary spoon to suck, and they woke up 75 minutes later.

(116 words)

b) Your editor now asks you to reduce the summary to about 75 words.
1 Underline the words/phrases you will keep.
2 Cross out the words/phrases you will cut.
3 Circle the words/phrases you will re-express.

2 Following these guidelines, write a summary in your own words of the article on page 178 (about 120 words).

SUMMARY WRITING GUIDELINES
1 The purpose of a summary is very important. For example, if you are a journalist, you might want to include an example or a quotation to bring the summary to life. However, if you are writing an official summary of a meeting for a report, these are often excluded.
2 In many summaries the following are often excluded: anecdotes, lists, figures of speech, unnecessary adjectives.
3 You may need to use words that are different from the original.

SUGGESTED PROCEDURE
1 Read and understand the text.
   Stage 1: What is the general meaning?
   Stage 2: Read again. What is really being said?
   Stage 3: What is the aim of each paragraph? Give each paragraph a heading.
2 Decide if there are any paragraphs you can ignore.
3 Underline/highlight the main points in each paragraph. (Will you include only facts or will you include opinions? Will you include only general points or will you include detail – quotations, examples etc?)
4 Make notes of the important points in your own words.
5 Put the notes in a logical order.
6 Do a first draft.
7 **Check 1:** Is the length appropriate? Have you included all the important points? If it is too long, what can you cut or combine? Are there any words/phrases that can go? If it is too short, what should you bring in?
   Check 2: Review the spelling, consistency of verb forms, vocabulary, sentence structure, punctuation etc.
8 Do a final version.

YOU
HAVE TO CATCH THEM
YOUNG ....

Bilinguals seem to hold the world in the palm of their hand. They cruise across frontiers with enviable ease, unburdened by phrase books or dictionary. They shift gear from one language and culture to another with an ease that makes monoglots despair. But how do bilinguals learn in the first place to operate in two languages?

To find out, psychologists at Barcelona University selected 30 babies aged four months – ten from families where only Catalan was spoken, ten where only Spanish was spoken and ten from bilingual Spanish-Catalan families – and read them a story in Spanish and Catalan. Psychologist Nuria Sebastián, who is from a Spanish-Catalan family, said: 'We wanted to see if babies of that age could distinguish between the languages.' Their recognition of a language was judged by the speed with which they looked to the source of the sound. The researchers found that all the babies could distinguish clearly between their maternal language and a foreign one.

'Using languages as similar as Catalan and Spanish meant we were testing their ability to make quite subtle linguistic distinctions – although we don't yet know if they were distinguishing by rhythm or by sounds,' says Sebastián.

The first experiment of this kind, it shows just how early the brain is able to respond to one or more particular languages. The study also showed that bilingual babies take longer to respond to voices than monolingual ones. 'We're not sure why but we think it is probably because they are having to decide which language to plug into,' says Sebastián, who hopes to follow this with further studies into the mechanisms by which children begin to handle two languages simultaneously.

Sebastián says: 'Neurologists know how messages travel through the brain. But very little is known about the different ways language is processed by monolinguals and bilinguals – and there must be differences.'

Infants learn languages better when they are young, she says, because the brain is so flexible. It is the first few months that seem to be crucial because there is a progressive reduction in the infant's ability to distinguish between two languages. At two-and-a-half months a baby can make this distinction. At four months it can only distinguish a foreign language from its mother tongue. At six months the baby can distinguish only between the vowels of its mother tongue and the foreign language. And by ten months babies have lost the ability to distinguish between foreign sounds.

It seems that the language an infant hears every day influences the structure of the developing pathways in the brain so that they are programmed to pick up only relevant sounds. After these pathways are set down, they become increasingly rigid. So if a child has not learnt a second language before this inflexibility sets in, it is unlikely to become truly bilingual. Several studies have shown three years to be a cut-off point.

Being bilingual does not only affect language use. In tests judging creative thinking power, bilingual children have performed better. If you ask them, say, how many uses they can think of for a brick, they tend to come back with more answers than the monoglots. Psychologists suggest that this is because they naturally distinguish word and meaning, so are relatively free from the conceptual constraints that language imposes.

Anecdotally, bilingual children have more sensitive communication skills. It may be that they have to learn very early to be aware of the listener's needs because they have to decide which language to speak. They soon come to see language as an integral part of the relationship.

However, even monoglot adults need not despair. They can still learn fast because they have advanced intellectual skills. But because they're operating on an analytic level, with most adults their speaking improves faster than their listening. In children it's probably the other way around, says Dr Winifred Strange, a psychologist at South Florida University. Her research has confirmed that it is the listening which a baby does, long before it can talk, that enables it to learn a foreign language much more effectively than an adult.

The lesson for adults who want to learn a foreign language fluently, says Strange, is to listen as much as possible – which can be as easy as watching television programmes from a neighbouring country. At the same time, don't assume your children are watching too much TV – they could be effortlessly equipping themselves with a valuable skill that no amount of homework will ever give them.

(755 words)

(From *The European Magazine*)

Unit 2 (page 30)

STUDENT B:

Respond to your neighbour's complaints about the noise in your house. You agree with, and apologise for, some things (e.g. your son does play his music very loud). However, you think that your neighbour is being a bit unreasonable about other things (e.g. your baby doesn't cry very much, really, and there's not much you can do about it!). Think about what you will say and/or suggest to solve the problem.

Unit 5 (page 68)

Answer: 3

Unit 7 (page 90)

Quiz answers

1b)   2b)   3a)   4b)   5a)   6b)   7a)   8b)

Unit 7 (page 99)

STUDENT B:

Unit 9 (page 120)

Quiz answers

1   a) True   b) True   c) False   d) True   e) False   f) False
2   *Ought* is followed by the *to*-infinitive. *Should* is often used instead.
3   They have two forms: both as an ordinary verb, and as a modal auxiliary.

4   1a) It is a fact that Mary is at the door.
    1b) I am certain that Mary is at the door; I'm expecting her.
    2a) I'm sure she's German.
    2b) I'm certain she is German; I have some evidence.
    3a) It is a fact that it is raining.
    3b) I can't believe that it is raining (but it is).
    4a) I think he is probably at home.
    4b) I have good reason to think he is at home.

We use modals to show our attitude to an event or situation.

5   (Possible answers)
    1   It isn't necessary for you to eat that.
    2   It's bad for you/It is forbidden for you to eat that./Don't eat that.
    3   I think it's important for you to phone him and apologise.
    4   It's necessary to wear a tie at that club.
    5   I strongly recommend that you try that new restaurant.

Unit 10 (page 131)

Coincidence

This was a subject which fascinated Carl Jung, who collected a number of examples so extraordinary that he felt there must be an explanation beyond mere chance. He called this phenomenon 'synchronicity', the simultaneous occurrence of two meaningful but not causally related events, and argued that clusters of events must indicate the presence of some greater force.

Every day literally thousands of events happen to us. We meet people, see people, talk to people and think about them. We observe thousands of different objects every day. Most literate people read thousands of words, in books, newspapers and magazines. Given that there are about five billion people in the world, it would be incredible if chance did not throw up an astonishing number of coincidences.

Unit 10 (page 135)

Answers

1   This may be because it is in one of the folk-lore cycles where white is associated with goodness and banishes the evil blackness.

2   A blockbuster was a massive bomb developed in the Second World War, which was capable of destroying a whole block of houses. Later the term was used to describe anything large and successful, especially a lavish musical or a big-budget film.

3   A normal dozen is twelve. A baker's dozen is thirteen, because, when baking a batch of loaves, for instance, he'll have twelve to sell and one for his own use. Another theory is that, because the penalties for supplying underweight loaves were so severe in the Middle Ages, bakers would bake an extra one in case they were accused of short measures.

4   It may be a mispronunciation of *le lieu*, French for 'the place'.
    However, it is more likely to be a shortening of *gardy loo!*, a warning cry that housewives made when they emptied chamber pails out of windows into the street, a corruption of the French *gardez l'eau*, meaning 'watch out for the water'.

5   Originally everyone in Britain pronounced the short northern 'a' of *cat* and *fat*. But towards the end of the 17th century in the south of England, it gradually changed to the long one of *car*. It is difficult to pinpoint one reason for the change, but it most likely happened because of fashion.

6   It is not certain why the number twelve was chosen. The practice dates back to the eleventh century when the King decided that a group of people was the fairest way to decide whether or not someone was guilty.

7   The Italian word *paparazzi* means 'buzzing insects'. The photographers often resemble flies as they swarm around a celebrity victim.

8   This means 'to tell someone to do something they already know'. At Easter and other festivals, ordinary eggs were pierced and sucked dry so that the empty shells could be decorated and kept without them going bad. The ideal members to undertake this task were the grandmothers, who had invariably lost all their teeth in such times and were thus less likely to crack the fragile eggshells.

9   By touching wood to obtain good fortune Christians used to believe they were symbolically touching the Cross. Nowadays, for most people, the original meaning has been lost, leaving only a superstitious gesture.

10   This nickname is a pun on the Latin name for it, the *humerus*.

Language Bank 4 (page 144)

STUDENT A:

Read the text. Try to guess which comparative structure completes gaps 1–11 and underline which nationalities (in italics) you think the article might be about. Then ask Student B questions to check your answers. Examples: *Is it **The earliest** risers'? Which two nationalities are likely to go to work by bus?*

A day in the life of a European

EARLY BIRDS

(1) *The earliest* risers are the Czechs although almost (2) .... number .... Hungarians get up before 6.00. The people who stay in bed (3) .... are the Spanish together with the other lie-in-beds, the Irish.

NIGHT OWLS

Despite their early rising, many Eastern Europeans stay up late but not nearly (4) .... late .... the Italians, (5) .... half of whom stay up beyond midnight.

NAPPING

Interestingly, the industrious Dutch are unveiled as Europe's (6) .... avid nappers, considerably (7) .... the allegedly siesta-loving Spanish, whereas the Irish are the people in Europe (8) .... prone to napping.

NEWSHOUNDS

(9) .... more of the Swiss will have read a newspaper .... the Norwegians but (10) .... a third of Greeks will have read a newspaper. The Danes were easily (11) .... avid radio listeners.

ON THE BUS

Almost as many *Swiss / Turks* as *Czechs / Serbians* are likely to go to work by bus but nowhere near as many *Finns / Swedes* – only 6.6% do so. Indeed the results seem to show that these days fewer and fewer Scandinavians are travelling by public transport.

EATING OUT

The *Swiss / Belgians* are by far the most assiduous restaurant patrons, closely followed by the *Bulgarians / Czechs*. The least likely to be found in a restaurant are the *Ukrainians / Portuguese* and *French / Russians*.

BAD TEMPER

The hottest tempers were found in *Turkey / Russia* but the researchers were more than surprised to find that it was almost the same number as the allegedly phlegmatic British!

HAPPINESS

Another surprise was that supposedly gloomy *Scandinavians / Eastern Europeans* felt a great deal happier than the *Spanish / Greeks* and *Russians / Armenians*, and quite the saddest nations in Europe were the *Danes / Italians* and *British / Swedes*!

(From *The European Magazine*)

UNIT 1 RECORDING 1.1

1 It was one of those situations where you're feeling a bit low, you decide to go shopping, so you go for a walk and you wander round the shops and you can't find anything to buy so you just see something and you think oh yes, I wish I'd got one of those, so I bought this hair curling tong and it wasn't because it didn't work properly or I couldn't work it properly or it wasn't good quality, it was simply that it just made me look stupid, just that.

2 Oh, well, yes, one thing I really regret is never, is never learning the piano when I was younger because lots of people I know, lots of people I met at college sort of seemed to have Grade 5 piano and it was like well how did you do that – 'Oh, just when I was a child' – and I just wish my parents had made us play an instrument because it would just be a really useful, I mean just like a nice recreational thing.

3 Oh, well, yes, one thing that I've always regretted is that I never actually learned a language to a level which I could actually communicate effectively in it – apart from English of course.

4 It would be nice to write a book – always wanted to write a book – and they're really successful, you know, incredibly sort of literary, sort of bestseller – well, not very literary probably, but a bestseller anyway, but not ...

5 Imagine if we lived in a world where there wasn't any crime.

RECORDING 1.2

Steve Jones
Extract 1
People often see genetics as some kind of new moral threat. Well I don't think that it is. I think it certainly poses moral questions but they're the same ones as are posed by medicine in general and indeed ... The commonest disease among white-skinned people is an illness of the lung – that's called cystic fibrosis – and it's extremely damaging, it's very unpleasant, your lungs become clogged up with mucus and in the end those with the illness die really quite unpleasantly and very young. For many years there's been an attempt to cure that by inserting the correct kind of DNA into the damaged cells of those patients. Many people have said that faces them with some kind of moral problem but surely it doesn't because now we can actually treat the disease in another way.

Extract 2
People sometimes say that scientists should make moral decisions when they're doing their research, well I think that's impossible: science itself is completely separate from morals, scientific fact would be there if there were no humans around to discover it, so there is no morals in science, there are enormous moral implications of what science finds out.

Extract 3
There's also the question about whether genetics should be allowed to make choices about the kind of babies we have. And clearly that is a moral issue which I think needs discussing. However, one of the things that persuades me that one should do that is that the people who are most enthusiastic for research on the kinds of tests for unborn babies, tests for shall we say cystic fibrosis or another ... brain, the people who are among the most enthusiastic for gathering money to support the research are parents who've already had children with that condition. Now it seems to me that they are the people who know, they are the people who should be allowed to make the moral decisions and it certainly isn't for me as a scientist to say that it should be done but I also think it's not for anyone who has never experienced it to say that it should not be done.

Extract 4
Genetic research is going at an incredible rate – it's almost impossible for me to look back as to when I started as a geneticist 25 years ago and to see what's happened. Certainly, 25 years ago, not in anybody's wildest dreams would we have imagined that we're cloning mammals for example, or we're moving genes from humans into other creatures, or that the entire subject has been completely revolutionised. Well, that doesn't worry me at all, that fills me with pleasure and excitement because the faster that science can go surely the better.

RECORDING 1.6

TONY ROBINSON: And then when I was 21 I was invited by this girl to her cottage for the weekend and I thought I'd play it cool and I was, I was stunningly cool until she plonked this half an avocado pear in front of me and she kept talking about art and politics and life and the kind of stuff that you talk about when you're 21, and I was listening, nodding – except I wasn't really listening, I was thinking what the hell do I do with this thing and I thought I'll just toy with my spoon until she starts and so I toyed and toyed and she said, 'Don't you like avocado pear?' and I said, 'Oh, yes, yes, yes, yes' and I even then I just fiddled a bit more until eventually she got this gravy boat and she tipped this stuff into it and I had no idea whether it was honey or, or gravy or, or what and still she was talking, I dipped my spoon in and I took a mouthful and it was salad dressing with garlic in it. I mean I'd just about started to be able to handle garlic – you know I was quite sophisticated by that time – but you know mouthfuls of salad dressing – a little bit on a bit of lettuce but this was like an eggcupful so she kept on talking – I don't remember anything about the conversation – and I thought I made a really good stab at it except that in the end she said to me: 'Well aren't you going to eat any more?' 'cause I'd had about, like, a quarter of a square inch of it and she took it over her own side and ate the rest, which I found fairly humiliating.

UNIT 2 RECORDING 2.1

Extract 1
Now, in 'Temper Temper', Katie Whittaker investigates the phenomenon known as the *furore brevis* – the Brief Madness.
A: 40,30 Warning, Mr McEnroe – misconduct
B: What was offensive about that? What did I do, what did I do wrong? I hit it like this? I mean, what? Like that? Was that abuse of ball? No, how do you know, were you even watching?

PRESENTER: How many of us can put our hands on our hearts and say we've never blown our top? That we've never shed our calm demeanour, cast caution aside and let rip in that most exquisite spasm of apoplexy – temper? Oh, we've all heard about road rage, trolley rage, you-name-it rage – that kind of sirocco fury you get when you spot your bus at the red traffic light beside you, with the driver immune to your frantic gestures to open the door; that burning frustration, simmering and threatening to explode as you wait for the shopkeeper to finish her conversation before she serves you. Despite living in a culture which positively encourages us to let it all hang out, a few of us still don't like to admit we lose our temper – but we've all been there. Certainly, as children, the stamping feet, clenched fists, wails of fury – but as adults? Well, that's a different story. Have you ever caught sight of yourself in the mirror while in the throes of a rage? The bright red face, the huffing and puffing – it's the ever-so-slightly undignified episode most of us would like to forget, and quite often do.

Extract 2

SPEAKER 1: You wake up of a morning in an angry mood and it just carries on through the day until it bursts.

SPEAKER 2: It lasts seconds. It's like being sort of trapped and wanting to get out. You feel very, very tense and you just want to throw something.

SPEAKER 3: Your heart rate starts to get faster, your hands start to sweat and you start to get agitated, and you know anything can happen then because your hands start to flex ready for a fight where anything that's at hand you start throwing.

PRESENTER: There's no doubt we do show our anger both physically and mentally. Our blood pressure rises, so does our heart rate and hormone levels. What's happening, in fact, when we fly off the handle, is that we're bringing a primitive instinct into play. It's the body adopting a fight or flight mechanism where we either stand our ground and fight or about turn and run.

Extract 3

DR WILLIAMS: Anger kills. Anger kills, whether you bottle it up or let it out. The research that's been done shows that people who lose their temper frequently, particularly at little things – traffic, things you see on the television, things you hear over the radio etc., read in the newspaper – have been found, in multiple studies both in the US and around the world now, to be at higher risk of dying, going from age 25, say, to age 50. Those of us who have this anger proneness, when we become angry our blood pressure goes up twice as much, our adrenalin levels, other stress hormones go up more. We believe that this excessive fight/flight, this more frequent fight/flight response, physiological response, is one of the pathways whereby people with this anger-prone personality are nipping out the lining of their arteries, suppressing their immune system, making cancer and other infectious diseases as well more likely. We are more likely to engage in risky health behaviour so we're more likely to consume more alcohol, we're more likely to be smokers, if we are smokers we're less likely to be able to quit. We even eat more. So there's a whole series of biological and behavioural characteristics that go along with this anger proneness that are perfectly plausible candidates to be shortening our life and raising the risk of all kinds of serious health problems.

RECORDING 2.2

A These two really determined ambulancemen went to a house in a small village and they picked up this perfectly healthy person and they put him on a stretcher and they rushed him all the way to hospital. Even though he protested the whole way they just ignored that. Got him to hospital and at the very same moment the real patient, who'd, like, driven all the way there suffering from anaemia, happened to have the same name and lived in the same village, and wasn't allowed to register because, technically, he'd already registered!

B A married businessman, yeah, who'd booked into a hotel with his mistress, had given the name of Scott Anderson. Now this was a false name, of course, and a rather unfortunate choice since a man of this name was wanted in connection with a murder. As a result the hotel staff contacted the police and later that evening armed officers crept into the bedroom to question him. As soon as they realised it was the wrong man they apologised and the man checked out the following morning. Later, hotel staff were trying to trace him, as he and the woman hadn't paid their bill for £100.

RECORDING 2.3

MAN: Oh, so you've decided to come back, then! That's very kind of you!

WOMAN: Is there a problem?

M: A problem? Oh no, no problem. I've just been trying to leave my own house for the last hour and because of you my son has now missed his dental appointment.

W: I'm terribly sorry. I didn't realise.

M: Sorry? Sorry? Is that all you can say?

W: Actually, I didn't see that notice before.

M: It's beyond me how anyone can *not* see the notice. It's large enough! In any case, anyone can see this is private property, if you can be bothered to look.

W: The thing is I was in a hurry because I had to drop my son off at school and there was nowhere else to park ...

M: I couldn't actually care less where you had to go. I've a good mind to phone the police.

W: Look I've said I'm sorry. Don't you think you're overreacting a bit?

M: Don't you dare tell me I'm overreacting.

UNIT 3 RECORDING 3.1

BERNIE: I can remember I've always had an association between certain words and certain colours. The strongest association I have with words and colours is days of the week. Whenever I hear somebody say a day of the week or if I see a day written down on a piece of paper, I immediately see a colour in my mind. It's a very strong association and it's not something deliberate but it's just something that happens, the colour comes into my mind automatically. Monday's a nice light sky blue, Tuesday's a lovely sort of silver colour, Wednesday's a very deep gold sort of rusty colour, Thursday I think of as a sort of a bold yellowy orangey sort of colour, very bright, very bold, Friday's black and Saturday's white and Sunday's a very, very dark brown. The colours are very very exact, very precise. I can see a very particular colour in my mind but I find it hard to describe that colour to somebody else. But it springs to my mind's eye immediately. I suppose one of the funniest things about this business of seeing colours in words is that for many years I thought everybody did it and I was quite surprised when I was a child and I started to say to people, 'What colour's Tuesday for you,' and they would just look at me in a very blank way. Another thing about the days of the week is you would also think perhaps I would associate days of the week that I liked with bright colours and days that I didn't like with dark and gloomy colours and it doesn't seem to work like that. I like Saturday very much, it's probably my favourite day, and I see Saturday as a nice white colour but I also like Friday very much and Friday's a much darker black. Tuesday's I normally don't like often – I've had bad things happen to me on Tuesdays – but Tuesday's a very bright silvery colour so that doesn't seem to explain the connection either, but it is nice when people say 'Monday' and you immediately see a nice light blue in your mind. Most people on a Monday just see misery, gloom, the start of another week.

RECORDING 3.2

ROGER MCGOUGH: I'm sometimes asked, 'Where do you get your ideas from in writing a poem?' Well I wrote a poem thinking about just that question. The poem's called 'Smithereens' ... (*Reads poem*)

RECORDING 3.3

Extract 1

INTERVIEWER: We're here this morning in Roger McGough's house and we're going to talk for a little bit about the craft of writing poetry. Roger, what kinds of poems do you like writing, comic poems, serious poems?

ROGER MCGOUGH: I write serious poems and I write comic poems, funny poems, but I see myself as a serious poet in the way that I think writing poetry is a serious business – it's very much a sort of quite a lonely, private affair – it's just yourself and in my case a pen and a paper – and ... some of the subjects you deal with are serious. I mean, over my life I've written poems about friends dying, about being in love and about being out of love, and all the things that we all live through. But of course the way you tackle it can sometimes be from a humorous point of view, which I do enjoy. I think generally when I write funny poems I'm probably writing for children and I do write a lot of poems that are published in children's books.

I: Where do you get your ideas from, is it things you see, things you hear, are they accidental or are they set off by something quite concrete?

RM: I think my ideas for writing poems can come from various ways. Poems of mine like 'The Identification' – it's a poem about a father identifying his son after an explosion, which is quite a popular poem and used in schools. And I actually got this poem from a television news item, where there's a father in Ireland, who in fact was an Anglican minister, who talked about his experience of identifying his son after an explosion – and I was moved by this and I tried to write down the father's reaction, how he felt. That may have been the starting point but of course then the poem took over and this is what happens in the best sort of writing. You may start with something but then the poem has its own life and goes off and you sort of control it like a shepherd guiding these words, these sheep into places.

I: Do you try and write a bit every day, I mean do you have a routine (a 9 to lunchtime routine) or do you write as and when the inspiration strikes?

RM: A lot of my life as a working poet consists of doing poetry readings as well, sometimes perhaps once a week, or once every two weeks I have a reading in the evening which involves travelling, going there, doing readings, staying over, coming back, so perhaps the day before or the day after I can't think creatively otherwise just thinking about what you're doing that evening and what programme to read and that sort of thing, but if I've got a clear day, I'll always come to my desk in the morning – I have a room – which you see here – where I work and inevitably all my other friends who are poets moan about the first few hours where you've got to deal with everyday business of tax forms and business and people sending you poems and young people send me poems and there's that sort of ... and you either sort of get that out of the way right away, and then the day's your own or put it aside to the end of the day but I tend to deal with it all, do the phone calls and then hope that a poem will come winging its way like an aeroplane across the sky ... I don't use, have never been able to type, I can't drive a car, I'm one of those sort of poets that Wendy Cope calls a TUMP (a TUMP is a Totally Useless Male Poet) – can't drive, can't type, can't use a word processor but I can write poetry and I like the idea, the feeling of the pen on the paper and the ink and I enjoy that – the crossings-out, transferring to another book, see how it looks there, go back and the whole process, I enjoy immensely the physical side of writing poetry.

Extract 2

I: But what is a poem as distinct from anything else, I mean, what makes it a poem, what are the elements of a poem that are unique over prose?

RM: It's got to be concise, there will be, in my case, but there doesn't have to be, rhythm and sometimes rhyme but if I write a line down and then this, then, line springboards me into the next line, if the next line rhymes, then it's going to be a poem, if it wants to extend itself into prose, that'll happen. But in my case it's always seems to be my mental make-up makes the poem.

I: People say that poetry is dead. Is it?

RM: It's very strange and I often do radio interviews – this has happened now for 20 years, this will happen next week. I'll go on radio and the news guy or the DJ will say, 'Roger, it's great to have you in the studio. Poetry's making a comeback, isn't it?' And well no it's never been away, I mean as far as I'm concerned it's always been popular and always will ... It's like everything else you know, if you're not interested in poetry, you don't know about it. But people who are, and there are many, many, many, many thousands in Britain, the poetry societies flourishing, local magazines are flourishing, lots of readings and it has been ever so (*Interviewer: You make a living from it*) I've been very lucky to have made a living, yes.

RECORDING 3.9

a Give me your wallet!
b He's going to kill us. He's going to kill us.
c Go on, give him the camera.
d Please, please let us go.

e I'm not afraid of you.
f I-is that g-gun loaded?
g I love you. I love you.
h You're not going anywhere.
i We're free!
j Why are we always robbed when we go on holiday?

UNIT 4 RECORDING 4.1

1 A: Shall we go?
  B: Go!? I've only just arrived!
2 A: It was a nice wedding, didn't you think?
  B: Yes, but I'm afraid I didn't like Lisa's dress at all.
3 A: Did you get a lot of work done while I was out?
  B: I finished it! I even managed to sort out my papers.
4 A: 'Bye. I do hope you'll enjoy the film.
  B: I'm sure we will. See you later.
5 A: Was the film good?
  B: It was absolutely brilliant!
6 A: How are you getting on with Hannah these days?
  B: I can't believe it. She's actually invited me to lunch!
7 A: Does this look OK?
  B: Yes, great. I really like you in red.

RECORDING 4.2

1 I think they must be going out together. Whenever I see him, he's with her.
2 I've told you over and over again not to do that. Stop it!
3 That was Joe on the phone. He's getting more and more worried about his job situation.
4 Nobody's helping me this time. I'm doing it myself.
5 No, I'm not the least tired. Let's go a bit further.
6 There was a big drama today! The producer just got up and walked out.
7 I did enjoy seeing you yesterday.

RECORDING 4.3

1 It was yesterday that Tim phoned.
2 It was me that Tim phoned yesterday.
3 It was Tim who phoned me yesterday.
4 It was London that Tim phoned from yesterday.
5 What Tim did was phone me yesterday from London.
6 Where Tim phoned from yesterday was London.

RECORDING 4.8

Extract 1

INTERVIEWER: As an Englishman living in Italy could you describe some aspects of Italian life that you find very different or very difficult to live with?

TIM PARKS: I think one of the things that's most perplexing to a foreigner is that the rules of operating in Italian society are *actually* very different from the written rules so that for example they will introduce a new law. I remember one year there was a tax on the use of your local GP – your local doctor – and I immediately rushed out and paid this and nobody else did because everybody else had a sense that maybe this tax wasn't *actually* in the end going to be enforced and very quickly the whole thing was removed. Well, I *mean* in Italy this kind of thing happens with great regularity. And in many areas of life you need a process of initiation from somebody else to understand the difference between the official way of doing things and the way things are *actually* done. Let me give a rather funny anecdote of that. I *mean*, Naples, for example, is famous for its chaotic traffic and for the fact that the people don't stop at red lights *and so on*. So I remember the first time I went to Naples I was thinking *well, you know* I wonder if it's really like this or if it's *just* folklore. And I'm coming in from the airport with a taxi and this taxi is running most of the red lights and I'm thinking, yes it really is like this and he's driving far too fast, and I was quite pleased that this was the case, and then he stops at a red light and I was somewhat shocked because there didn't seem any difference between this light and the others and I said to him, *you know*, 'Why have you stopped?' and he said, '*Well* it's a red light. Can't you see?' and I said, '*Well you know* you ran through all the others,' and he said, 'Yeah but this is a light that you stop at and we know that in Naples' so *you see* you begin to realise that really you'd have to live there to know where you have to stop and where you don't and I think that's true of many aspects of Italian life in a different way. *I mean* it seems a kind of facetious example but even for example getting a job at the university there's an official set of rules for how that's done but everybody knows that basically it operates in a different way from that. So those kind of things can be difficult but also they can be fun.

Extract 2

1 I: Do you think a person can have the traits of two different national characters?

TP: I think, I think you can up to a point – different areas of different national characters float to the fore. But that brings up the whole question of whether national character exists anyway, which is an interesting one. One of the things that has always been problematic to me was whether a national stereotype exists, like whether when I'm dealing with an Italian I can assume certain things from the start. And obviously when you go there you go there with a lot of preconceptions of how Italians are and then you have the problem that all the people you meet are different and have different ways of operating. So that it really is problematic sometimes and you begin to think that perhaps national stereotypes are like caricatures in that they have an element of truth and for that reason a caricature is always recognisable, but they're not actually what people are.

2 For example, the Italians and English have a mutually self-defining way of looking at each other. The Italians for example think the English are wonderful for their sense of civic duty, they're organised, they're slightly reticent, they believe in privacy, they generally pay their taxes and behave quite reasonably in certain situations and of course they're sportsmanlike etc. But the English are awful in other ways – they eat terrible food, the weather's awful and so we might go there occasionally but Italy's better in the end. And the British think of the Italians as wonderfully warm, beautiful women, wonderful landscape, great clothes, great art, great design – but those Italians, you know, can you really trust them, they might be a little perverse, they might be trying to fiddle you etc. etc. so again one will go on holiday but England's better in the end. And I think these traits which to a certain extent do exist in both nations are then exaggerated in order to define yourself by what you're not so I think there is an element of that. Having said that …

RECORDING 4.9

1 A: Did you enjoy the film?
 B: Well, I didn't go in the end, actually.
2 A: Rumour has it that she actually walked out of the meeting!
 B: Really! Why?
3 A: I'm intending to do my tax return this weekend.
 B: Yes, but will you actually *do* it?
4 A: Surely it isn't going to rain again!
 B: Actually, I'm afraid it is.
5 A: Have you got a second, Jim?
 B: Well actually, I'm afraid I'm just on my way out.
6 A: That's our new neighbour, Harriet Walker.
 B: Oh yes, I know her. Her son's in Hannah's class actually.

UNIT 5   RECORDING 5.1

1 ... but some of the beer ones are very good. There's the famous Guinness one, for example, which is maybe a bit clichéd now but when that first came out that was, I thought that worked very well – the dancing, the *(it had that song didn't it?)* the bloke in the kind of black trousers and blue shirt, and he sort of, he dances up to this pint of Guinness and there's this music going in the background which I won't try and ...

2 If you're standing in a supermarket and there's three brands of washing up liquid, then I'd, I remember picking up a Persil bottle only because I'd seen an advert and I thought God I'm actually responding to the advert here, aren't I, picking it up, but I mean it wasn't ...

3 I don't mind being manipulated by adverts – it's a way of getting to use and try new things. You see them advertised and you think – oh yeah, I'd like to try that, so it's a way of trying something new.

4 There was the Benetton one – that was a few years ago now – but I thought that was – that was quite offensive – *(which Benetton advert was that?)* well there was a whole series they ran – there was one that showed a man dying of Aids ... they were all very strong images but quite sort of disturbing as well *(but it just seems that they're designed to shock)* designed to shock ...

RECORDING 5.2

Trevor Beattie
Extract A
I think pretty clearly it's ads which stand out from the crowd, those are the most successful. There are so many ads out there, there are millions of ads around the place, and only a tiny percentage of those ads I think get noticed. So, with everyone shouting it doesn't always pay to shout louder to get noticed, you have to employ different means of getting your, getting your message across. The most successful ones are the ones which get their message across very clearly through the clutter.

Extract B
If the ad stays in your mind and the product is intrinsically woven into the ad, then the product will stay in people's minds as well. Where the ad stays in people's minds and they can't remember the product, the ad's no good, it's redundant, it's a waste of money, waste of everyone's time. It's a bad ad. And if people say, 'I saw a great ad last night Trev, don't know what it was for but there's this funny thing happened,' it wasn't a great ad, it was a bad ad. If

they, if they can describe the ad without saying the name of the product, it's a bad ad.

Extract C
It's the difference between art and selling. I'm selling, I'm not in the business of self-gratification. I'm not in the business of, 'I've done this thing, you can think of it what you will, but it is my art.' Rubbish, I want people to understand my message. It's vital that they understand everything I say about this product. I don't want any mystery about it. I want them to know what this product is and what it does and why they should buy it. It's not a mystery and it's not art and it's a communication. We're in the business of communicating to other people, sharing ideas with other people. They should know what we're talking about. And my target audience is essential. I need to know exactly who I'm talking to. Whether it's half the population of the world or whether it's seven people in Birmingham, I need to know what those people are like so I can talk to them.

Extract D
Yeah, I wouldn't advertise the Conservative Party, I wouldn't advertise in support of fox hunting, I don't smoke but I feel a bit odd about cigarette advertising. However, I disagree with the ban on cigarette advertising because it's a legal product and any legal product should be allowed to advertise so my view on that is ban the product, don't ban the advertising. It doesn't make any sense to me at all.

Extract E
All advertising can achieve is to, with a bit of luck, encourage you to buy the product once. If the product is rubbish, you won't buy it again. No matter how great the advertising, if the product doesn't live up to it, and it doesn't live up to your personal expectations, you won't buy it again. You won't get, you can't, won't get fooled again, you won't be fooled twice ... if fooled is the right word. But I really, really don't like this notion that people are brainwashed by advertising, that they put their arms in front of them and they, 'Oh I don't know what to do – this advert's told me to buy something I don't really want, oh my god, here comes my money!' – I don't think so. I don't think people part with their money if they don't want to, people have got a lot more sense than that, you know.

RECORDING 5.3

1 A: That was the last train!
 B: Was it?
2 A: He has a way with women!
 B: Does he?
3 A: I've never seen an octopus before.
 B: Haven't you?
4 A: Nice day!
 B: Is it?
5 A: He'd already gone when I got there.
 B: Oh, had he?

RECORDING 5.4

1 A: Mr Baker wants to know how you're getting to the conference.
 B: Oh, so he expects us to be there, does he?
2 A: No, thanks. I went to the Taj Mahal last time.
 B: Ah, you've been to India before, have you?
3 A: Sorry I can't cook this evening. I sprained my wrist playing tennis this morning.
 B: Really! You hurt yourself, did you?

4 A: You know you really are a bore!
  B: Shut up, will you!
5 A: I'm afraid Sue can't come this evening.
  B: She's not well, is she? Tell me the truth.

UNIT 6 RECORDING 6.1

Brenda Kean
Extract 1
Well, women you know – they say necessity is the mother of invention – and women are very good inventors. It was a woman that invented the circular saw and without the circular saw would we have all the buildings that we have? It was a woman also who invented the Mars Bar ice-cream which has brought delight to the lives of so many of us in recent times.
About six years ago I became a professional photographer specialising mainly in travel and wildlife. I was asked one day by a manufacturer in Sweden to photograph some day-old chicks – little hen, little fluffy hen chicks – for Easter cards and I found I couldn't use studio lights as the chicks would get too hot – so I took them out into my sun-lounge and set them up in a little scene and I tried using flash on my camera, but this caused very bad shadows behind the chicks and also gave them white eye, where the, the little eyes of the chicks reflected back white instead of black. The night before we'd had a Chinese meal, and it'd come in its own little container with a silver foil lid – so I took, I washed the lid, this lid and I fashioned it into a hood shape and attached it to my camera with some elastic bands. Then I bounced the flash up into this lid first before it reached the chicks and it worked really well and that was the basic idea of Quasar Flash Bouncers, and this now has expanded into three different types of bouncers for different cameras.

Extract 2
Well, the next step is to try and protect your invention because you want to stand on the rooftops and say to everybody, 'Hey world, look – this is my invention and it's going to change your life,' but if you do that somebody's going to steal the idea off you.
Now the, in England – well in most of the world – you can be protected with patents. So you take out a patent – you go to see a patent agent and they advise you. And there are three routes then for exploiting your patent. You can sell the idea on to another company to make it for you. Now this gives the least return and, but it also involves the least risk, but if an invention goes on to make millions of pounds and the idea is sold cheaply, then someone else gets the profits, having taken most of the risk. You can license another company to make it for you, which means that they pay royalties for each one that's sold, or you can make it yourself and this is the route that I chose because I also wanted the intellectual challenge of setting up a business and challenging myself to see if I could do it and this gives you the best money returns because all the money comes to the inventor in that case.

Extract 3
I've found in life that there are two kinds of thinkers. First of all there are the people who think in straight lines, that see a problem, see a solution, go to it straight from A to B without a moment's hesitation or deviation from the plan. And then there are people who think in circles, who look round a problem, under a problem, who question, who don't take no for an answer and I think the inventor falls in this category. I've been described as a mono-maniac with a mission and in truth a successful inventor must be that. You must have this commitment and not be swayed or deviated from your path, so initially you think in circles, and then you've got to be very single-minded.

Extract 4
Well, I'd like to invent something simple that everybody could use that would perhaps save lives or enhance the quality of life for millions of people. I'm thinking, perhaps, mainly of things like the cat's eyes that you get in the middle of the road, or a new non-skin-puncturing injection system for giving medical injections or perhaps these new glasses that don't need, you don't need to go to a qualified optician to have, which are going to make a tremendous difference to people. As regards what invention have I, do I admire the most I think I would have to say the dishwasher because I loathe washing up. The invention I'd most like to be invented is something that empties the dishwasher and stacks it all away neatly in the cupboard and wipes all the kitchen surfaces down.

RECORDING 6.5

A: I thought we were going to ask Michael and Jean over tonight.
B: Well, the problem is I can't get away before six and now I haven't got transport either.
A: It doesn't matter. I'll come and pick you up from work in my car.
B: And who's going to do the cooking?
A: I am. I always do, anyway.
B: Well, that's great if you don't mind. Why don't you just do pasta and salad for a change?
A: Leave it all to me. See you at six in front of the entrance.

UNIT 7 RECORDING 7.1

Professor David Crystal
1 English has over the past two or three hundred years repeatedly found itself in the right place at the right time. If you go back to the beginning – why does a language become a world language? The answer is nothing to do with the nature of the language as such. No, no, a language becomes a world language for one reason only and that is the power of the people who use it and power here means political power, military power if you will, originally, economic power, cultural power possibly and various other kinds of power. There's nothing particularly attractive about the pronunciation system of English, it's not easier or more difficult than most others. In grammar it has an awful lot of grammatical construction, well over 3,000 identifiably distinct grammatical features in English to be learned, you know, it's quite a lot of grammar, well up on the scale of grammatical learning in any context. Its spelling is very difficult in many ways, so I think, you know, there are difficulties with learning English. But all of this is beside the point, because if somebody is waving dollar bills under your nose and saying, 'If you learn English you are going to get a lot of these,' you will assimilate even quite a complicated language in order to get at some of those dollar bills, and the real reason why one learns English is because of the accessibility to the power structures of the world that it guarantees.

2 English has always been a vacuum cleaner of a language. It has sucked in vocabulary from every other language it has come into contact with since it was Anglo Saxon right from back in the 8th and 9th centuries. It was always borrowing, borrowing, borrowing, well stealing of course, because when you borrow words from other languages you don't give them back and it's been that way all the way through. And the thing is this, that if you come from another language background and you approach English, you'll probably find that some of the words from your mother tongue are already in English and it gives a kind of familiarity to the language, a kind of welcome, you know, some of your words are already there. And certainly over 150 languages, major languages around the world have had their words loaned into English in this way, so I think the range and versatility and size of the vocabulary is quite a plus as far as English is concerned.

3 Standard English of course exists at the moment in the form of standard written English, standard printed English. It has done for many decades now and when one looks at the way English has moved around the world one doesn't actually see very much change in the nature of that standard English. If you go for newspapers in Britain or America, or Australia, or for that matter in Athens, or Cairo, or Tokyo, any place which has an English language newspaper and you compare the language as it turns up in those newspapers around the world, you will find precious little difference in the language of those newspapers. At a spoken level, however, it's a much different scenario, very different scenario and very interesting because of course it is in speech that identity is most readily expressed. The way in which you express your identity in speech is through accent and dialect. And as the language has spread around the world the most noticeable thing everybody's seen in the last 20 or 30 years is the growth of these new Englishes, as they're called, so that in, it's not just America and Britain any more but in West Africa and East Africa and Singapore and Malaysia and India and Bangladesh and Sri Lanka and all of these other places you are now getting these new varieties, localised varieties of English. Chiefly in vocabulary, hardly at all in grammar but quite substantially in pronunciation.

4 Now half the languages of the world dying is really quite a dramatic thing and it's a matter of great concern, a concern that many people are still not fully aware of. Most of these peoples are dying for reasons perhaps so many and varied that it's impossible to generalise about them. But there's one very important point to realise and that is it isn't just English which is at the heart of the matter here. If you take, for example Brazil, where the number of Brazilian indigenous languages is now perhaps a couple of hundred or less, whereas a couple of hundred years ago there were a thousand or more languages spoken in that part of the world. Well, yes these languages have died but not because of the influence of English, English has no place in Brazil, it's because of Portuguese.

5 Bilingualism is the answer. If I were a member of a minority language community or even a majority language community that was not a world language, I would want obviously access to the rest of the world by using the lingua franca that happens to be in vogue at the moment and it seems to be English. I would want to learn English, at the same time I would not want to lose my mother tongue because it's part of me.

RECORDING 7.2

Well I have a friend who, who was in London at the same time I was and he's an actor and he, we passed a haberdashery and he said, 'Let's go in and let's pretend we're British,' so I thought all right, this is fairly juvenile but what the hell let's do it. So we went in and he just laid it on so thick he became extremely cockney and said, 'I'd like a shirt please ... blue ... blue's a nice colour, I like blue,' and the, the salesman was very solicitous and very polite and helped him select a shirt and he paid for it and he wrapped it up and as he was handing it to my friend he said, 'Enjoy your stay in London, sir.'

RECORDING 7.4

Otherwise I just noticed various expressions which I found interesting like the use of the word 'right', which seemed to follow just about every, or actually precede just about every sentence when you would ask somebody something usually the word 'right' would come along and then they would say the rest of the sentence. 'Which way is it to the train station?' 'Right, well you take a left over there.' Now that could be confusing if in fact you were worried about left and right but you would hear 'right' before that, before, right before that answer.

UNIT 8 RECORDING 8.1

MARK: At the age of 13 she went to her first Olympics. I was probably 9 years old then and that's probably my strongest memory of sort of the competitive side of Sharron. My mother and father went to the Montreal Olympic Games together and me and my twin brother went and stayed with some family friends and I remember sort of staying up till 3 o'clock in the morning to sit and watch the swimming events and that was when she became very very popular.

SHARRON: My brothers saw how hard I worked and even as youngsters I think appreciated that, but they would tend to be left a little bit to their own devices, they didn't have this really sort of passionate positive force behind them, which I had which was dad, because he was so sort of preoccupied with me. But it's only now I suppose that I actually, you know, realise how much they did all sacrifice for me.

M: I didn't really have my own life – it was, it was more of a shadow life – I didn't see it any different from anyone else's, I didn't know that other boys or you know all my school friends or whatever did anything different in their free time. I didn't know that they sort of all went out together as a family at the weekend – we went out together as a family but it was to go along to a swim meet.

S: I don't think they've ever begrudged any of it to me because I think they've realised how hard I worked. I mean you know he channelled all his energies into me and all his ambition went into me and therefore Mark and Tony definitely got a poor second as far as his attention was concerned and he never realised that but he did, whereas my mum always treated all of us as equal.

M: Maybe it was 11, 12 I started to feel the difference, I started to feel like, you know, oh, well, you know, Sharron went over to Spain, Sharron went over to America, Sharron went over to there and a lot of the family money was being spent on Sharron's sport ... maybe I was a little bit jealous, a little bit envious underneath, which might have been sort of part of the reason why I became a little bit of a troublesome youngster, had to get punished a little bit more than most people did.

S: He had this incredible determination, I mean he just, he has this incredible ability to apply himself to something and give 100%. I mean I had swimming 24 hours a day 7 days a week. He didn't want to, anyone to think he was giving me an inch because I was his daughter, so I'd have to train through anything, I mean, I broke both my arms when I was eleven, he wrapped them in plastic bags and I trained with two broken arms.

M: Being that Sharron was always successful and did so well I always wanted to be sort of, I wanted to come forward, I wanted to, I wanted my father to be very proud of me ... one of the things I always seemed to do when I was younger was seem to fail at things. My father would sort of say, 'Oh, he's got in trouble again. Get in your room' and all that sort of stuff.

S: I think in hindsight he probably realised he did push me too hard. He killed a lot of my enthusiasm for the sport. He was without doubt a better coach than he was a father.

M: I think the price was the family ... unfortunately the price was the family ... my brother as well as me and my mother. You know, it was always a funny time and I do feel that there's still always the funny feelings within the family, whether it be from me or whether it be from my sister or from Tony about sort of like I wish we'd all stayed together as a family, you know, and that's something now that we're coming back to. I still love my dad and I still loved him then – he sort of went away at the age of about 14, and I don't think I saw him again till I was sort of 17 or so, so those three years in there were my fondest memories. I know it sounds really strange because my father wasn't around but they were some of my fondest young memories I've got because that was my start of my life, when I was independent.

S: I wouldn't change anything because that would be being really two-faced about it. You know I have a good life, I earn a good living, I want for very little, I'm very happily married with a little boy, and, you know, the majority of that has come because of swimming, even to the extent that I've met my husband because I was an athlete ... but there's no doubt about it that my father did push so hard that he knocked a lot of the love of the sport out of me. I mean, one of the saddest things I think was when I won my Olympic medal *(+ background commentary)* in Moscow. I touched the wall, I turned around, I looked at the scoreboard, I saw that I was second and the first feeling I had was not joy and adulation, it was relief because I could pack it in.

UNIT 9 RECORDING 9.1

Obstinately he made his way to the house, with quick, pathetic, persistent glances of appeal back at her. But she never looked around. Her defiant but anxious young body stung him into love and repentance. He stopped. 'But I never meant ...' he muttered, waiting for her to turn and run to him. 'I didn't mean ...'

She did not turn. She had forgotten him. Along the road came the young man Steven, with something in his hand. A present for her? The old man stiffened as he watched the gate swing back, and the couple embrace. In the brittle shadows of the frangipani tree his granddaughter, his darling, lay in the arms of the postmaster's son, and her hair flowed back over his shoulder.

'I see you!' shouted the old man spitefully. They did not move. He stumped into the little whitewashed house, hearing the wooden veranda creak angrily under his feet. His daughter was sewing in the front room, threading a needle held to the light.

He stopped again, looking back into the garden. The couple were now sauntering among the bushes, laughing. As he watched he saw the girl escape from the youth with a sudden mischievous movement, and run off through the flowers with him in pursuit. He heard shouts, laughter, a scream, silence.

'But it's not like that at all,' he muttered miserably. 'It's not like that. Why can't you see? Running and giggling, and kissing and kissing. You'll come to something quite different.'

He looked at his daughter with sardonic hatred, hating himself. They were caught and finished, both of them, but the girl was still running free.

'Can't you see?' he demanded of his invisible granddaughter, who was at that moment lying in the thick green grass with the postmaster's son.

His daughter looked at him and her eyebrows went up in tired forbearance.

'Put your birds to bed?' she asked humouring him.

'Lucy,' he said urgently. 'Lucy ...'

'Well, what is it now?'

'She's in the garden with Steven.'

'Now you just sit down and have your tea.'

He stumped his feet alternately, thump, thump, on the hollow wooden floor and shouted: 'She'll marry him. I'm telling you she'll marry him next!'

His daughter rose swiftly, brought him a cup, set him a plate.

'I don't want any tea. I don't want it, I tell you.'

'Now, now,' she crooned. 'What's wrong with it? Why not?'

'She's 18. 18!'

'I was married at 17 and I never regretted it.'

'Liar', he said. 'Liar. Then you should regret it. Why do you make your girls marry? It's you who does it. What do you do it for? Why?'

'The other three have done fine. They've three fine husbands. Why not Alice?'

'She's the last,' he mourned. 'Can't we keep her a bit longer?'

'Come, now, Dad. She'll be down the road, that's all. She'll be here every day to see you.'

'But it's not the same.' He thought of the other three girls, transformed inside a few months from charming petulant spoiled children into serious young matrons.

'You never did like it when we married,' she said. 'Why not? Every time, it's the same. When I got married you made me feel like it was something wrong. And my girls the same. You get them all crying and miserable the way you go on. Leave Alice alone. She's happy.' She sighed, letting her eyes linger on the sunlit garden. 'She'll marry next month. There's no reason to wait.'

'You've said they can marry?' he said incredulously.

'Yes Dad, why not?' she said coldly, and took up her sewing.

His eyes stung, and he went out on to the veranda. Wet spread down over his chin and he took out a handkerchief and mopped his whole face. The garden was empty.

RECORDING 9.2

A: I'm beginning to get worried about Simon. It's nearly seven and the train should have got in by six thirty.

B: Well, he may have missed it.

A: No, he can't have. He phoned me from the station – he had plenty of time to catch it.

B: Well then, it must have been delayed for some reason otherwise we would have heard something.

RECORDING 9.3

1 I could have gone to university if I'd worked harder.

2 Did the person who phoned have a northern accent? Ah, in that case it will have been Tim.

3 What beautiful flowers! But you really shouldn't have bothered.

4 You might have told me you'd be this late!

5 He can't have failed. He was the cleverest in his class!

RECORDING 9.6

A: Well I disagree with you, actually. I think it's a very good idea that students should be made to pay for their education.

B: Why? Because I mean, surely people that are gifted – are clever – but don't have the means to pay for it will be disadvantaged by that.

A: Well, they're not expected to pay straightaway. I mean, if there's a limit set once they've left university – they've got their degree, they've got their qualification and then they go on into these great jobs and they start earning a great salary then surely they're in a position to pay back their tuition fees.

B: Well that's fine if you can expect to get a good job at the end of it but these days it's not so easy and if you're going into something that isn't law or medicine or something highly paid, it may be a very long time before you could pay it back – it might put you under a lot of, a lot of stress – and you might consider not even considering a course that would, would lead to that.

C: But hang on, I mean all that students pay for when they're at university is drinks – they don't buy books, do they? They spend all the time in bed – they don't get up in the morning to go to the lectures.

B: Speak for yourself! That's not true for everybody.

A: I think that's true for most of the students.

B: I don't think so. I entirely disagree.

A: Ah you've got to admit that it is true for a lot of students, though, isn't it? I mean, probably fifty per cent of student life is spent messing around and not actually getting down to any serious study.

C: Yes, why should the country pay for that?

B: Well, no, that's a completely separate issue, I think. I mean, what goes on once they get to university is a different matter. We're talking about the education that they receive while they're there, not what they choose to do outside that. And if they're not being rigorously enough assessed so they can go, they can spend all their time partying and drinking, then …

C: That's what it's like, isn't it? Why should the government and taxpayers have to pay for that?

A: Absolutely!

B: Well, I still think it's a separate issue. I don't think it's related in any way to whether grants should be given to students or not.

A: All the same, why should people who haven't been to university have to pay taxes to help pay for the education of those who do go to university, and if they're on very low wages themselves? You know, some people in certain low-paid positions – why should they have to fund somebody who's going to go on and become a doctor or become a lawyer? I mean, let's face it, those who do go to university do come up in higher paid jobs generally, don't they?

UNIT 10 RECORDING 10.1

Richard

As far as religion goes, yes, I believe in God, otherwise I don't think there would be any meaning to what we do, but quite what form that God takes and – well, I can't really answer that. I don't believe in the church, particularly, but I think that's a different issue. I'm not religiously motivated, no – something I dislike in people is piety, and others telling you how you should live your life according to their morals. And I don't, I think to some extent one should teach correct ways of doing things but I think the answer to life really is there are many ways of doing things. And that's the humanist approach, not so much a religious one. Well, a humanist approach is recognising that, that the essence or the definition of mankind is that we are, we are, we are varied and variable and it doesn't matter what your, your, cultural background, your political background, you know, your religious background – all these things are diverse and so narrow, narrow religious ideology has no place for me but a broad understanding of people I think is essential to a religion.

Gillie

I'd like to think that I didn't strongly believe in something like astrology but I must confess that I flirt with it. When I read descriptions of Capricorn I have to admit that it's surprisingly close to me – I'm a plodder, I'm the one that goes up the mountain, I have a great sense of duty and responsibility, I have the work ethic very much in my heart – fun is always the last thing on my list.

Another thing is my health. Yes, I mean I have an arthritic hip and the doctors – Western medicine – tell me that the only thing available is that I will have to have a hip replacement so I must admit I will search out anything that isn't going to demand somebody attacking my hip with a pickaxe. I have been to things like meetings on how magnets can cure arthritic hips and I'm afraid it didn't cure mine and I believe, I believe that there are alternatives to knocking my hip-bone out yes, I do. I'd like to think you know that the fish oil that I take is going to cure my arthritic hip so yes I think I wouldn't, I mean I'm not denying Western medicine, I'm just saying I think there are plausible and workable alternatives in terms of medicine.

Ruth

When I got to about 13 I know that I started thinking about what the hell I was doing on the planet for anyway – why was I here and I did actually go through about a four-year phase where I explored religion quite heavily, so you start to think to yourself – well, if I am doing all these things, who am I doing them for and what sort of, what sort of other goals should I achieve if there is a Creator? I mean, I certainly think that there should be a reason, even if it's one that – which you create it in your own mind. I know that religion means different things to lots of different people. I soon started to sort out for myself that, that provided I had my own set of reasons for going forth in things that I wanted to do, that, that I was justifying why I was alive, and in that sense you actually set yourself certain goals and you think, well, I can achieve perhaps three or four things that I'm really pleased with that, that, that I know I could look back on my life and say I have done that instead of achieving nothing at all – then that would justify why I've been alive and having people remember you for doing certain things – I think that's important, too.

RECORDING 10.2

Rosie

Well, I reckon it's going to be like, probably like money 'cause like I reckon that money's like really important 'cause when you want to go out at night, see your mates and stuff you always need to have lots of money and especially if you're like a young person and that. I'd like to earn a lot of money basically – yeah, have a nice car, you know, have a nice life – spend as much money as I want and not have to worry about it really.

Kate

Well I think one of the most important things for me personally has to definitely be my friends. Without my friends I'd be lonely, unhappy, upset etc. etc. and I think that friends are just one of the most important things to have. I think it's vital if you're a young person to try and make the most out of your life, and have as much good time as you possibly can before you have other restrictions later on in life.

Cliff

Your health, family. Well, general condition of yourself – looking after yourself, eating the right foods, fitness, working out.

RECORDING 10.3

Success

We used to go out walking hand in hand
You told me all the big things you had planned
It wasn't long till all your dreams came true
Success put me in second place with you
You have no time to love me any more
Since fame and fortune knocked upon our door
I spend my evenings all alone
Success has made a failure of our home
If we could spend an evening now and then
Perhaps we'd find true happiness again
You never hold me like you used to do
It's funny what success has done for you
You have no time to love me any more
Since fame and fortune knocked upon our door
I spend my evenings all alone
Success has made a failure of our home

PRONUNCIATION: PHONEMIC CHART

CONSONANTS				VOWELS		DIPHTHONGS	
symbol	key word	symbol	key word	symbol	key word	symbol	key word
/ p /	pen	/ s /	soon	/ iː /	sheep	/ eɪ /	make
/ b /	back	/ z /	zero	/ ɪ /	ship	/ əʊ /	no
/ t /	tea	/ ʃ /	fish	/ e /	bed	/ aɪ /	write
/ d /	day	/ ʒ /	pleasure	/ æ /	bad	/ aʊ /	now
/ k /	key	/ h /	hot	/ ɑː /	calm	/ ɔɪ /	boy
/ g /	get	/ m /	come	/ ɒ /	pot	/ ɪə /	here
/ tʃ /	cheer	/ n /	sun	/ ɔː /	saw	/ eə /	there
/ dʒ /	jump	/ ŋ /	sung	/ ʊ /	put	/ ʊə /	tour
/ f /	fat	/ l /	led	/ uː /	boot		
/ v /	view	/ r /	red	/ ʌ /	cut		
/ θ /	thing	/ j /	yet	/ ɜː /	bird		
/ ð /	then	/ w /	wet	/ ə /	China		

WEAK FORMS AND STRONG FORMS

This is a list of 'grammar' words (with phonemic symbols) that have both a 'weak form' and a 'strong form' when speaking.
Examples:

*Oh, yes it **has**.* (/hæz/ is a 'strong' form because *has* is stressed.)

*Where **has** he gone?* (/əz/ is a 'weak' form because *has* is not stressed.)

*It's **his** problem, not mine.* (/hɪz/ is 'strong' because *his* is stressed.)

*What's **his** address?* (/ɪz/ is 'weak' because *his* is not stressed.)

	Weak form	Strong form			Weak form	Strong form
a/an	/ə, ən/	/eɪ, æn/		must	/m(ə)s(t)/	/mʌst/
am	/(ə)m/	/æm/		not	/nt/	/nɒt/
and	/(ə)n(d)/	/ænd/		of	/əv/	/ɒv/
are	/ə(r)/	/ɑː(r)/		our	/ɑː(r)/	/aʊə(r)/
as	/əz/	/æz/		shall	/ʃ(ə)l/	/ʃæl/
at	/ət/	/æt/		she	/ʃɪ/	/ʃiː/
be	/bɪ/	/biː/		should	/ʃ(ə)d/	/ʃʊd/
been	/bɪn/	/biːn/		some	/s(ə)m/	/sʌm/
but	/bət/	/bʌt/		than	/ð(ə)n/	/ðæn/
can	/k(ə)n/	/kæn/		that	/ð(ə)t/	/ðæt/
could	/kəd/	/kʊd/		the	/ðə, ðɪ/	/ðiː/
do	/d(ə)/	/duː/		them	/ð(ə)m/	/ðem/
does	/dəz/	/dʌz/		there	/ðə(r)/	/ðeə(r)/
for	/fə(r)/	/fɔː(r)/		to	/tə/	/tuː/
from	/frəm/	/frɒm/		us	/əs/	/ʌs/
had	/(h)əd/	/hæd/		was	/w(ə)z/	/wɒz/
has	/(h)əz/	/hæz/		we	/wɪ/	/wiː/
have	/(h)əv/	/hæv/		were	/wə(r)/	/wɜː(r)/
he	/(h)ɪ/	/hiː/		who	/hʊ/	/huː/
her	/(h)ə(r)/	/hɜː(r)/		will	/(ə)l/	/wɪl/
him	/(h)ɪm/	/hɪm/		would	/wəd, əd/	/wʊd/
his	/(h)ɪz/	/hɪz/		you	/jʊ, jə/	/juː/
is	/z, s/	/ɪz/		your	/jə(r)/	/jɔː(r)/
me	/mɪ, mə/	/miː/				

NOTE:
When grammar words are at the end of the sentence, they are sometimes stressed and so the strong form is used.
Example: *Yes, we **are**.* /ɑː(r)/